A History of Horseley, Tipton

200 Years of Engineering Progress

Eur. Ing. J. S. Allen

Produced and published by Landmark Publishing
Waterloo House, 12 Compton, Ashbourne, Derbyshire DE6 1DA, England
Tel 01335 347349 Fax 01335 347303 e-mail landmark@clara.net

1st Edition
ISBN 1-901522-90-3
© J. S. Allen

Designed by Samantha Witham
Printed by MPG Books Ltd, Cornwall

The right of J. S. Allen as author of this work has been asserted by him in accordance with the Copyright, Design and Patents Act, 1993.

All rights reserved. No part of this publication may be reproduced, stored in a retrieval system or transmitted in any form or by any means, electronic, mechanical, photo-copying, recording or otherwise without the prior permission of Landmark Publishing Ltd.

British Library Cataloguing in Publication Data: a catalogue record for this book is available from the British Library.

A HISTORY OF HORSELEY, TIPTON

200 YEARS OF ENGINEERING PROGRESS

Eur. Ing. J. S. Allen C.Eng, F.I.C.E., F.Weld.I.

Foreword

The Industrial Revolution in Britain led to the formation of many new companies to develop new industries and related engineering activities. The exploitation of the power available from water and steam, the increased demands for coal as a fuel, the development of iron as structural material and the rapid introduction of the railways and canal systems of transport provided many opportunities for entrepreneurs to set up such companies. Few of these companies survived into the twentieth century, so that the story of the Horseley Company of Tipton, from its formation in 1792 to its closure in 1992 is a unique historical record.

The long established Horseley family estate was purchased in 1792 by three entrepreneurs to develop coal mining. The first requirement was to extend the canals to provide transport to the immediate areas required. Following the successful developments in iron making by Henry Cort in the 1780s, the Horseley Company moved into iron making around 1808 and started manufacturing marine steam engines and iron boats in about 1817. The first iron steam boat, launched in 1822 was called the *Aaron Manby*, after the then Leading Partner and pre-dated Brunel's *SS Great Britain* by over twenty years. The company started making cast iron bridges in 1816 with a Swing Bridge in East India Docks, London and provided many bridges over the following years for the canal railway systems and for countries overseas.

The tracing of the history of the Horseley Company by John Allen is a true labour of love. Mr Allen has spent his whole professional life working for the Company and its successors, from Articled apprenticeship, to Structural Engineering, to retiring as Welding Technologist for the NEI Group of Companies in 1988. Mr Allen is a highly respected figure in the field of welding and steel construction with an international reputation for expertise on submerged arc welding. It was my pleasure to work with him on many welded steel construction projects in the 1970s including road and rail bridges and our paths have crossed since on numerous occasions. Having served as President of the Newcomen Society Mr Allen is a recognised authority on the history of Engineering and Technology. He has devoted himself to his account of the history of the Horseley Company with the same meticulous attention to detail as in his responsibilities for the many constructions completed by the Company under his stewardship.

Professor F. M. Burdekin
FREng., FRS, FICE, FIStructE, FWeldI.
Department of Civil & Structural Engineering,
UMIST,
Manchester

Contents

THE HORSELEY STORY	6
Prehistory	7
PART 1 THE EARLY HISTORY OF THE HORSELEY COMPANY TO 1865	8
The Partnership of Dixon, Amphlett And Bedford	8
The Establishment of the Horseley Colleries	10
The building of Furnaces	12
The Building of the Engineering Works	15
The Building of Marine Steam Engines and Iron Boats	19
Locomotive Engine Building	21
Bridge Building	25
Conclusions	26
Acknowledgements	26
Appendices	28
Robert Stephenson and the Horseley Company	37
Notes and References	39
PART II THE NEW WORKS	43
Chapter 1. 1865-1885	43
The New Horseley Works	43
The Horseley Company Limited	45
Spon Lane Foundry	47
Chapter 2. 1885	55
Joseph S. Keep	55
Spon Lane Works	56
Works Developments	56
Chapter 3. 1906-1919	71
The First World War	71
Chapter 4. 1919-1928	85
The Post War Years and Thomas Piggott	85
Chapter 5. 1928-1932	104
The Fusion	104
Chapter 6. 1932-1939	109
Horseley Bridge & Thomas Piggott Ltd	109
Chapter 7. 1939-1945	124
The Second World War Years	124
Chapter 8. Thomas Piggott & Co., Ltd.	134
Chapter 9. 1945-1992	150
The Post War Years	150
Notes & References	171
Acknowledgments	172
Index	173

THE HORSELEY STORY

The lives and hopes of many people have been affected by the events described in these pages. This book sets down the history of an industrial area and of those involved at Tipton in Staffordshire. It was known over the centuries as Horseley. In ancient times it was a purely agricultural area with farms, a windmill and a waterwheel driven forge. The ancient border of Tipton and of Dudley with its castle were not far away and this border had seen the arrival of coal mining on very shallow and often outcropping seams in very early times. As the coal on the outcrop became exhausted the mines were taken deeper and slowly moved away from the borders towards the centre of Tipton. Water became a serious problem to the mines and the first successful atmospheric steam pumping engine was built by Thomas Newcomen and his assistant, John Calley in 1712. Others were to follow.

The first coal mines on the Horseley Estate were sunk some eighty years later in 1792 and the first part of the book discusses these mines and the important engineering history which was to follow. Firstly by the erection of blast furnaces with a Boulton and Watt steam blowing engine in 1809 followed by the building of an extensive engineering works which was in production by 1815.

There are no Company records from this early period and it has been necessary to draw the story together from a variety of secondary sources. Nevertheless it has been possible to build up a quite extensive picture and to learn a great deal of the engineering work carried out at the first works by which it was to gain a most impressive reputation. Not only were locomotive engines built but steam engines for ships were constructed and the first iron steam boat completed. Many cast iron bridges were made and many of these remain today in excellent condition.

The second part of the history deals with the building of the new works in Horseley Road some half mile away in 1865 and continues to the sad ending in 1992 when along with many other established engineering concerns it was to suffer work difficulties, the arrival of the accountant mind and be closed down.

This second part of the history is based upon extensive company records which were saved at the time of closure. The events are dealt with in a sequential manner and the reader will for example, follow the changes from the use of horses through to steam and then to electricity. Changes in plant and in transport will be noted and the influence of the Company Directors can be followed. Slow social changes occurred and these were greatly influenced by the two world wars.

The Company gained an unrivalled reputation for its works which were carried out throughout the world and many projects are discussed. About 1929 there was an amalgamation with Thomas Piggott and Sons of Spring Hill, Birmingham who were from 1822 large diameter steel pipe and gas holder builders. This was to signal many changes as the two works became one organisation based at Tipton.

Prior to the closure the Company, having rebuilt much of the works and installed modern plant, had reached a very high standard of technical excellence and apart from traditional structural steel and bridges work there was extensive work on Lloyds Class 1 pressure vessels and on nuclear work in a variety of exotic materials.

Over almost two hundred years the Horseley Company has affected the lives of a great many people but there was always a great sense of belonging and many instances of three generations of a family being employed over a period of a hundred years. The text gives many references to those involved and local families may well recognise earlier members.

PREHISTORY

The company is sited in Tipton (alias Tibbington) in Staffordshire, upon part of the ancient Horseley estate. In 1302 there is reference to a watermill in a suit involving Thomas de Horsley[1] and a grant of 1320 has the signature of John de Horseley.[2] The subsidy rolls of 1327 and 1332 include the name of Ph'O De Horseleye (Philip de Horseley). By 1696 the area was well-defined and marked on a county map produced by Robert Morden, but still rural in 1769 other than for mills, smithies and windmills.[3] Details of the area become well-defined[4] on a plan of 1792 of the Horseley Estate (Fig. 1) which includes an area of 113a 1r 0p of particular interest purchased from 'Finch's Devisees' containing a windmill, blade mill and pool, for it was here the works was to be built. Whether the blade mill which was formerly a corn mill was on the site of the Domesday mill is uncertain, but it was of ancient origin. Parkes[5] identifies its history from 1708 and at the time of the 1792 plan it was identified as Finches Mill[6] having previously been Partridges Mill. Another part of the estate had belonged to Thomas Dudley[7] of Shutt End, Kingswinford.

There is no evidence in 1792 that there was any other form of industry on the estate but within a few miles there was extensive mining at Dudley and Wednesbury where the thick coal seams outcropped. The Birmingham Canal company sought and obtained power in 1783 to extend their canal and the Act[8] which approved the Broadwaters Branch also approved 'Six collateral cuts' and the first of these was to be into the Horseley Estate…

'through the lands of Thomas Dudley and John Finch Esquires, near Partridges Mill Pool … terminating in a Meadow called Brookes Meadow, belonging to the said Thomas Dudley.'

The planning of this branch appears to indicate that mines were about to be sunk in the area. The Branch was commenced, but by 1785 had only been completed for a short distance, and it was not to be built into the Horseley Estate until after 1792.

PART I

THE EARLY HISTORY
of the
HORSELEY COMPANY
TO 1865

THE PARTNERSHIP OF
DIXON, AMPHLETT AND BEDFORD

The Horseley Estate was purchased for £10,000 in 1792 by Edward Dixon of Dudley and Joseph Amphlett of Dudley, bankers, and William Bedford of Birmingham, solicitor, and on 18 July 1792 articles were signed under the style 'Dixon Amphlett and Bedford' with the purpose of working the mines under the Horseley Estate. Joseph Amphlett[9] was appointed Chief Manager and Director with a salary of £200 a year and authority to spend £600 in repairs at Horseley House, Tipton, which is shown as the Mansion House on the 1792 plan, reached by two tree lined drives and with attached orchards and gardens.

Amphlett had an ironmonger's business in High Street, Dudley between 1780 and 1796. There is reference[10] to his having tested iron produced by Henry Cort in 1785. His knowledge of the coal, iron and nail trade obviously fitted him for his appointment at Horseley. Unfortunately, he was to die on 14 January 1801 and left to his daughter by his first marriage and his son equal shares of his one-third share in the Horseley partnership. Edward Dixon[11] had been a partner with John Finch in the banking business. He became High Sheriff of Worcestershire in 1799 and died on 10 August 1807 aged 66. The third partner William Bedford,[12] a solicitor of Birmingham, as the survivor was to play a leading part in the concern. He died in 1832. He was connected with the Birmingham Canal Navigation Company and in 1792 was engaged as their solicitor.[13]

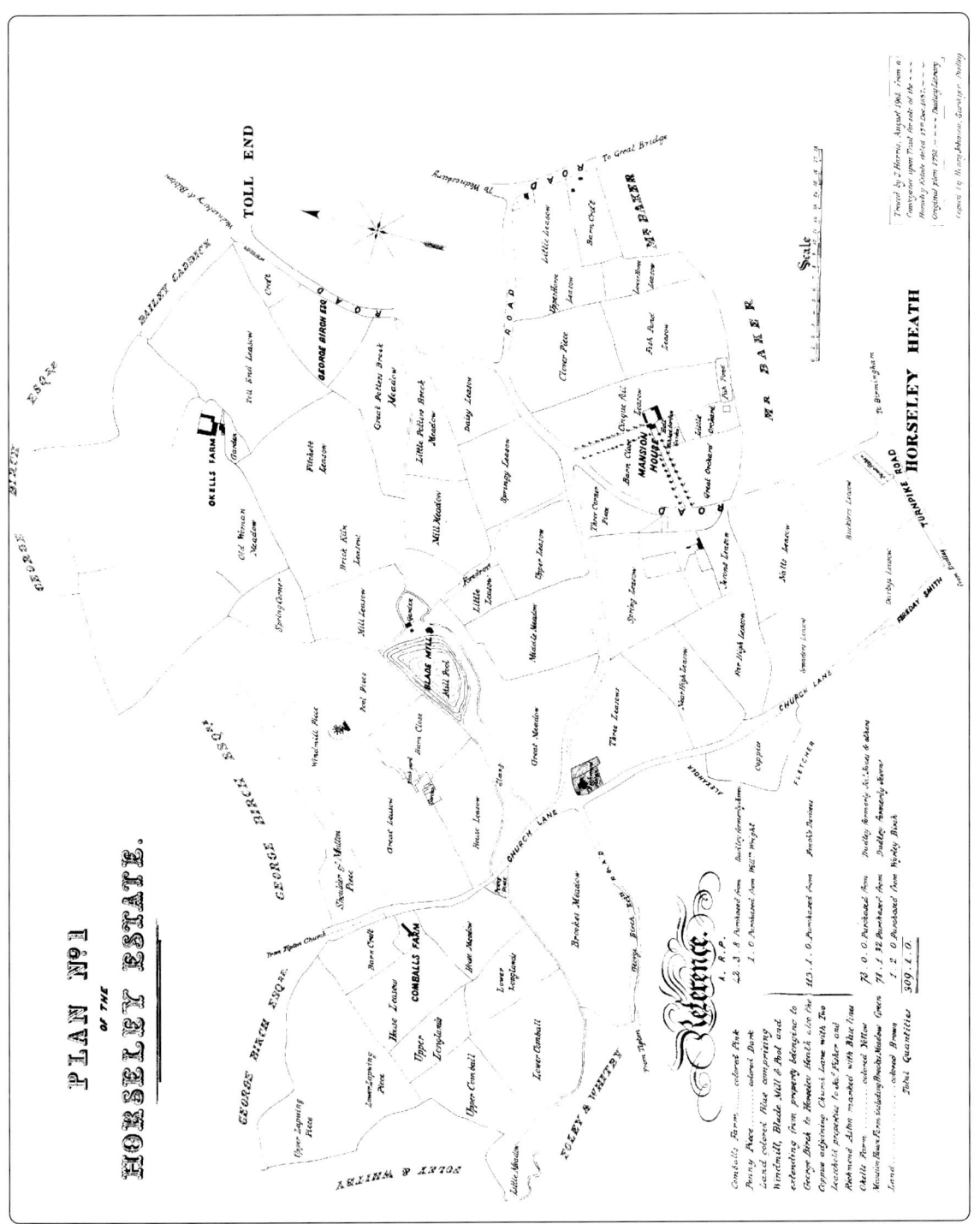

Fig. 1. Plan No. 1 of the Horseley Estate, 1792

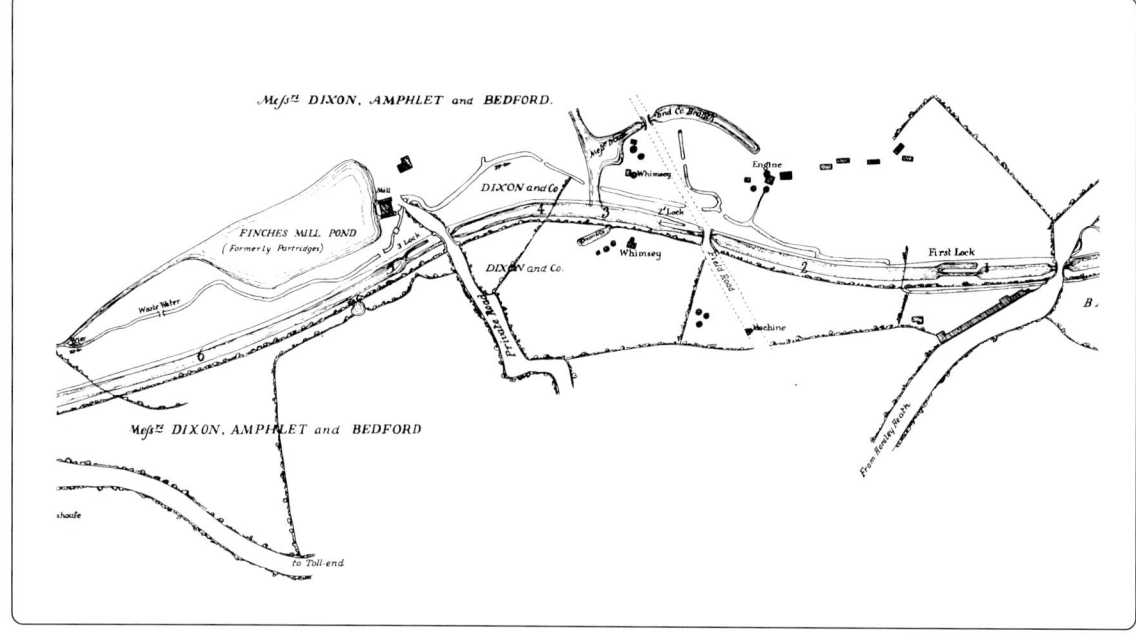

Fig. 2. Canal plan showing the earliest coal working, c. 1797

THE ESTABLISHMENT OF THE HORSELEY COLLERIES

On the formation of the partnership Joseph Amphlett took up residence at Horseley House, Tipton, described in 1798 by Shaw[14] as 'an excellent square house, pleasantly situated at a proper distance from the coal works'. The completion of the canal into the estate was of prime importance and the partnership approached the canal company on 16 March 1792 as 'they were about the immediate erection of considerable works upon the adjoining lands'.[15] The Canal Company decided[16] to

'level and make estimates of the expense of executing the same both with and without locks and to stake out such branch in the line which will be most commodius to the mine and land owners.'

The partnership first proposed (3 August 1792) that the branch should be built with two locks, but one week later suggested that the required rise was 15 feet and since this cut 'would be made much more commodius . . . by three locks' they would offer to pay

'one fifth part of the whole expense of erecting such locks and will give the Company satisfactory security that no such locks shall be at any time or in any manner injured by the working of their mines.'

The Canal Company agreed to a branch with three locks each of 5 foot rise and sent their engineers to Tipton to agree a price they would pay for the purchase of the land. A price of £84 per acre was agreed and the articles[17] indicated that the canal should be completed in two stages, firstly to a meadow near Partridges Mill Pool and secondly when called upon by the partnership 'the length of a boat into Brookes Meadow'.

The initial work was in hand by October 1793 when surplus bricks were being disposed of from the site. By 1795 the partnership were complaining to the Canal Company over a bridge on the canal where it had been found that[18]

> 'owing to the extra swell of the water in that part of the canal, some of the highest Oxfordshire Cabins had been obstructed in their passage under it.'

It was agreed that the arch of the bridge would be raised. This reference indicates clearly that extensive trade was already being undertaken, and at about the same time the partnership were building wharfs and requested that the water be drawn out of the canal for that purpose. At the end of that year, a meeting with the Canal Company surveyor was requested and agreed in order to ascertain the amount of land taken for the canal.

The earliest reference to a mine pumping engine on the Horseley Estate occurs in November 1796, when the Canal Company examined whether feeders could be provided to supply the top lock on the Horseley Branch – then known as the Toll End Branch – and

> 'to ascertain the quantity of water raised by the Engines of Messrs. Dixon & Co . . . and into what parts of the canal such waters are discharged . . . and also what quantity of water is likely to become requisite . . . when the Collierys' shall be in full working.'

Mr. Bull of the Canal Company made his estimates of the quantity of water being raised by the engine(s) but it does not survive and so no indication of the engine(s) size can be deduced at this time.

Trade from the estate increased further and in 1796 the turn out from the Toll End Branch into the main canal was improved.

In 1797 Mr. Robins of the Canal Company made a survey of the land taken in the building of the Canal and details of the costs for the 15 feet of lockage were assessed at £1,369 5s 3d by Mr. Bull of the Canal Company. One-fifth of this sum, £273 17s 0d was to the account of the Partnership in accordance with their agreement. Mr. Bull noted that at that time (5 July 1797) the third or top lock was not completed.

The Partnership's account against the Canal Company amounted to £393 14s $2^3/_4$d being the cost of the lands, bricks supplied and damages to land charged at 84/- per acre per annum. This account remains[19] and is the earliest known communication extant from the Partnership and written from the 'Horseley Colliery' showing that the workings were known by that name from their commencement.

A most informative plan[20] of the early workings on the Horseley Estate has been produced (Fig. 2) from three separate sheets of the original Canal Survey. The eastern section represents the situation in 1785 and shows the first section of the canal to be built. The brook which flowed from the Mill Pool has been diverted to the south of the canal. The centre section of the plan is undated but probably made in 1797 as referred to earlier. It shows clearly the first mines to the east of the Mill Pool with three pairs of shafts, two pairs each having a whimsey and the third a pumping engine which is pumping into the brook. Other rectangular buildings are shown as is a weighing machine on a field road which represented the land access. A small canal arm has been built to serve one pair of shafts and a significant arm and basin to serve the other two. The three locks are shown, the top one being adjacent to the old mill. The western section of the plan was made in 1809 and represents the later extension beyond the 'length of a boat into Brookes Meadow' which was to join with the Upper Level. It shows three more locks, four arms to serve other coal pits and a feeder into the canal, known from later evidence to be from another pumping engine.

As mining continued at the Horseley Collieries, difficulties were encountered with the sinking of the locks. In 1802 the middle lock had cracked, by 1804 one lock had sunk by about one foot and representatives of the Horseley Collieries believed the locks would sink four or five feet below original level! By 1808 the third lock had been raised two feet and the second lock had sunk a similar amount.

In 1808 the Canal Company made proposals to extend the canal to the upper or Summit Level and in 1809 the Horseley Colliery Company were paid £961 4s 0d for their section of canal. A price of £130 per acre was agreed for the land and the conveyance was completed on 5 October 1809 and signed by members of the families of the two original partners together with William Bedford. A through route was then established.

From later evidence[21] it is confirmed that two engines at Horseley were of Newcomen type and a Birmingham Canal Navigation survey of 1827 gives their capacities and working hours:

a) Pump diameter 12 inches stroke 7' 0" working at 8 strokes per minute for 6 hours per day lifting 3.16 locks per day.
b) Pump diameter 9 inches stroke 5' 0" working at 10 strokes per minutes for 22 hours per day lifting 5.82 locks per day.

THE BUILDING OF THE FURNACES

The first iron furnaces on the Horseley Estate were built between 1808 and 1809 for new lessees. William Bedford complained of delay by the Canal Company in completing the new extension to which Mr. Hood retorted[22] that 'the bricklayers he had engaged had been enticed from their engagements to erect iron furnaces upon the estate for the lessees.' The furnaces were to be blown by a Boulton & Watt Engine and a significant letter was sent from the Horseley Collieries on 18 March 1809 to Boulton and Watt signed by H. Golding for the Company. The letter asked 'when the engine you have underhand for the works will be ready as it will be needed immediately'. The partners are listed and were: Richard Harrison of Wolverton, Near Stoney Stratford; John Oliver, Banker of Stoney Stratford; Richard Kitely of Stoney Stratford; and Joseph Smith of Coseley, near Dudley.

Joseph Smith wrote to Boulton & Watt on 23 October 1809:

'As you intimated to Mr. Golding a wish that your man should be present at the setting on of the Engine, I hereby inform you we shall be ready by Wednesday morning, if not tomorrow night. If he comes, I could wish for him to be here tomorrow as our furnace is quite ready for the blast, and the sooner the engine starts the better.'

A pencilled foot note reads 'G. Taylor is directed to go over this day (Tuesday)' and so on 24 October 1809 the engineering side of the Horseley Company was founded.

From drawings in the Boulton & Watt Collection[23] it is learned that the engine had a steam cylinder of 43 inches diameter by 9 foot length. The beam was of cast iron $4\frac{1}{2}$ inches thick where the link spindles were to fit, 25 feet centres in two sides each cast full length. The engine house was 36 ft by 14 ft inside, 40 ft by 20 ft outside and 42 feet from base to eaves with some 16 feet underground. The entablature beam was supported on tapered cast iron columns. The cistern was 7' 6" by 9' 0" and 8' 0" deep.

Visiting the area in 1821 Joshua Field[24] went to Horseley and recorded the following observations in his diary:

> 'The blowing engine has a cylinder of 42 (sic) inches made about 14 (sic) years back by Boulton & Watts, working two Blast cylinders of 6 feet diameter each, one at the end of the beam 7' 0" stroke, the other half or 3' 6'. These both blow into a cylinder 6 feet diameter having a fly piston, then into a water regulator 30 ft x 10 ft x 6 ft deep, made of cast iron covered by brick and standing in a brick cistern.
>
> There is a small rod from the fly piston to the hand gear with levers etc., so contrived that the engine will stop at the end of each stroke until the piston has descended a little way, then it permits the engine to take another stroke. So if only one furnace is on the engine will make a long pause between each stroke, if two on less pause; if three on no pause at all. The apparatus is very simple and called the Catterack. There is also a safety valve which is lifted should the piston ever rise up too high which lets the wind escape.
>
> The oldest engines have only the valve and work at the same rate at all times and allow the spare blast to escape but this is a very wasteful plan. Some have the Catterack simpler by making it stop only at the top of the stroke so the piston moves down and up when a double pause is made, this is as good as the other if the regulator is large. At these Works the wind was formerly let into the water regulator at one end and out at the other, but was found to carry water with it into the furnaces which reduces both the quantity and quality of the iron. It has been altered by draining all into the stand pipe leading to the furnaces and the objection obviated. This engine works also a pump to raise water for a small water wheel employed to draw the waggons with two barrows upon them up a sloping railroad to the top of the furnaces. The machinery to do all this is very complicated and requires a man to be at the top always, the same thing is done infinitely more simpler at other works.'

Details of the extent of the works in 1813 is given in the Tipton Rating Book:[25]

Horseley Colliery Company
2 Furnaces
1 Puddling Furnace
1 Finery
3 Cupolas
2 Engines
6 Pitts
House and office

Other pits on the estate continued under the style Dixon Amphlett & Bedford and did not cease trading until 1875. It continued as an Estate and earlier this century E. W. Peacock of Dixon House, Tipton, was Estate Manager and E. G. Amphlett, J. P. of Worthing, Sussex, as direct male descendant held the one-sixth share handed down from his great grandfather. The engineering activities of the Horseley Company from which the present company descends, flows from the new lessees who became a separate concern which will be considered further.

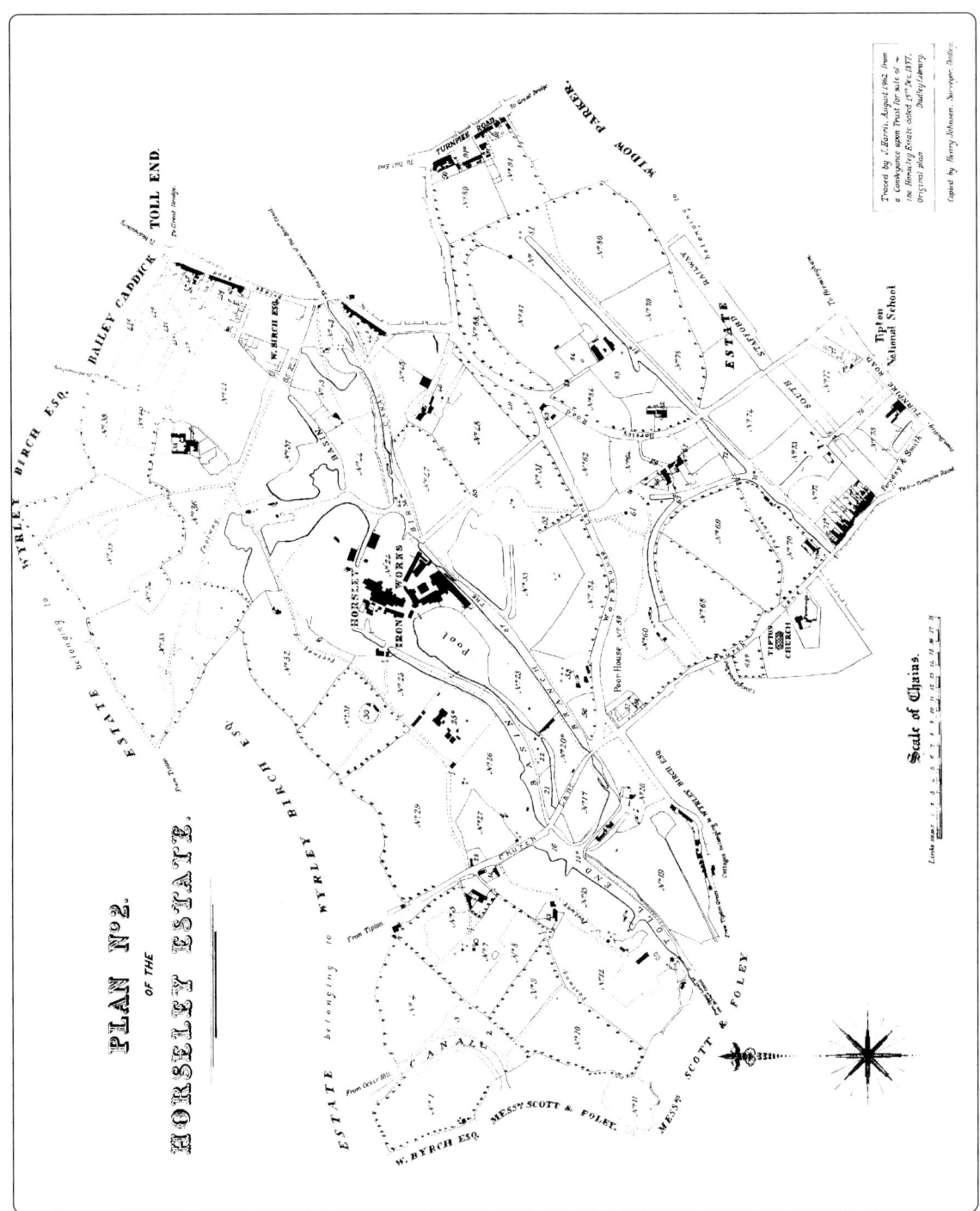

Fig. 3. Plan No. 2 of the Horseley Estate, 1857

THE BUILDING OF THE ENGINEERING WORKS

The furnaces and foundry being established, the lessees turned their attention to the building of an engineering works. How the partners from Stoney Stratford became involved at Tipton is not known but it may be assumed that they provided capital. The local man, Joseph Smith, is better known. He had taken a lease of 11 acres of the Great Coal Land[26] at Sedgley from Joseph Lane in 1808. At the same time he had leased[27] 4 acres in the Priests Leasowe. Significantly, a map of 1812 by Sheriff indicates the workings at Priests Leasowe and shows them under the style 'Manby and Smith'. Aaron Manby[28] was to join Smith at Horseley about 1813 and was to take a leading hand in the development of the engineering works. Manby had gained experience in banking on the Isle of Wight, but at Wolverhampton he was allowed credit by the Canal Company in 1809 and in 1812 wrote[29] to the President of the Board of Trade seeking orders for munitions. At this time he was still with Smith at Wolverhampton. On 1 January 1813 he leased a house on the Dudley-Wolverhampton Turnpike Road for 14 years and in the same year he took out a patent (No. 3705) for making bricks out of refuse slag from blast furnaces. In this patent he is described as an Ironmaster of Wolverhampton.

Certainly by 29 August 1815 Manby was at Horseley as Managing Partner. The Yorkshire Ironmaster Thomas Butler[30] of Kirkstall Forge, Leeds visited Horseley where he recorded 'those well managed works' were in charge of Aaron Manby. Butler also noted:

> 'they make most of their metal in (to) castings-make prepared plate out of waste castings, price £6.2.6 (ton), pay Quarter Day, 2 months bill, sometimes forge pig.'

During his visit he saw two furnaces in blast. Butler does not mention the engineering works and the Tipton Rating Books of 1815 show[31] similar entries to those of 1813 except for the addition of two more houses and two meadows.

It would seem that the Engineering Works was built between 1815 and 1816, and the first reference to them is made by a German Engineer, John George Bodmer who visited[32] on 20 and 21 November 1816. He recorded:

> 'I went with Mr. Aston (Agent of the Canal Company) to the Horseley Iron-works, where I was received in a very friendly manner and after I had given up my letter of recommendation, I went for a meal and booked accommodation at an Inn. After dinner and after Mr. Aston and his agent had gone home, I went with my landlord – a good John Bull – to the Horseley Ironworks where the poor man twisted his ankle when jumping over a pile of coke. But then Mr. Peyke, a relation of Mr. Mennlin came and showed me with the utmost cordiality everything noteworthy in these fine works.'

Next day Mr. Peyke took him again to Horseley where he noted 'everything is illuminated by gas'. It is known from later evidence that the gas works was in the new fabrication works.

Bodmer also made a plan of the works but most unfortunately this has not survived. In the obituary of Manby's son it states that his father had 'established a large engineering factory at Horseley, a few miles from Birmingham'. Manby had also been a member of the Institution of Civil Engineers.

Fortunately a very detailed description and plan[33] of the works was made by Joshua Field when he visited the works on Thursday 23 August 1821. Field was met by Aaron

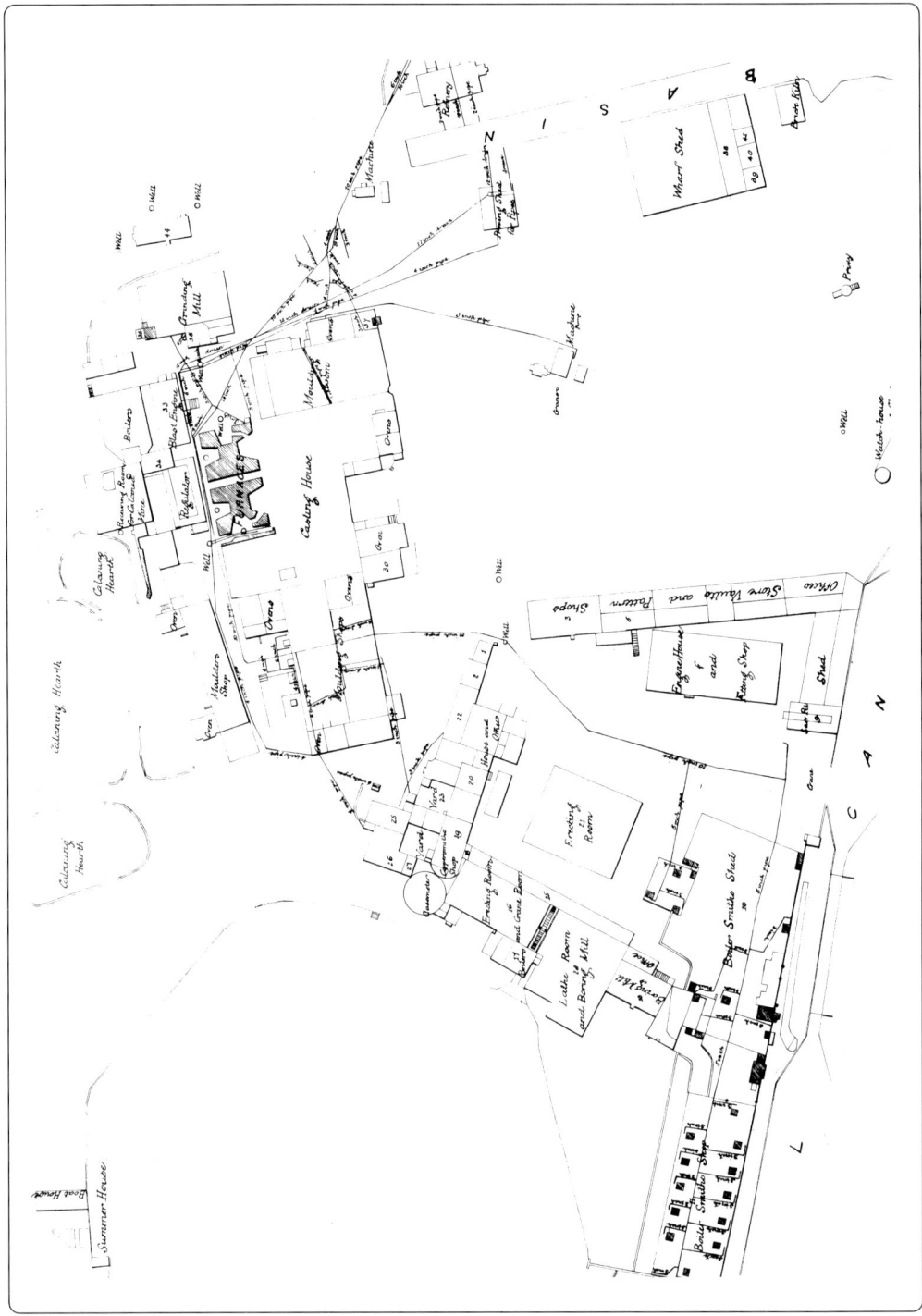

Fig. 4. Detailed plan of the Horseley Works, 1849

Manby who, feeling rather unwell, arranged for Mr. Davis the foreman of the engine factory to show him round. His detailed report is given in Appendix 1 and discusses the furnaces, the work in hand and the separate engine factory driven either by a steam engine or a 25 foot diameter water wheel from the ancient mill pool. He also describes the gas works by which the works was lit. His small plan of the works is shown by other evidence to be quite accurate in detail.

The works would seem to have altered little in the ensuing years. A map of Tipton by Pigott Smith made in 1825/6 shows an outline similar to Field's sketch and Wm. Fowler's map of Tipton of 1849, which is in fact the Tithe Award Plan, shows a similar outline.

A plan[34] of the Horseley Estate in 1857 was made when the estate was the subject of a conveyance upon trust for sale. This plan (Fig. 3) is accompanied by a schedule which details the occupiers of all the areas and relates to areas by the field names of the 1792 plan. It is fascinating to study the developments over the 65 years and to appreciate how the peaceful agricultural scene has been transformed into an industrial area. Most of the areas with pits are noted as being 'in hand', clearly those being operated by the original Dixon Amphlett and Bedford Parnership successors. The 'Horseley Ironworks, cinder mound, private canal, pool etc' is shown to be in the hands of 'Messrs. Bramah & Others' to whom it had been leased.

This plan is also important, as it shows the location of two other furnaces built near to the works on land sold to John Colbourne and Sons. From other evidence,[35] they are known to have been in operation since 1849 and must not be confused with the 1809 Horseley Furnaces which appear to have been in work until 1842, when only one was at work and 1843 when both were out. In 1852 they were available to let upon application to Messrs. Broad & Tierney.

It would seem that the whole Horseley Works ran into financial difficulties about 1846 and fell into the hands of the Stratford Bank from where it was rescued by three local ironmasters: J. J. Bramah, Deeley and Cochrane. The change in ownership was anticipated on 14 February 1844 when an advertisement appeared in the Wolverhampton Chronicle giving notice that the whole of the works would be offered for sale by the month end or in early March. The notice refers to "the whole of the truly valuable and important MACHINERY, ENGINES, CRANES, FORGE MILL and ENGINE PATTERNS, GASOMETER, &c at those celebrated works known as the Horseley Ironworks, Tipton."

There follows a detailed list of the machinery and installations at the works and a reference that a catalogue would be available from a Mr. Danks of High Street, Dudley.

It follows with a note - "N.B – The Assignees would still be willing to treat for the disposal of the entirety of the Machinery and Works, so as to obviate the necessity for a sale in lots; and this being a most desirable investment, considering the capabilities and well known celebrity of the Horseley Works, as to the erection of new docks, &c. on the Lancashire and Cheshire coasts at Liverpool will create a demand for Staffordshire castings, which may be here produced of superior qualities and at a moderate expense, it is to be hoped that some capitalist will turn his attention to this opportunity in which case application to treat may be made to JOHN WILLIAMS, Esq. Friary, Handsworth near Birmingham."

However shortly afterwards a further short advertisement appeared on 13 March 1844 informing all concerned that the sale would not take place as the whole works had been sold on 5 March to Messrs. Bramah and Company of the Woodside Ironworks, Dudley as a going concern and would operate as the "Horseley Iron Works".

Only some 18 months later a further advertisement appeared in the Wolverhampton Chronicle for 19 Nov. 1845 giving notice of an auction sale of "The ENTIRETY and LEASE of those well known and justly celebrated WORKS situated at Tipton carried on for many years by Messrs. York, Harrison and Co and lately by Messrs. Bramah, Cochrane and Deeley by whom great improvements and additions have been made, and known as the Horseley Iron Works." The advertisement then gives very detailed information on the works and its equipment which although it repeats some information in the 1843 advertisement it is more detailed and was as follows.

"The entirety comprises immense Founderies, calculated to carry on that department to any extent, and fitted with large and small double and single sided iron cranes, with blocks and chains complete, stoves, air furnaces, cupolas, pipe pits, &c.; to these are connected two blast furnaces, with a most powerful engine, cylinder 42 inches diameter, 8 feet stroke, with three oblong flue boilers, 24 feet by 6 feet, 6 inches long, with blowing apparatus complete, a portable bright ten horse engine, which has been used for drawing up the materials to the furnaces, extensive smith's shops, with numerous hearths, double and single cranes, boshes, bellows, &c. a four horse portable engine, and a regulating damper complete, three large punching presses, gasometer punching press and countersinking machine, immense and powerful wood wharf crane with iron column, gear and chain complete, bed and side lathes, boring mill, large and small planing machines, drilling machines, with driving apparatus complete, a marine engine, slotting machines, screwing machines, travelling winches, with rochet tramways for lifting great weights, to which are annexed immense pully blocks, with ropes complete, a twenty horse power horizontal high-pressure engine, with cylinder 17 inches diameter, large face plate lathe, capable of turning 20 feet diameter, with planed iron beds, one single and two double-sliding rests driving apparatus complete, a six horse house engine, boring and turning mill, double and single weighing machines, cranes, loam and blacking mills, refineries, pattern makers' shops, and lathes, immense range of fitting and workshops, which are fitted up with work benches, vices &c., extensive warehouses and sheds, pipe proving machine; stables most convenient, and extensive offices, which are fitted up with every convenience, furnace and foundry, wharfs and yards. Also a very large inner yard, for engineering purposes, surrounded by workshops and warehouses, with large entrance folding doors. In the centre of the works is a gasometer, for making gas for lighting the whole premises. The whole of these extensive works are enclosed by a wall, except such parts as are bounded by the canal, and are capable of any extent of business either in the foundry or engineering departments, and are most complete in all respects, and may be put in full operation in a few days. There will also be included in this sale the Horseley House, which is in every way fit for the residence of a principal, or manager, it comprises dining, drawing, and breakfast rooms, kitchens, entrance hall, numerous bedrooms, ale and wine cellars, garden, vinery, and pleasure grounds, stables, and coach houses, and about fourteen acres of meadow land. The approach is by a handsome carriage drive from the main road leading from Tipton to Walsall, &c.

The principal part of the machinery was manufactured by Messrs. Sharp, Roberts, and Co., and by Nasmyth and Co. More full descriptive particulars will be given in the catalogue, which will be ready in a few days, and will be sent to any part of the kingdom on application.

The whole of the said works are held for a term of 21 years from the 25th day of March 1844 (determinable at the option of the lessee, at the end of the first seven or fourteen years), at the low rent of £250 per annum.

The whole of the said works, house, land and premises will be offered for sale in the first instance as an entirety, and if not sold the foundries with the house and land will then be put up separately, and if the same shall be sold, the machinery, engines, shop fittings, and erections belonging to the engineering department will be sold by auction on the premises on the 8th day of December next, in lots.

For further information, apply to WILLAM WILLS, esq. Solicitor, Waterloo Street, Birmingham; SAMUEL DALTON, esq. Solicitor, Dudley or to the Auctioneer."

Exactly what was the immediate result of this auction is not known but certainly by 1849 the works were leased to Messrs. Broad and Tierney and they may well have taken the lease in 1845. The information that the works were held on a lease of 21 years from March 1844 is significant and no doubt influenced the building of the new works in 1865. A very detailed plan was made around 1849 of the engineering works and the furnaces. (Fig 4) and this even shows the underground air and water mains. It is possible to compare the list of plant above with this plan and also to compare with the description given by Joshua Field in 1821 given in Appendix 1.

Clearly the works was fully equipped to manufacture all types of engineering product. The works continued under Broad and Tierney until a decision was made to build a new works some half a mile away – the site of the works discussed in the second part of this book.

The new works were built about 1865/66 and some of the plant transferred from the original works. All the cast iron work of the new works was produced at the old and some of this still survived. When the old works were finally cleared they were demolished. They may well have been severely affected by mining subsidence. Its effect had been a problem from the early days. So ended the first phase of the Company history.

THE BUILDING OF MARINE STEAM ENGINES AND IRON BOATS

One of the chief products of the engineering works in its early days was the building of marine steam engines.[37] The earliest traced was for the Prince of Coburg, built in 1817. Details of all known engines are given in Appendix 2.

Manby was deeply involved in the construction of these steam engines and on 9 July 1821 he took out a patent (No. 4558) for an oscillating marine steam engine and for the use of an intermediate agent (oil) for getting up steam. His subsequent French Patent included both the oscillating engine and an iron ship. Field during his visit to Horseley in 1821 had referred to iron barges then in use for seven years without repair.

Manby's interests became centred more in France and with Captain (later Admiral Sir) Charles Napier formed a company to operate steam packets upon the Seine between Rouen and Paris and immediately began to build their first iron boat at Horseley. Although registered on 30 April 1822 as *Manby* she was generally known as *Aaron Manby*. The boat was 106' 10" by 17' 2" by 7' 2". Burthen, exclusive of engine room 115 $^{23}/_{94}$ tons, 1 deck and 1 mast. Field had seen the vessel under construction during his visit and had drawn the position on his plan and described her in his report: see Appendix 1.

The engine was of 32 Horsepower and the vessel had Oldhams patent[38] paddles fitted either side. The engine had two oscillating cylinders about 27 in diameter by 3 ft stroke and used steam 2 lbs per sq in above atmospheric. On completion the vessel was dismantled and sent to London by canal where she was re-assembled at the Surrey Canal Dock, Rotherhithe. The first river trials were on 9 May 1822 and a detailed report was printed[39] in the *Morning Chronicle* of 14 May. The public were 'much gratified and astonished' by the iron boat and she was described as 'the most complete piece of workmanship in the iron way that has ever been witnessed'. After completion of trials she sailed from London to Rouen arriving 27/28 May after touching Bolougne on 18 May. The fascinating story of her races with vessels of the 'Societe des transports acceleres par eau' are fully detailed by Chaloner and Henderson'.[40] She was sold in 1830 and in 1836 was on the Loire and was only broken up in 1855. A remarkable life for the first iron steam boat.

The hull of the second iron boat for Manby & Napier was built at Horseley in 1822/3 but was engined by Manby from his works at Charenton, Paris to which he had transferred his interests. This vessel was the *Commerce de Paris* and was similar to, but of slightly greater burthen than the *Aaron Manby*. The engines were of 50 horsepower, high pressure. Fuel 657 lbs/hour. Correspondence exists between Horseley and the Grand Surrey Canal and Docks Co. in connection with the hire of an area to build the vessel, eventually agreed at £40 per two months and pro-rata for extra time.

Manby had now severed his connection with Horseley and no further engines were built at Tipton for him, and other orders were much reduced. This had a severe effect upon Horseley, not only by lack of orders but by the significant numbers of men enticed by Manby to move to France. Men were also taken from other Midland works. Such was the concern over this, that by February 1824 a Select Committee had been set up to study 'Artisans and Machinery'. Their report confirmed that three manufactures at Paris were

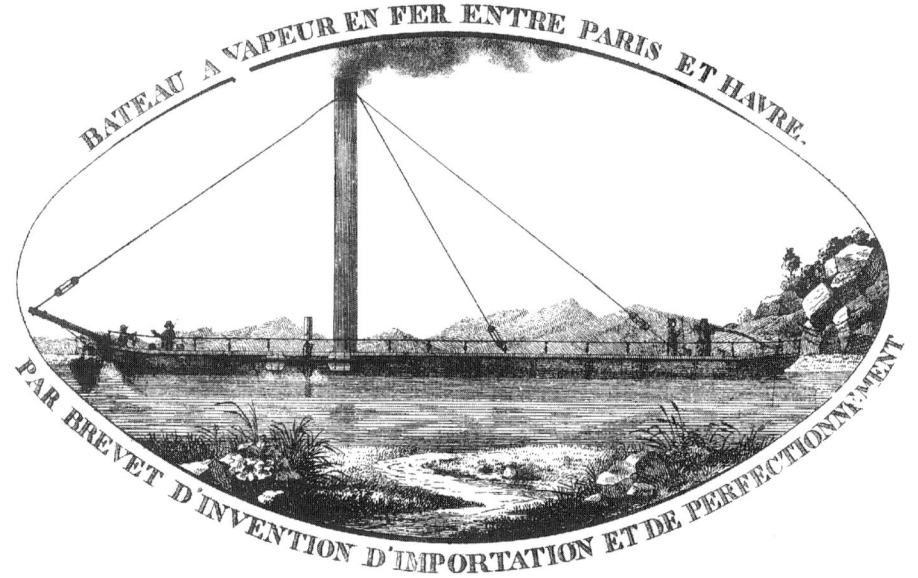

Fig. 5. Aaron Manby, *1821*

run by Englishmen, that at Charenton by Manby who employed many Englishmen. A William Turner of Wolverhampton and a Thomas Lester who had worked at Horseley gave evidence and Manby was reported to have been convicted of enticing workmen. The most important and relevant report was made by Richard Harrison and John Yorke, two of the Horseley Partners. This is quoted in Appendix 3.

Some indication of the dangers of work at that time can be deduced from the statement that 'out of a fund for widows of those who sustain accidents 14 widows are now receiving 2/-d a week from our works'.

A serious stoppage of work had taken place in 1822 when the colliers struck, and had stopped the ironworks and this in turn all the other works dependent on them. Other documents concern this dispute when a number of public statements were issued by both sides. One signed by the Horseley Coal and Iron Company and others, offers the miners 3 shillings per day plus two quarts of good drink for six days per week making 18/- per week. The men gradually returned to work and it was stated

> 'that the Country is again blazing with furnaces–but from the dreadful state in which bankruptcy has involved many of the colliery companies and coal masters, the mining district around us cannot be said to wear a pleasing aspect . . .'

It may have been these difficulties which had encouraged the artizans to venture abroad, where many settled permanently. The Civil Register of Charenton 1825-29 lists[41] the birth of 40 children to the workers at the 'Founderie Anglais' and many of these would be from Tipton. There are many local names among the families and three men married French girls. One was James Davis a relative of Mr. Davis the engine shop foreman at Tipton.

LOCOMOTIVE ENGINE BUILDING[42]

St. Helens and Runcorn Gap Railway

Following the decline in orders for ship's engines the company turned its interest to the building of locomotive engines. Their first were for the St. Helens and Runcorn Gap Railway and were quoted against a specification issued by their engineer C. B. Vignoles in 1832. It read as follows:

> 'The wheels to be 54 inches diameter, Axles 5 inches diameter, cylinders 13 inches, stroke 20 inches, weight with water in the boiler not to exceed 8 tons, the Engine to work with coal and the 4 wheels to be moved. The Boiler guaranteed to generate steam to a power of not less than 2,500 lbs at a velocity of 10 miles per hour giving a capability to the Engine of Drawing 150 tons including its own weight and that of the tender at a rate of 5 miles per hour, up an inclination of 1 in 400.'

Horseley quoted £455 on 26 March 1832, some £200 less than the next competitive price and they obtained an order for three engines, delivery to be on the first's of August, September and October of 1832.

Horseley had obtained the services of an engineer Matthew Loam, the son of a Cornish Beam engine builder and he designed the engines, the first being *Greenall* after the Railway's Chairman, the second *St. Helens* and the third possibly *Runcorn*. They were not particularly successful and on 26 November 1833 C. B. Vignoles was to record:

> 'These engines produced sufficient steam (of which there is indeed at present no possibility of any maker falling short) but they were most complete failures

in the mechanical arrangements, and from that and the low price at which they were taken, it has occurred that for the first week or two after their working on the railway we have seldom or ever had more than one out of the three at work together, the others being laid up for continual repairs. I do not state this as a reproach against the Horseley Company, that concern are sensible that cheap engines do no credit either to makers or to companies.'

On 12 April 1833 the following spares were ordered from Horseley:

'One set spare wheels

Three dozen tubes

Tools for putting in do.

One set screwing tackle for all the gauges of bolts belonging to the engine.'

Some time during late 1832 Loam left to join the new Vulcan Foundry and Isaac Dodds[43] joined Horseley where he was to design the fourth engine for the railway and which was ordered on 26 April 1833. This locomotive was named either *Monarch* or *Mersey* and was a much heavier machine[44] with horizontal inside cylinders working rocking-shafts at the smoke box end of the frame, on the end levers of which were coupled the connecting rods, acting upon outside crank-pins.

A dispute occurred over engines Nos. 2 and 3 which were said not to have 'double tires' to their wheels as fitted to engine No. 1 and Horseley were asked to put them in the same condition as No. 1 which had worked well. When accounts were not settled the Horseley agent John Pollock attended the Railway Company's meeting on 8 November 1833 and claimed that:

'. . . the new engine has been tried on the Liverpool and Manchester Line and its efficiency has been so satisfactory as to cause an order to be given to us to place an engine on that line as soon as possible. An accident occasioned by a piece of wood placed higher on the road than, according to our information, was allowed has caused us to overhaul the whole engine but it will be ready in a few days.'

Fig. 6 Star *Locomotive, 1833-4*

Fig. 7. Swannington Incline Engine, 1833

The accounts were agreed on 30 June 1834 and on 10 August 1835 the railway company agreed to sell engines Nos. 1 and 2 and they were advertised in the *Leeds Mercury* in September and October as having cylinders 12½ by 20".

The Liverpool and Manchester Railway

The locomotive on the Liverpool and Manchester Railway to which John Pollock had referred was offered by Horseley on 18 November 1833 on a 'sale or return' basis. This was to be the *Star* and was stated[45] to have solid plate frames with the horn plates welded on, the boiler made to expand and contract on the frames, horizontal cylinders outside and the motion given to the valve by a return crank, working the eccentric-rod to an arc or link moving by a reversing lever, the position of the eccentric-rod in the arc, which gave the forward or backward motion, and also varied the stroke of the valves.

A pencil drawing[46] of the *Star* subsequently inked in was discovered from which the principle dimensions can be scaled:

'Driving wheels	5' 0" diameter
Leading wheels	3' 0" diameter
Wheelbase	5' 8"
Boiler	3' 6" diameter by 8' 6" long
Chimney top above rails	11' 10" by 11" diameter
Cylinders	Approximately 11" diameter by 18" stroke'

By 15 December 1834 the engine was recorded[47] as 'now putting together on the railway'. However, during her trials a sad accident occurred, the circumstances being recorded[48] on 2 March 1835:

> 'Read Mr. Dixon's Report of the state of the Way, also his account of the accident to the Engine of the two o'clock train from Liverpool on Saturday last. Owing to the switch leading out of the St. Helens junction line being left wrong placed the Horseley Engine the STAR which was proceeding with the train to Manchester was jerked off the rails and ran across to the opposite side of the road when she came into collision with the Caledonia Engine and Tender. Ralph Thompson the Company's Engine man was thrown off and killed on the spot, a working mechanic belonging to the Horseley Company was also thrown off and had his foot badly crushed by the Engine. The Company's fireman and Barnsley the Horseley Company's Engineer escaped without much injury. The Engine having broken loose from the train, the coaches kept the way and after about $1/2$ hours delay, were forwarded to Manchester by another Engine.
>
> The Caledonia Engine was considerably damaged by the collision and her tender was literally broken to pieces. The Horseley Engine was a good deal damaged, her frame being twisted and one of her cylinders and some of the steam pipes being broken.'

This was a great misfortune to the Horseley Company as the engine had been working well and had been offered at £970. The Liverpool and Manchester Railway declined to purchase the engine but agreed to pay for the damages–a sum of £179 4s 5d plus £9 14s 1d interest being agreed against the claim by Horseley for £492 2s 8d.

The Dublin and Kingstown Railway

Horseley then offered the engine to the Dublin and Kingstown Railway, a company with whom they had previously had contact, having offered to supply a locomotive on 2 September 1833. Vignoles had issued a specification for this but Isaac Dodds commented in detail on it (see Appendix 4)[49] in a most informative manner. Horseley offered an engine with:

Cylinders: 11 inch diameter by 17" stroke, inside frames.
Wheels: 4 at 5' 0" diameter on straight axles.
Boiler: 3' 7' diameter by 10' 6" long including firebox and chimney box.
Tubes: 100, $1 1/2$" to 2" diameter.
Boiler Pressure: 50 lbs per sq in.
Dodds patent slide valves.
Price: £800.

No decision was taken on orders in November 1833, but T. F. Bergin the D.&K.R. Secretary observed that Tayleur & Co. were 'out of the question as I find Loam not young Stephenson, would have the direction'! Orders were eventually placed elsewhere and the next contact was over the *Star*, which they purchased for £700 on 14 August 1835. After delivery the pair of 'small wheels' were found to be unsound, with their spokes loose and so Horseley were directed to supply a new pair. The account was settled in January 1836.

The Locomotive was modified in 1838 by the D.&K.R. and probably had a further pair of wheels fitted. She fouled points shortly after and was damaged, derailed again in May 1839 and again in 1840. Parts of the locomotive were later built into a new engine the *Belle isle* which was still at work in 1870.

Leicester and Swannington Railway

Horseley supplied a stationary winding engine to the Leicester and Swannington Railway to operate the Swannington Incline which was at a slope between 1 in 17 and 1 in 24, and length of 33 chains. This engine was designed by Robert Stephenson.

Advertisements were placed for the engine, and the order given to Horseley on 23 April 1833 at a price of £750. It started work on 25 November 1833 with a cylinder $18\frac{1}{4}$" in dia and stroke 3' 6", working pressure 80 lbs per sq in and embodies one of the earliest known applications of the piston slide valve. Another feature is the 'gab' motion wherein the movement of the valve is controlled by hand when the engine is being 'manouvered' and the eccentric subsequently engaged by means of a slot in the end of its rod. There is some fine embossed decorative work on the castings of the engine.

The engine shaft broke on 29 November 1833 and a new one of 'best wrought iron' fitted. Isaac Dodds had to attend himself on 15 January 1834 in connection with a failure of the boiler which he judged could be repaired in a week for about £10. The boiler was replaced in 1839 and Stephenson stated that corrosion had been caused by failure to clean out the boiler at short intervals.

The engine was later modified and then worked until 1948 and in 1952 it was removed to the York Railway Museum where it may be seen in motion.

Horseley also carried out repairs to the *Comet* and the *Phoenix* locomotives at Tipton. These had been supplied to the Leicester and Swannington Railway by Robert Stephenson and both he and his father George were involved in discussions on the failure of these and other engines of the Company. They judged it due 'entirely from the nature of the water and its effects upon the Tubes and Boilers'. The repairs proved difficult and time consuming and Horseley had to threaten legal action to get settlement of £800.

BRIDGE BUILDING

It is for bridges, mainly cast iron, that the Company is most well known. The earliest traced[50] was a swing bridge built at East India Docks, London in 1816. Another early bridge of 1820 still remains over the Grand Union Canal at Brentford. Many roving bridges cast between 1824 and 1836 exist on the Birmingham Canal Navigations and are of differing pattern, all remaining in excellent condition, many showing grooves where the ropes of countless barges have rubbed away the metal (see Appendix 5).

Each bridge consists of two main castings each side joined by a central locking plate. The main castings also contain the hand rail section and must have proved difficult to cast with their combination of thick and thin iron. The decks are formed from smaller cast flanged plates which were bolted in place to present a smooth surface to the underside of the bridge. This profile is a feature of another series of identical bridges on the Coventry and Oxford Canals built 1832-34, which may well have been designed by C. B. Vignoles (see Appendix 6). One of these was moved by the present company in 1969 to a new site within the city of Coventry from nearby Sowe Common.

One of the most famous bridges is the 1829 Galton Bridge at Smethwick, designed by Thomas Telford with a span of 150 feet. It remains as an industrial monument after being in continuous use until about 1970. There is a delightful bridge over the river at Hampton Lucy near Stratford on Avon built at the charge of the Rector in 1829 having cast tracery reminiscent of church windows. With the coming of the railways very many bridges were

Fig. 8. Cast iron bridge on the Oxford Canal, 1832-4

built including one at Nash Mills[51] on the London-Birmingham Railway in 1836 the subject of a well known engraving. A section of the G.W.R. Shifnal Bridge is preserved at Tipton and this includes the company name and the date of 1848.

CONCLUSIONS

The versatility of the facilities and skills of the Company are reflected in the many types of construction in which they became engaged. It was a self-contained unit producing from its own raw materials iron, cast and wrought and turning these into many final forms. In addition to the principal products discussed many other fields were entered. There are references to many early connections with the gas industry[52] in which Aaron Manby was concerned including the first supply to Cheltenham, in pumping plant[53] and numerous other mechanical and constructional forms.

The history recounted shows clearly the rapid change from the agricultural to the industrial environment in this part of the Black Country. This change involved the building of the canals, the introduction of gas and then the coming of the railways. On all these developments the Company was proud to cast its name for posterity – HORSELEY.

ACKNOWLEDGEMENTS

Help has been received from many authorities, in particular British Waterways Offices at Gloucester and Wolverhampton and the BTC Archives at London. The writer is particularly indebted to the following individuals, G. E. C. Townsend, the late W. K. V. Gale,

Fig. 9. Galton Bridge, Smethwick, 1829

Fig. 10. C.I. Roving Bridge on Oxford Canal – 1832.

D. M. Huffer and the late J. S. Roper. His colleagues John Harris and Robert Wild traced the early plans and Miss Anne Greenway kindly typed the drafts. To these and many others the author offers his sincere thanks.

APPENDIX 1

Diary of a tour made in 1821 by Joshua Field through the Midland manufacturing districts: extract relative to visit to Horseley

On Thursday 23 August 1821 Field arrived at the Horseley Iron Works, to be met by Aaron Manby,

'who expressed himself very glad to see me having heard of me before, and being himself rather unwell deputed Mr. Davis, the foreman of the engine factory to walk over the works with us and he would join us afterwards. Horseley Iron Works belongs to a company of three or four individuals of which Mr. Manby is one and has the management. At this work there are three Blast Furnaces, two of them at work from which the iron is wholly cast into goods . . .'

The three furnaces tap into a large foundry where the largest casting can be made. Here were large columns for the London docks and many castings for the Calcutta Mint Rolling Mill for Rennie, beds, large wheels, shafts; the latter are rough turned to see that they are sound. These castings are not all made from the blast furnace but in a mixture of $1/2$ Shropshire iron of which they use a great quantity from Lightmoor Furnaces belonging to the Colebrook Company. Almost all the castings are made in dry sand. The flasks are not nailed but cast with grating about 6 ins square and 4" bars, the sand is red and seems very strong. There is a separate small foundry for green sand castings, 2 large cupola and several smaller furnaces blow from the blast engine. A 6H engine is placed near the foundry which drives three lathes roughly made and having no change of motion to them. These are employed in cutting off the heads of rollers and shafts and trying the bearings, turning the ends of columns etc. also working mill for beating loam and grinding coal into dust.

The former operation is done by a pair of rollers about 2' 6" diameter, $1^{1}/_{2}$" thick having pins standing about 3" through them thus, which rolling in the loam, knead it and mix it well. The coal dust is ground by a pair of horizontal stones on the floor above. It is said that the loam is beat much better this way than any other.

There is a Finery fire at which they refine all the waste castings and sell it in that state to the neighbouring ironmasters.

The Engine factory is parted off from the rest of the Works and none admitted except on business. It consists of a large yard with several shops and sheds but much of the work is performed out of doors. The castings are all done at the other part of the works and only fitted up here.

A large water wheel of about 25-ft diameter x 2-ft wide originally drove the lathes but being short of water, a small boat engine is attached to it of 6H Power to aid it. When there is water it is let on the wheel; when we were there, there was no water. The engine has a cistern two side beams and an horizontal or upright cone about the angle of ours, the enduction passage going through the small end. The boring bar and lathes are connected by a train of wheel works on the other side of the wall. The large boring bar is about 1-ft diameter and 12-ft long, hollow and is slit along one side by which the head is moved with a rack coming out at the end and attached by a swivel so the rack stands still. The largest cylinder it has bored is 8-ft diameter. There is no provision for holding the cylinder but by temporary means.

This bar was in motion so I judge there is no means of throwing it out of gear. There are two lathes besides it one hook and only one motion. A plate chuck which applies to every purpose, a strong cast iron bed full of chase mortices forms the floors; by these holes the back centre and the rest are fixed anywhere they may be required.

There is also a machine to screw bolts and tap nuts. It is merely a chuck with a square to hold the tap or the bolt head. The dies are held in a square hole in the middle of a bar which slides laterally up to the chuck. This is moved by hand until the screw is stuck. The taps are very long and very taper, so once passing along cuts the nut. This machine was so covered with grease it was hardly possible to see how it performed. The screws were tolerably good.

There is also a little engine with swaying cylinder about four horse power. An air pump is worked between them in a cistern below the ground. They have late made one from the same patterns for a small boat at Dublin, only the air pump is kept above the floor and fixes on the 'A' frames. The valves are all contrived in the gudgeons of the cylinders.

Mr. Manby has taken a patent for it but considers the patent of no value having heard since that the same thing has been done before him; he however intends to adopt it for boats in consequence of its simplicity and is now making one of 32H power for an iron steam boat building for the service.

This iron boat has the bottom and stern up, is 17 ft wide, 106 ft long, quite flat at bottom with angle iron, the plate is $\frac{1}{4}$ cross seams but with a bar inside, the fore and aft seams lap'd, square tuck like a ships boat. The ribs are made of common square angle iron. She is to have a Keelson of wood and beams for the engine, wood beams and deck also wood, is expected to draw very little (1' 6") water and intended to carry goods from Rouen to Paris. The paddles are to be upon Mr. Oldhams plan to have two wheels on each side one before the other, each wheel to have two feathering blades. The total width is not to exceed 23 ft., the size of the bridges, so the wheels will not be more than 2' 6". The vessel is to be put together at Brentford and worked over the season.

The two boilers are made thus open under the fires (sketch).

The small double engine is intended to drive a punching and cutting machine of the ordinary kind such as it used by every Boilermaker in Staffordshire.

There were some workshops upstairs which we did not see, but suppose there was nothing worth seeing as Mr. Manby wished us to see everything. The patterns are kept in a yard parted off with sheds round two sides of it in tolerable order. Our pattern of the press is there in good order and may be had at any time.

There is a very compact gas work at this place. It consists of three pairs of oval retorts and the tar passed through two round ones at the end by which it is mostly made into gas. The gas is purified by passing it through dry lime. The pipe from the retorts into the main is done neater than commonly.

A short cut comes up from this canal up to the works. Mr. M. has several iron barges which have been at work seven years without any repairs and says wood barges would have cost much to repair them and would be worn out in that time.

The d slides are made of iron and a metal face on the cylinder; this Mr. Davis considers the best way. They are not all decided upon any kind of valve, making them in many ways. The engine working the lathe is an upright one about the angle of ours having the eduction pipe going through the small end.

APPENDIX 2

A. Engines for steam boats supplied by Horseley under Aaron Manby

Date	Name	Owner	Vessel Size	Notes
1817	Prince of Coburg	Henry Smith. Built at Gainsborough	75' 6" x 14' 4" x 5' 10" deep Burthen 71 $^{67}/_{94}$ Until 1819 then 52 $^{58}/_{94}$ tons	Vessel owned by Smith & Manby to 1 June 1819 when Manby sold his share to Smith. Sold to Ward and Fitzhugh in February 1820 to become first steam vessel on Cowes-Southampton route. Engines removed in 1828 and hull used until 1846 as floating blacksmith's shop at Southampton, where there is a painting of the hull in Tudor House Museum.
1818	Albion	Henry Smith		
1819	Maria	Henry Smith	Tug	
1819	Favourite	Henry Smith	Tug	
1820	Leeds	Gutteridge		
1822	Medina	Ward & Fitzhugh		Second vessel for their service Cowes-Southampton. Sold in 1825 to Liverpool owners who removed her engines.
Circa 1821	Small boat at Dublin	Charles Wye Williams		Williams was manager of City of Dublin Steam Packet Co. Vessel driven by paddle wheels.
Prior to 1821	Genie Du Commerce Ville de Rouen Duc de Bordeux	Societe des Transports accélérés par eau		3 engines supplied to French Company at 2 Rue de Valois, Nr. Place Carousel, Paris.
1822	Ville de Paris	Societe des Transports accélérés par eau		Fourth vessel for French Company. J. J. Magendie, Managing Director wrote to Horseley 25 Feb 1822 urging completion. Engine 50 H.P.
1822	Union	G. Jennings		Built Rotherhithe by Wm. Evans. Dover-Boulogne till 1825. Sold, then Portsmouth-Ryde route.
1822	Aaron Manby	A. Manby and Charles Napier	106' 10" x 17' 2" x 7' 2" deep	See text.

B. Engines for steam boats supplied by Horseley after Aaron Manby's departure in c. 1822

Date	Name	Owner	Notes
1826	*Earl of Malmsbury*	Ward & Fitzhugh	Built at Cowes and was third vessel in fleet. Went to Plymouth 1858.
1826	*George the Fourth*	Ward & Fitzhugh	Built at Cowes by Wm. Evans as fourth vessel in fleet. Broken up 1853.
1825	*Emulous* *Gunga Saugor* *King of Oude* *Courier*	J. W. Taylor	Four built by Wm. Evans at Rotherhithe for the Indian Trade. After *Emulous* arrived in Calcutta, Taylor became bankrupt.
?	*Marquess of Wellesley*		Vessel built complete by Horseley, assembled Liverpool and operated on River Shannon "Light boat . . . composed of very thin sheet iron", Mallet I.C.E. 30.5.1843.

APPENDIX 3

Evidence of Richard Harrison and John Yorke to the Commission on artisans and machinery 1824

'I am one of a firm of considerable extent, in which a large capital is employed. Before the establishment of the one particular concern at Charenton, the party conducting it had great opportunities of knowing our best men, in fact, he was a partner in our concern; and from that circumstance he has been of course able to seduce and entice, in a very improper and most dishonourable way, our men to a greater extent than from other works, of which he had not the same knowledge; we have lost, I should think, about 50 men, or thereabout. Before this establishment at Charenton was formed, we had orders to a very considerable extent for steam engines for France; . . . since they have been in a state capable of manufacturing steam engines themselves, we have not had an order for one. Before that, we made, I should think, 20 engines for France, and they have now, to my knowledge, turned out about 4 engines of considerable power. At Charenton they have 5 or 6 others in hand, and have orders for a great many more; and it is my firm belief; that but for that those engines would have been manufactured in this country; if it had not been for the men being seduced over and English Artizans manufacturing them in Paris- I am convinced that if the English Artizans were to be brought home, the work must stop . . .'

APPENDIX 4

Report by Isaac Dodds in 1833 on a specification for the first locomotives on the Dublin and Kingstown Railway

Report made during Dodds' employment at the Horseley Coal and Iron Co. Tipton and comments on a specification by Charles B. Vignoles, C.E. who was engineer for the railway. Report presented to the Science Museum by Major S. Snell

Cylinders	Dimensions of which we perfectly agree.
	We recommend perfectly horizontal cylinders with either parallel motion or guides, but if parallel motion we would adopt our improved motion as the most likely one not to be deranged by the compound jolting occasioned on the railway at quick speeds.
	Vertical cylinders in our opinion are objectionable in as much as they can't have their piston, piston rod and parallel motion or cross head balanced conveniently, consequently always producing accelerated and retarding motion, thereby causing a jolting which in locomotives is highly detrimental and in a short time draws upon it most expensive keeping up of wear and tear; that is, in the down stroke you have the whole gravity of the above named machinery attached to piston, beside one part of the Bell Crank, plus the steam power on piston, and in the upstroke you have the power of the steam on underside of piston minus the gravity of the above appendage and having no means of balancing this, the disadvantage becomes immediately apparent; taking it for granted that you are already aware that the cranks do not balance each other in any more than two points in describing their circle, as has been asserted by some but which need only have one moments consideration to prove it false.
	The jerking of piston rod etc., is most likely to be done away with in perfect horizontal cylinders and no crank'd axles with a proportionably long connecting rod.
Slide Valves	The patent slide valve as manufactured by us, is perfectly adjustable both as regards wear of packing and also to take the passages at such cuttings off of the steam as may be deem'd prudent and can be done with the least possible delay decidedly better in our opinion, than in any other valve now in use, and is considerably less liable to friction than any other valve either circular or D shaped as it has so much less rubbing surface; but our patent

equally extends to the packing of D-valves or otherwise providing they use the inclined plane or cone.

Instead of eccentric motion we would advise an elliptical motion which could be brought adjustable close to the engine, although multiplicity of workmanship we condemn where a simple motion can be given to the valve without great rubbing surface as in the eccentric and by allowing the steam to remain on the piston during the time of the elliptical pin passing its major axis and being cut off almost instantly when it passes its minor axis. You save condensation by its rapid transit, and also have the privilege of working expansively as the piston can have any lead as is now the case with eccentric motions which can as before stated be regulated at pleasure.

Wheels

The wheels we see nothing to object to, but as you are aware of our manufacture of wheels that is all done by shrinking, turning etc., and no wood, the nave only being cast iron, spokes and tires wrought iron, which have since you saw them been tried and from their simplicity and easy mode of repairing them in any part renders them an advantage which in use must shew its superiority over others; as spoke or spokes, tire or tires or if necessary a nave, now the whole or any part of these might be applied without materially altering the effect of the wheel, altho' in case putting a single spoke or two in you might put them in in two pieces without taking off the tire.

Wheels & Connecting Rods

We advise the cylinder so adapted as to lead the motion to the centre of large wheel and therefore would not have the small wheel axle bearings outside of the wheels as the advantage you would gain by having small bearings would be overruled by the machinery being thrown farther from the centre of engine and consequently reduce its stability unless extra strength and stays, consequently extra weight would necessarily be wanted, the working part of the machinery being all outside of the wheels and so low as to be immediately within reach of engine (attendant) whether in motion or at ease, would be an advantage and always be at pleasure, within sight for either repair or lubrication. Yet all could be partially hidden as well, in case the framing need not be crank'd; small wheels may be made to either of your dimensions say 3' 9" or 4' 0".

Axles

The axles of driving wheels of best faggotted wrought iron, perfect in every respect and to be 5" diameter but

	would advise them a little tapering to the ends or neck, maintaining a uniform strength throughout; smaller axles 4" diam. and so constructed, this in a great measure does away with the tremulus motion so observable in motive power. Oilers in all cases to be used in a most improved manner.
Framing	This in your description in the specification is unobjectionable.
Springs	These are well -do- -do- -do-
Fire Box	We would say use rolled copper or rolled brass as in case you use cast you will have to cast it thick to ensure its soundness and even in its annealed state its liability to breakage is much more than rolled material and its tenacity is very slight. Copper fire boxes in round or semi-round shapes wear exceedingly well. A fire box, the material being good and well manufactured will wear out some parts of the shell of the boiler that is, where fire box and boiler are connected and also where chimney end and boiler are connected, those parts have very frequently fail'd before the interior of fire boxes.

We would say, put in stays to the fire box and let them be screw'd at both ends, as you seldom see any circle box but will, when it does give, give at the interior plate. That is where without stays, more especially any part near the bottom where it is likely to be acted upon by mudded or impure water. |
Tubes	The tubes we consider (in) your specification quite sufficient.
Safety Valves & Gauges	We agree with your specification as it regards the safety valves, but would advise a mercurial thermometer instead of the mercurial barometer.
Eccentric Elliptical Motion	The eccentrics we would advise to be laid aside, although we would recommend them preferable to any other mode except the elliptical motion as we have had these at work a few months in a locomotive we are satisfied of the effects and there is no likelihood in ordinary working for these to be deranged and by this method the engineer does not clash the two engines together, but the motion is given moderately and so taken of as required.

APPENDIX 5

Some roving bridges supplied[54] by Horseley to the Birmingham Canal Navigations.
- 1829 Spon Lane Junction.
- 1848 Spon Lane Roving Bridge.
- 1828 Smethwick Junction.
- 1828 Smethwick Roving Bridge.
- 1848 Winson Green Roving Bridge.
- 1828 Aston Top Lock Birmingham.
- 1827 Roving Bridge near Nile St. Birmingham.
- 1827 Deep cutting junction – King Edward's Road over Tindal Bridge.

APPENDIX 6

Some roving bridges[55] and other work on the Oxford Canal supplied by Horseley, c.1831-33:

- Bridge No. 8   Sowe Common, Nr. Coventry (Removed to Coventry City Centre by Carter Horseley in 1969).
- Bridge No. 32   Brinklow Arm.
- Bridge No. 39   All Oaks Lane, Easenhall (Ferris Field Arm).
- Bridge No. 45   Newbold Arm, Nr. Rugby.
- Bridge No. 53   Rugby Wharf Arm.
- Bridge No. 93   Braunston, at entrance to Barlow's Dock.
- Braunston –   Double span bridge across junction of branch to Birmingham.

Horseley were paid £419 12s 10d for three bridges in October 1832 and £693 19s 8d (presumably for the remaining five) in January 1833, i.e. approximately £140 each.

They also supplied an iron aqueduct for the Shilton Valley at £222 13s 6d with delivery from Horseley at £9 9s 4d. For work on the canal by Vignoles Horseley supplied rails for £749 6s 7d, guards for £774 15s 9d, iron boats, 10 off for £1,382 5s 8d at £16 6s 0d to £17 10s 0d per ton and a pair of iron lock gates for Napton top lock for £30 in March 1832.

The total received for ironwork of all kinds by Horseley was £4,302 1s 10d plus small sums for fitting and supervisory work.

APPENDIX 7

Particulars of gas holders built by Horseley Company prior to c. 1865

a. **Great Britain**

1854	Birmingham Gas Light Co.	No particulars.
1864	British Gas Co.	60' 0" dia. x 20' 0" deep
		62' 0" dia. x 20' 0" deep
1846	Bow Gas Co.	No particulars.
1857	Bristol United Gas Co.	109' 0" dia. x 24' 0" deep
1859	Crystal Palace Gas Co.	137' 0" dia. x 28' 0" deep

1860 Croydon Gas Co.   Telescopic 76' 0" dia. x 18' 0" deep.
78' 0" dia. x 18' 0" deep

1863 Commercial Gas Co.   Telescopic 100' 0" dia. x 26' 0" deep.

1855 Dover Gas Co.   No particulars.

1855 Faversham Gas Co.   30' 0" dia. x 14' 0" deep

1848 Surrey Gas Light Co.   77' 9" dia. x 20' 0" deep
80' 0" dia. x 20' 0" deep

b. Overseas

1863 Berlin Gas Co.   98' 0" dia. x 24' 10" deep
100' 0" dia. x 25' 10" deep

1852 Milan Gas Co.   99' 3" dia.

1859 Zeitz Gas Co.   No particulars.

APPENDIX 8

References* to furnaces and production at the Horseley Company to 1865

TIPTON RATING BOOK, 1813	Horseley Colliery Co. 2 Furnaces, 1 Puddling Furnace, 1 Finery, 3 Cupolas
THOMAS BUTLERS DIARY, 1815	Horseley 2 furnaces (2 in blast). Harrison, Oliver, Kitely & Smith & Co.
PIGOTS DIRECTORY, 1818/19/20	Horseley Company, Tipton
JOSHUA FIELD, 1821	Horseley Ironworks 3 furnaces tapping into a large foundry 2 at work.
LIST SUPPLIED TO MATTHEW BOULTON, 1823	2 furnaces: annual production 4,368 tons.
ASSAY OFFICE, BIRMINGHAM, 1825	Horseley 2 furnaces (2 in blast). Oliver & Co.: Output 90 tons per week. Yearly 4,940 tons. (Remarks: 20/3/1826, castings).
BOULTON & WATT, 1825	Information as above. (Remarks: casting trade)
J. SMART, WOLVERHAMPTON, 1827	Horseley Coal & Iron Company. Horseley Ironworks, Near Birmingham.
PIGOTS BIRMINGHAM COMMERCIAL DIRECTORY, 1829	Horseley Iron Company. Horseley Iron Works.
LIST SUPPLIED TO MATTHEW BOULTON, 1830	2 Furnaces: annual production 4,680 tons.
PRIORY OFICE LIST, 1839	Horseley Company, Works Horseley. No. of furnaces 2 standing, one in blast. Output 60 tons per week, 3,064 tons per year. Remarks: castings, cold blast.

PRIORY OFFICE, 1841	Horseley Company 2 furnaces.
MINING JOURNAL, 1842	Horseley Company 2 furnaces, one working. Output 55 tons per week.
PRIORY LIST, 1843	Horseley. 0 in blast 2 out of blast.
BENJAMIN BEST, MIDLANDS MINING COMMISSION REPORT, 1843	Horseley Company 2 furnaces.
OXFORD, WORCS. & WOLVERHAMPTON RAILWAY REPORT, 1845	Horseley Company: 100 tons per week
COMMISSIONERS REPORT ON IRON IN RAILWAY STRUCTURES, 1849	Horseley Iron Works. Part cold blast, part hot. Iron £3-£6 per ton. Wrought iron £7-£10 per ton.
ROBERT HUNT, 1849	Horseley: 3 furnaces.
W. FORDYCE, 1860	Horseley: Colburn & Sons.
THE ENGINEER, 11 JANUARY 1861	Colburn: Horseley. 4 furnaces, 3 in blast.
THE ENGINEER, AUGUST 1861	Colburn: Horseley: 4 furnaces, 2 in blast.

*Information provided by W. K. V. Gale).

ROBERT STEPHENSON AND THE HORSELEY COMPANY

Communication by Michael R. Bailey MA. D. Phil.
Past President of the Newcomen Society

In the early 1830s Robert Stephenson was impressed with the Horseley Company and particularly with Isaac Horton, a boilermaker employed there. In a letter, dated 12 November 1833 to the directors of the Leicester & Swannington Railway, Stephenson wrote, 'The Horsley Iron Company have one of the best boiler builders in England in their manufactory named Horton. With this person's workmanship I am well acquainted'.[56] The earliest reference I can find to Stephenson dealing with Isaac Horton is in December 1829 by which date he had completed two 'high-pressure' boilers (probably 35 p.s.i.) for the 'Liverpool No. 1 Engine'.[57] This refers to the large winding engine installed within the Moorish Arch at Edge Hill to haul trains to and from the Crown Street terminus of the Liverpool & Manchester Railway. Although the boilers were delivered in good time, the engine itself, from Robert Stephenson & Co., was shipwrecked on its delivery voyage.[58] The entry for the boilers in the Stephenson company books records an invoice from 'Isaac Horton of West Bromwich', as if on his own account. Stephenson's letter to the Leicester & Swannington therefore suggests he later went to work for the Horseley Company in Tipton but, as the Horseley Company itself is occasionally referred to by the railway as being in West Bromwich, he may actually have worked there for a longer time, perhaps in a similar capacity to an ironmaster. It is possible that Stephenson became acquainted with Horton and the Horseley Company by introduction of the Dudley firm of Joseph and William Bennitt which regularly supplied iron, and particularly 'best RB boiler plates' to the Stephensons' Newcastle works in the 1820s and 1830s. It is possible that the Bennitts were rolling plate for Horton and, in turn, for the Horseley Company.

In the 1830s Robert Stephenson was the Consulting Engineer to the Leicester & Swannington Railway. In that capacity his directions were sought regarding serious failures to the fireboxes of the (R. Stephenson & Co.-built) locomotives. From 1830, the emergent locomotive industry had produced a demand for substantial quantities of copper plate for fireboxes which proved difficult to meet. Its consequent expense, at £7 per cwt, compared with a price of just 10/-per cwt for wrought iron and the Stephenson Company consequently adopted the latter for its earliest production locomotives.[59] Wrought iron being less conductive than copper, it was soon apparent that fireboxes were overheating, leading to progressive deterioration by 'burning away'. This was made worse by inadequate wash-out practices and the later hard water problem experienced on the Leicester & Swannington line. The fireboxes on the Liverpool & Manchester line were being replaced after, typically, 20,000 miles and, as early as the autumn of 1830, the Stephenson Company sub-contracted the manufacture of two experimental copper fireboxes to see if their longer life and better reliability would off-set the initial cost. By May 1832 the Stephenson Company had concluded that 'no more inside fireboxes to be made of iron as we think of trying copper.'[60]

In spite of this resolution, copper plate was in such short supply that the Stephensons could not obtain enough to meet its locomotive commitments and wrought iron continued to be used. This included the first two locomotives for the Leicester & Swannington line, the *Comet* and the *Phoenix*. It could thus have been anticipated that trouble would be

Horseley C.I. bridge on Birmingham Canal near Oldbury

experienced with these fireboxes, but whether the railway's directors were warned in advance is not clear.

By November 1833, the fireboxes were already in need of replacement and the railway company approached a Leicester boiler-making firm, Ryde & Coleman, to quote for the provision and fitting of copper fireboxes. The quotation for the first firebox, 12cwt & 18lb of "best, hard rolled copper", was £7 per cwt plus £34 for labour, a total estimate of just over £119.[61] Robert Stephenson's advice on the firm and its estimate were sought and, in his reply, he was careful to stress the very new and particular problems that would arise. It was this letter to the railway's directors (above) in which he offered his preferential opinion about the Horseley Iron Company. He continued:

'The replacing of the fireboxes is a difficult operation requiring very great care and if the engines were my own I would have them repaired by the Horsley Company at an extra charge of £5 or £10. Their prices are I believe generally low.'

Stephenson's warnings about the difficulties of providing copper plate, manufacturing a firebox and installing it within an existing boiler shell were well founded. Although the Horseley Iron Company was clearly well experienced in iron work, the working of copper plate to the particular tolerances required was a new skill that few smiths had yet acquired. In spite of Stephenson's views about Isaac Horton, the difficulties that the Horseley company appeared to have experienced are borne out by the subsequent serious delays in getting the locomotives back into service. On its return from the Horseley Company, Stephenson himself inspected the *Phoenix* and reported 'that the repairs have been done in an inefficient manner'.[62] The Horseley men came over to Leicester to rectify the problem but Stephenson felt 'confident it will not put the firebox into the state in which it ought to have been delivered'. After several months during 1834, in which attempts continued to put the new fireboxes into working order, the Leicester & Swannington directors felt obliged to return to their original view that Ryde & Coleman should be engaged to install new copper boxes.

So bad were the railway's problems due to poor availability of the locomotives in the summer of 1834 that it was obliged to consider using horses for its motive power. The withholding of payment to the Horseley Company and the consequent threat of legal action, referred to by Mr. Allen, (p. 25, above) may be seen against this background.

NOTES AND REFERENCES

1. Parkes, *History of Tipton* (1915), p.15. Variations occur in the spelling of Horsley, Horseley, Horseleye, etc.
2. Parchment at Wombourn Wodehouse.
3. See Tipton Tithe Assessment Book for 1769. Wombourn Wodehouse.
4. Horseley Estate-Plan No. 1. Total area 309a 1r 0p. 121a 1r 0p includes Comballs Farm, Mansion House Farm and Brookes Meadow purchased from Dudley formerly Jeavons; 73a including Ockells Farm bought from Dudley, formerly Jas. Jones and others.
5. Parkes, op. cit.(3).
6. John Finch, glass maker and banker of Dudley died 23 December 1791, aged 56; and lived at Horseley House, Wolverhampton Street, Dudley. His father also John Finch was an ironmonger and merchant, born c.1705, died 1 January 1759. The Finch family were Quakers.

7. Thomas Dudley (1749-3 September 1826). Member of ancient family of Dudleys who were much involved in mining.
8. Act 23 Geo. III Cap 92, 24 June 1783.
9. Joseph Amphlett baptized 3 May 1757 at Hadzor, 4th son of William Amphlett of Hadzor, Worcs., who was High Sheriff of Worcestershire in 1745. Joseph Amphlett married first wife Mary Bree on 1 May 1778, and she died 29 January 1784, aged 27. His second marriage was to Mary Davis Dixon, eldest daughter of his partner, on 16 April 1792. Amphlett settled £2,000 on her as a marriage settlement and her father Edward Dixon a like sum. She died after two years on 21 October 1794, shortly after birth of their son Edward at Horseley House, Tipton.
10. R. A. Mott, 'The Coalbrookdale Group Horsehay Works, Part II', *T.N.S.*, Vol. XXXII, p.48.
11. Edward Dixon was the son of Joseph Dixon of Dudley, hop and cyder merchant. Edward Dixon's entry into the banking business was 1780 when the Universal British Directory has 'E. Dixon, banker, Dudley'. In July 1803, Ed. Dixon & Son were bankers in Dudley and in 1805/6/7 the style was Edward Dixon, Son & Co. Dixon was married to Phoebe Davis, 18 June 1767 and they had five children. His wife died in 1812, aged 60.
12. The Bedford family were from Pershore and Droitwich. His mother was Elizabeth Yeend, daughter of John Yeend of Pershore. He married in 1784 Lydia, eldest daughter of Rev. Richard Riland, Rector of Sutton Coldfield.
13. BTC Archives, BCNI Book 6. Now Public Record Office, Kew.
14. J. Stebbing-Shaw, *History of Staffordshire* (1800). The House was variously styled 'Mansion House', 'Dixon's Hall', 'Horseley Hall' and 'Horseley House'. It was demolished about 1820, due to mining subsidence and its fine oak staircase transferred to Ellows Hall, Sedgley. In 1915 the old stables remained in ruins, but the servants' cottages had been put in good repair and were tenanted. The main drive commenced near the entrance to Tipton Cemetery and is now Clarkes Grove.
15. BTC Archives, BCNI Book 6.
16. Tipton Library, BCN Letter Book, 23 March 1792.
17. British Waterways Board, Gloucester Office. Memorandum of Agreement, 16 October 1792.
18. BTC Archives, BCNI Book 7A.
19. British Waterways Office, Gloucester.
20. Plan traced by John Harris, 1964.
21. *The Engineer*, 6 June 1879, states Horseley have two Newcomen engines at that date.
22. BTC Archives, BCNI Book 8, p.162.
23. Birmingham Reference Library. *Boulton & Watt Collection*.
24. J. W. Hall, 'Joshua Fields diary of a tour in 1821 through the Midlands' *T.N.S.*, Vol. VI, pp1-41.
25. Tipton Rating Book, Tipton Public Library: old chest.
26. Wombourn Wodehouse Collection, Bundle 39. Lease of 21 July 1808 of lands containing both coal and ironstone. Smith had authority to sink mines, erect steam and fire engines, gins and other machinery and to make carriages, rails and roadways for a term of 14 years.
27. Wombourn Wodehouse, op. cit.(28).
28. Aaron Manby was born 15 November 1776, at Albrighton near Shifnal, East Shropshire, the second son of Aaron Manby of Kingston, Jamaica. His mother was Jane Manby, a daughter of Joseph Lane whose other daughter was Mary Lane. Manby's elder brother was Joseph Lane Manby and their father died whilst they were under age. See W. H. Chaloner

and W. O. Henderson, 'Aaron Manby, builder of the first iron steamship' *T.N.S.*, Vol XXIX, pp77-91, and Wombourne Wodehouse Collection, Bundle 11.
29. P.R.O., **BTI**, Vol. 70, Dossier No. 19.
30. A. Birch, *Edgar Allen News*, Aug. 1952, pp.209-10; and September 1952, pp.231-3.
31. Parkes, op. cit.(1).
32. W. O. Henderson, *Industrial Britain under the Regency* (1968). Copy of transcript by C. Matchoss at Bolton Metropolitan Borough Library.
33. J. W. Hall, op. cit.(24).
34. Dudley Library.
35. Although Field states there were three furnaces at Horseley other evidence refers to only two furnaces at the Horseley works. A report by *Robert Hunt* in 1849 gives three. It might be deduced that this represents the first of the Colbourne furnaces also known as Horseley Furnaces. Later references e.g. *The Engineer*, 11 January and August 1861, refer to Colburn (sic) having four furnaces and it would seem that they may have operated the original furnaces at Horseley too, leaving the Engineering Works to operate separately.
36. Plan kindly loaned by W. K. V. Gale (Past-President).
37. The writer is greatly indebted to G. E. C. Townsend, Esq., TD, B.Sc.(Eng), F.I.C.E., sometime Divisional Engineer (River), Port of London Authority, London EC3, for information on the marine engines and the details of the iron vessel *Commerce de Paris*. Mr. Townsend compiled his information from the following references:
    1. G. A. Prinsep, *An account of the Steam Vessels and of Proceedings connected with Steam Navigation in British India* (Calcutta, 1830).
    2. *Fifth Report of the Select Committee on Roads from London to Holyhead, Steam Packets*, Sessional papers of the Houses of Parliament (1822), No. 417, Appendix 1, List of all Steam Boats built since 1811 *etc. Joshua Field*, Appendix 8 (14), Answers by William Evans to questionnaire.
    3. A manuscript volume of Returns by the *Registrar-General of Shipping, 1813-1829*, in the library of H.M. Customs & Excise, in particular a statement of the Names and Tonnages of Steam Vessels registered at the Ports of the UK, in the last 5 years etc., dated 21 January 1829.
38. John Oldham (Patent 4429. 9 June 1820). Paddles restricted to 2' 6" width. They can be seen on the illustration of the Aaron Manby. They enter the water edgeways and twist to give drive.
39. Chaloner & Henderson, op. cit.(28), fully describe the vessel and its history and quote the report given in the Appendix.
40. W. H. Chaloner and W. O. Henderson, 'Aaron Manby builder of the first iron steamship;, *T.N.S.*, Vol. XXIX, pp.77-91.
41. Information kindly provided by E. Davies of Montevideo who studied the Registers.
42. This section is based upon a study of the Directors Minute Books of the various railways at BTC Archives, Kew. Significant assistance was received from the Science Museum, London, in particular Lt. Col. T. M. Simmons and Mr. Ironmonger. Considerable help was given by F.. Craven of London. The Dublin and Kingstown Railway information was taken from the Minute and Letter Books at Dublin together with information from K. A. Murray of Dublin.
43. Matthew Loam (1794-1875), born Ludgvan, Cornwall. Served four-year apprenticeship as carpenter, then under Arthur Woolf at Gwennap and became chief assistant in erection of his engines. In 1825 he was manager of J. & S. Seaward, London, and in 1827 joined

Horseley. Left to join Charles Tayleur in 1833, until 1841. Isaac Dodds was born in 1801, but following the accidental death at Hebburn Colliery of his father Thomas Dodds, Isaac was brought up from the age of four by his uncle Ralph Dodds, the viewer at Killingworth when George Stephenson was building his first locomotives and joined in a patent with him in 1815. Isaac Dodds joined Robert Stephenson at Forth St. in 1823 and opened his own works at Felling in 1825, but he was to sell this and accept an offer from the Horseley Coal and Iron Company. Vignoles noted on 26 November 1833 'that concern (Horseley) is now managed by a more able Engineer who has been familiar for some years with the construction of locomotives'. Whilst at Horseley Dodds took out three patents: No. 6470 (1833) Improved valves for steam engines; No. 6755 (1835) Machinery for cutting out and shaping gun stocks; No. 6826 (1835) Improvements in fire arms and the boring of cannon. Dodds lost an eye in an accident at Horseley and left the Company in 1836.

44. Dodds' Obituary, *Institution of Civil Engineers Proceedings*, Vol. LXXV, Part 1.
45. Op. cit.
46. Drawing discovered by R. Taylor of Sheffield in a copy of John Guest's *Relics and Records of men and manufacturers of Rotherham* (1866). Considered to be compiled by Guest himself, an acquaintance of Dodds. Mr. Taylor considered it to be copied (and probably reduced) from a maker's drawing. P. C. Dewhurst in a private communication also considered that the drawing derived from some original drawing.
47. Directors' Minute Book, Liverpool and Manchester Railway Company.
48. Op. cit.
49. Document presented to Science Museum, London, by Major S. Snell.
50. A. W. Skempton, 'Engineering in the Port of London Authority', *T.N.S.*, Vol. 50 p.100.
51. An accident during the setting up of the cast iron ribs cost the life of the Horseley Foreman and injured seven of his men. Mr. Stephenson stated that 'the loss would fall wholly on the Horseley Iron Company and that the accident would not in the least delay the completion of the Kings Langley Contract by Messrs. M. & L. Cubitt'. Directors' Minute Book, 1 March 1837. BTC Archives.
52. Appendix 7 gives list of gas-holders built before 1865. Compiled from Company Booklet.
53. Six sets of pumping machinery for the water stations were supplied to the London & Birmingham Railway at £595 15 0d per set. Directors' Minute Book, 19 April 1837. BTC Archives.
54. Information from British Waterways.
55. Information from British Waterways and D. W. Hadley, 'The Role of Iron in Reconstructing the Oxford Canal', *Journal of R.C.H.S.*, Vol XXIV, No. 1 (March 1978), pp.9-15.
56. Leicester & Swannington Railway, Minutes of Board of Directors, December 13th 1833, Public Record Office Reference Rail 359/9. Letter shown dated 12 November but this is clearly error for December.
57. Robert Stephenson & Co. accounting book for 1823-1831, page 228, retained in the Science Museum, London.
58. Bailey, M. R., 'Robert Stephenson & Co. 1823-1829', Newcomen Society Transactions, Vol. 50, p. 127.
59. Bailey, M. R., 'Robert Stephenson & Co. 1823-1836', unpublished MA Thesis, Newcastle University, 1984, pp 298-301.
60. Robert Stephenson & Co. Order Book No. 1, March 1832-October 1833, retained in the Science Museum, London.
61. Op cit (1), 29 November 1833.
62. Op cit (1), 17 March 1834.

Part II

The New Works
1865-1992

The Horseley Company of Tipton, Staffordshire has been considered and the early history and first works discussed. This concluded at 1865 when the owner of the company, Robert Broad was considering the construction of a new works on a site some half mile from the original works. This site was between the Dixons Branch of the Birmingham Canal Navigation and the line of the London and North Western Railway towards the lower end of Horseley Road, Tipton.

Chapter 1
1865-1885

THE NEW HORSELEY WORKS

The building of this works was foreshadowed in 1864 when Robert Broad purchased the site in two parcels. The first on 4th April from George Parker and Mrs. Louisa Parker for £1,886-14s.4d.and the second on 26th June from Thomas Dudley and Samuel Brandram for £3581.17s.6d., a total of £5468.11s.10d. No doubt the facilities of the first works had become outdated and the owners were not interested in the blast furnaces preferring to concentrate on fabrication and foundry work. The lack of rail access was a factor and the change in the essential transport system from water to rail is significant although supplies were received via the canal, particularly of pig iron, coal and coke well into the mid twentieth century. This, then modern, works with pattern shops, foundry, boiler and fitting shops and offices was built by David Murray to the design of the engineer William Dempsey, Gt. George Street, London and a local architect John Weller of Wolverhampton. The architect's fees amounted to some £400 which included some 21 visits and the submission of final drawings to Mr. Broad on 8 January 1868.

Although the foundry was demolished in the 1950s many of the original buildings remained, but sadly in early 1991 it was decided to demolish the original office block to improve access and use only the more modern offices built behind. After final works closure in 1992 the whole of the site was cleared and is now covered by an estate of small houses.

The cast iron columns, beams and other ironwork for the new works were cast at the old foundry, but the new foundry Pattern Book which details patterns from January 30 1866 to July 1879 shows that a number of items for the structures and plant were cast at the new works. This vital document was presented by colleagues H. Hirons and W. Wheale.

Archives are few from the period 1866-1873 but the Pattern Book gives many details of the contracts undertaken. It records only the foundry work and the pattern descriptions so that details of the structural and boiler work are not known. The front leaf of the book is headed 'Horseley New Works Pattern Book' in red ink and commences on 30 January 1866. The first entry is for pattern number 573 – 2 small girders – to order number 11440. Clearly they were following the system from the earlier works.

Orders were executed for countries world wide and during the first year alone, work included a Berlin Water Tank, Vienna Gas Holder, Calleo Roof – South America, work for Bombay and Argentine. At home there were orders for Thurlo Park Bridge, Birmingham Proof House, Portsmouth, Aberystwyth, Chester, Conway and a gas holder for Croydon. An order from Crystal Palace Gas Works was undertaken, the first of a great number to follow in subsequent years.

Work for railway companies-London & North Western Rly., London Brighton and Millwall extension, London & South Western, South Devon at home and the Egyptian Agricultural and the Central Argentine abroad, was undertaken. The principal business however was with the gas companies world wide either for items of gas plant or for gas holders up to 100 feet in diameter; over 60 different companies being recorded up to 1873.

The book records the order numbers for the different jobs and assuming that consecutive numbers were given to every job an indication of the total number of orders for the years can be deduced. The size of the orders cannot be judged but reference to the dated list may give an indication of the varying work load.

Order No.	Date	Total Number
11,440	Jan 1866	
11,705	May 1867	265
211	May 1867	
4801	Jan 1873	3809
1	Jan 1873	
2303	Feb 1877	2303
A1	Feb 1877	
A2620	Jul 1879	2620

THE HORSELEY COMPANY LIMITED

The new registered company is noted in January 1874 following eight years of operation as a private company, when the page is headed 'The Horseley Co. Limited.' All the Board Minute Books to 1943 and many other records survive from this date so that it is possible to consider primary sources. The promoters of the Horseley Co. Limited met at the Birmingham Joint Stock Bank Ltd. on 28 November 1873 attended by solicitors when it was agreed that the title was acceptable. Robert Broad was to be Chairman for five years at a salary of £1,200/year, F. E. Muntz, Joint Managing Director at £300/year for the first year and £500/year afterwards. Other directors were to have £500/year.

On 22 December the new directors met at Horseley, they were:-

- Robert Broad, Ironmaster, Tipton
- George Frederick Muntz, Chairman of B'ham Joint Stock Bank Ltd.
- Frederick Ernest Muntz, Gloster Terrace, Hyde Park.
- John Cochrane, Hyde Park Gate, London, Ironmaster.
- James Holcroft, Stourbridge, Iron & Coal Master.
- John Scrivenor Keep, Birmingham, Director Midland Wagon Co.,
- Thomas Short, London and Birmingham, East India Merchant.

John Cochrane had chaired the meeting at Birmingham and was elected vice-chairman at this Directors' Meeting with Robert Broad as the Chairman, both being joint Managing Directors. Two of the staff from the old company were retained in their positions. John Spencer as Secretary and George Edward Jones as Works Manager. John Spencer later became the founder of Spencer's Tube Works.

The purchase money for the works was £40,000 with £46,714. 5s.2d. the value of the plant and stock. The nominal capital was £150,000 in 7500 shares at £20. A total of 2500 shares were issued to Robert Broad.

Having requested an overdraft of £20,000 from the bank on security of the title deeds the company was to start trading formally on 1 January 1874 and issued quotations for a number of structures. Sadly Robert Broad died suddenly on 2 January 1874.

At the funeral, which started from his house Vectis Lodge, Augustus Road, Edgbaston, the mourners were W. Dempsey who had designed the Works and H. E. Wallis. Amongst the pall bearers were E. Muntz and V. W. Houghton with John Spencer and G. E. Jones from the Works. The coffin was borne by ten of the principal workmen from Horseley and amongst the large procession were a great number of workers from Tipton.

A special meeting of the Board was convened on 5 January at which a letter of condolence was agreed to Mrs Broad and a letter to the Company's customers conveying the sad news. John Cochrane was elected Chairman of the Board and Thomas Short, Vice-chairman.

Later the Company insured the offices, pattern shop, patterns, stores and stables for £5,000 and purchased the mines beneath the works for £500 an acre from Dixon Amphlett and Bedford. The bank increased its support by another £10,000 and 'additional siding room and railway accommodation' was agreed with the LNWR, and was to be shared with Thomas Stonehewer. It was he who occupied an area to the east of the works towards Great Bridge and this was separated by a heavy brick wall. The area was later taken into the Horseley Works.

In order to assist the financial aspects of the Company two loans were accepted and these allowed the Bank's main loans to be cleared, They were each for £10,000 from Mrs.

The Works from Horseley Road, Tipton. An early view.

Broad and Charles Holcroft the brother of Director James Holcroft. The document confirming these loans is dated 3 Feb. 1874 and refer to 'Robert Broad having erected and built . . . an iron foundry with the necessary shopping, buildings, machinery erections, plant, three steam engines, five boilers, four large foundry cranes with engines attached – all known as "The Horseley Works".'

In 1876 a steam rivetting machine was ordered for the boiler shop at £270 with a cover and traveller at a further £400. It was reported that two boilers in the Boiler Department were badly worn and agreed that one new one should be made immediately.

Stern measures over the starting time in the Foundry were introduced in September 1877 when '...they should start work at 6 a.m. as others do in the neighbourhood, even if it means the closing of the Foundry'.

In June 1877 a meeting was held at which Joseph Keep acted as Chairman. They had to consider a letter from John Cochrane from London. He had written a year before stating he wished to seek some other occupation. It was then arranged that he give more time to Horseley in return for £200 in place of the £100 director's fee and also that he could take contracts on his own account. This did not work as '...those I speak to look upon me as part of the Horseley Co.' He wished therefore to resign. The resignation was accepted 'with much regret'. In his letter of confirmation to John S. Keep, John Cochrane stated that he wished he may '...often be of service to your Company and that our future relationship may be of the most satisfactory character'.

In January 1878 it was announced that there had been negotiations for some six months with Peter Duckworth Bennett, Ironfounder of Spon Lane, and Houghton Street, West Bromwich with the purpose of securing his business and appointing him Managing Director of Horseley. Bennett had been articled at Oak Farm Iron Company, near Dudley, becoming manager of the Construction Department. In 1847 he was with Cochrane and Co. at Woodside, Dudley where he later took charge of the Drawing, Estimating and Construction Offices. He became Chief Engineer at Fox Henderson and Co. of Smethwick and then moved to Spon Lane. The man in charge of the transport horses was named Checketts and lived in a house adjoining the stables in Houghton Street.

SPON LANE FOUNDRY

With agreement Bennett became Chairman of the Company and of the Board. A number of documents exist from which the early history of the site of the Spon Lane Foundry can be established. The earliest reference to the lands is 1783 when John Nock of Birmingham, a Brass Founder mortgaged the estate. There is no evidence of industry until 1792 when:- George Timmins, Button maker of Birmingham; William Whitehouse, Whitesmith of Birmingham; William Smith, Toymaker of Birmingham; obtained a lease referred to in 1798 when they and others set up the Spon Lane Brass Foundry. The foundry was sold in November 1824 to Edwin Bullock and leased in 1831 to Thomas Pemberton a Birmingham Brassfounder.

By 1850 Edwin Bullock is described as an ironfounder indicating a change of use. An excellent plan of the works at this date exists. The value of plant, tools and stock was £14,821.5.7d. but the Spon Lane Foundry was apparently not a success for by 1879 work

The main fabrication race with the foundry in the background

Above: The Dixons Branch canal showing the rear of the foundry and the delivery of coal and iron by barge. The two pit head gears of the colliery at the end of the branch will be seen

Below: The Antofagasta Railway Viaduct in Bolivia, 1889. 800 feet long, 310 feet high

was falling off and in December all work stopped. Some of the larger machines were to be transferred to Tipton. In May 1880 consideration was being given to the disposal of the property. The sale was complex due to some land being freehold and other leasehold. It was suggested by the advisers, Joseph Cooksey and Son that it be offered in three lots. These lots included the foundry buildings, fitting shop, pattern shop and engine room. The total area was 14,508 sq. yards. The value was considered to be – Lot 1 – £1150, Lot 2 – £900 including the large wharf crane, Lot 3 – leasehold section, £4,700 and freehold section £2,800. The total value being £9,550.

These lots excluded all the cranes, steam engines, boiler fittings and steam and feed pipes; shafts and pulleys; blast fans; cupolas; covered platform supported on cast iron pillars with the iron steps thereto; two double hoists; slack drying store; slack grinding mills; also the steam travelling crane and railway in the adjoining yard. (Slack drying and grinding would be for coal slack to provide dust for foundry blacking.)

It was decided to offer the property to A. Kenrick and Sons and if they did not wish to proceed to sell by auction. Kenrick did not wish to purchase and so it was offered to the Midland Railway Co., who also declined. It was then offered for auction at the Great Western Hotel, Birmingham on 23 June 1881 but no bids at all were made. In October Kenrick expressed an interest in the freehold portion and were advised the price would be £1,300 which they declined.

The problem remained and by July 1882 a proposal to break up the cranes, carriages, rails and grates valued at £1,600 but which for scrap would only be worth £400/500 was made and agreed. By May 1885 consideration was being given to turning the property into dwellings or use for other purposes. In June Alldays & Onions were offered the

The widening of the Charing Cross Railway Bridge for the S. E. & C. Railway, 1884/5

property for £9,000 but declined to make a counter offer and so the matter remained unresolved.

Progress and work at Tipton

At Tipton work continued and in 1878 a decision was made to build a new company strong room on the embankment path of the L.N.W.R., for which an annual rent of 2/6d would be paid. It was from this strong room that the books and documents by which this paper is prepared were recovered in 1987.

The Company's contracts continued to be varied with a heavy dependence upon the gas companies but tanks, roofs, warehouses and bridges became more frequent. Major orders in 1878 included 4 gas holders at Manchester, Ryde Pier on the Isle of Wight, Heaton Norris warehouse followed in 1879 by Harwich Pier. In 1881 a gas holder was built at Poplar, an order for two was received from Tipton Gas and also for three bridges for the London & South Western Railway Co..

In 1882 a large jetty at Port Elizabeth, South Africa was built and a quotation made for Blackfriars Bridge, London which was similar to Putney Bridge which had already been quoted. There were to be 3 spans of 185 ft. and 2 of 175 ft., weight 5100 tons priced at £120,000. These quotations involved co-operation with John Cochrane & Son who would do all the site work – a situation which occurred quite often showing that whilst he had left Horseley, significant contact and co-operation was maintained with John Cochrane. Also in 1882 a bridge was built over the River Itchen, near Southampton and another over the River Aire for the Hull, Barnsley and West Riding Junction Railway.

In 1883 two gas holders were supplied to the Gas Light & Coke Co., for Horseferry Road, Westminster; one for the Bilston Gas Light & Coke Co., and ironwork for Huddersfield Warehouses for the LNWR. In 1884 two major contracts were obtained, Charing Cross Bridge and Medway Bridge at Rochester. Both bridges were to be erected by John Cochrane. The precaution was taken of insuring his life for the period of the work. The Charing Cross Bridge order came from Cochrane and was a widening of the original structure. Total weight 5,000 tons, value £66,000. Some 10,000 tons of old rail was taken in exchange at £4 per ton as part of the contract. It was stated that Mr Cochrane had '...fixed the existing bridge and knows all the circumstances'.

The principal contracts in late 1885 were Rugby Station Extension, warehouses at Huddersfield, Monument Lane Station and Brunswick Dock, Liverpool and the gas works at Birkenhead. In October 1885 a most important matter was discussed. Edward Harry Woods, Engineer of Westminster was involved with a projected railway in the Argentine Republic. Three other firms were forming a consortium to offer various items such as locomotives, wagons and bolts. This involved a premium of £500. The railway was to be in the Tucuman Principality and be a loop line of the Central Northern Railway. The metre gauge single line would be 81 miles long with 19 miles of branches. The matter was agreed and Horseley joined the consortium.

State of Trade and Practice

When Peter D. Bennett took over in 1878 he complained of the '...direful state of trade' but when orders came '...nothing is wanted but organisation energy and determination to get the work out of the place'. However it was considered that the appliances '...for punching Gas holder sheets are very inferior and behind-hand and to enable us to hold our

The swing bridge at Littlehampton

own against competitors we shall require to possess ourselves of modern and efficient machinery'.

The works manager was relieved of the need to study correspondence and deal with estimating so that he could '...devote time getting the work through the Drawing Office and the Shops. However the Chief works are and have been insufficiently occupied; valuable workmen have, unfortunately been walking about for want of materials and their labour therefore lost'.

In December 1878 it was reported that although orders for gas plant fell off at this time of the year '...Gas companies are now still further deterred from making extensions by the partial success which attends the experiments with the new Electric Light'. A further sign of the times is referred in February 1879 when in addition to wrought iron for a contract, 1,100 tons of steel joists 11 in. x 5 in. – conditional upon its acceptance by the engineer – were purchased.

At the end of the year it was reported that the '...iron Market has been in a most excited state, and the higher rates which now rule for all kinds of iron compel us to ask much higher prices for our work. This, however has the effect of keeping back orders and we do not therefore participate in the so called "improved" state of things'. Trade was even more difficult in April 1881 and indirect costs were cut by amalgamating '...the duties of time and Storekeeper', superannuating John Evans and dispensing with the Secretary '...whose duties can be perfectly performed by the other existing officers. Then there is the question of John Davies -an old attached servant of Mr. Broad – for whom one feels every sympathy and interest – whom we can perfectly well do without — I advise him having 10 shillings per week allowed him for the present.'

The weather in late 1882 had, for three months, been very inclement which had hindered progress in the yard as '… so large a portion — is uncovered and exposed to the weather. It follows that our returns are diminished and our finances in a less satisfactory state than they have been for several months past. Then again the nature and requirements of our business are undergoing an entire and radical change. Wrought iron girder work is now required to be executed with a refinement and precision that were undreamt of a few years ago. The rivet holes in a very large and increasing number of cases have to be drilled instead of being punched as heretofore; and drilled too in a manner that involves special and higher class machinery and increased skill all round. The edges and ends of plates and bars have to be planed and shaped and the whole brought up to a class of work that was formerly most unusual if not unknown.

We are gradually adapting ourselves to the changed and changing state of things but in the meantime it is inevitable that only a less quantity of work can be turned out and it is only by the adoption of new methods and better and increased appliances that we can come up to the excellence that is required and that it is our interest and aim to acquire. And it is also only by these means that we can turn out refined work equal in quantity to the plainer and rougher work of former times.

I am adapting as fast as possible the parts of the original but inefficient Multiple drilling machine to the modern requirements and I hope to bring ourselves up to the highest standard of the times.

The new vertical casting pit is making very satisfactorily but it is unfortunately not deep enough for some columns we have to cast for the London & North Western Railway Company.'

A further indication of increasing sophistication occurs in November 1883 when it was decided to purchase a 50 ton testing machine from Buckton & Co. at Leeds which cost over £300. This machine survived in the Fitting Shop until the mid-20th century.

In September 1885 it was reported that the wrought iron departments were fully employed but the foundry only partially so. '…The slackness in the Foundry is partially explained by the fact that a great deal of the work which was originally done in cast Iron is now done in Wrot Iron and this added to the circumstance of the low price at which castings are being done in the North of England makes it very difficult for us to obtain orders for castings'.

Changes in Directors

The next changes after those due to the death of Robert Broad occurred in March 1875 following the resignation of Thomas Short in February. Charles Holcroft of Dudley and Samuel Rogers of London were elected. John Keep became Vice-Chairman in June 1875. F. E. Muntz became ill in 1881 and went to the South of France for three months. He was forced to resign on medical advice in October 1882, but remained an ordinary director. James Holcroft resigned in April 1877, and although he was not a director Herbert Bennett resigned in April 1884, a matter '… accepted with much regret'.

Accidents

One of the tragedies of the heavy iron and steel industries is that of accidents which due to the weight of the materials being handled are often severe or fatal. Horseley was not without such problems. Two men both lost an arm in October 1878 due to a girder slipping. On the Ryde Pier site, two men were seriously injured and in May 1879 a man was killed in the works when a bar of iron fell onto him from a wagon and in December another man was killed at Manchester Gas Works. In 1880 there was a fatal accident at the Commercial Gas Works.

In considering the Employers Liability Act of 1880 in 1881 it was stated that in the last four years at the works there had been 20 accidents of varying severity with one fatal and on site nine injuries with two fatal – which confirms the details reported above. It was first proposed that the men should pay one penny per week with a similar sum from the company. With an average of 600 men this would provide £260/year total which was considered to be sufficient to cover the likely legal costs under the Act. It was then decided to seek insurance to cover the possible costs on the basis of 470 men and 60 young persons and a policy for £122 2s.11d/year from the company agreed, with contributions from the work people as follows:-

        1d per week for 280 men over 20 years of age
        $1\frac{1}{4}$d per week for 190 men over 20 years of age
        $\frac{1}{2}$d per week for 45 young persons
        5/8d per week for 38 young persons
        553 Total workforce

In July 1881 another fatal accident occurred at the Commercial Gas Co., at Poplar. A man was refilling the boiler of a travelling crane when he fell 45 feet into the tank. His funeral expenses were paid and his wife given £10 to assist her in emigrating to America. Another man died in 1882 at Liverpool Alexandra Dock warehouse through tripping over a rope and another at Dudley Gas Works in 1883. There was a fatal accident in the Works when a painter fell from the roof and another man had his leg amputated when it was badly crushed. Horses were used in the Works and one was lost in 1884 when a heavy casting fell on him.

Company Staff

When Spon Lane Foundry was taken over Herbert Bennett was appointed Manager at a salary of £300/annum. In April 1878 an advertisement for a ledger clerk brought in about 50 applicants out of which 12 were interviewed and a man called Osborne was appointed at £120/annum plus a second class railway ticket from Birmingham. The Chief Draughtsman at Spon Lane was to transfer to Tipton and be replaced by a junior '… a thoroughly efficient draughtsman required at £150/annum.'

Works manager George E. Jones resigned in 1874 to be replaced by Walter E. Wood with a minimum salary of £800/annum. The Secretary, John Spencer resigned in March 1876 to be replaced by Robert Leach at a salary of £200. His duties were fully specified in the Directors Private Minute Book.

Works Manager Wood was in trouble in December 1876 over an error in some cast iron columns and following a letter from John Cochrane he submitted his resignation, but appears to have worked for three months afterwards. His successor was J. Ellis.

Secretary Leach was in serious trouble in September 1877 over '…so gross an act of insubordination'. The precise nature of the problem seems unclear but salary cheques in advance and sums owing for coal are mentioned. He was replaced by M. Holmden in October 1877 who was dismissed in 1881 and replaced by Thomas Hughes in 1882.

New Works Manager Ellis survived only briefly. He was informed that the conclusion was '…that his experience was not such as the necessities of the case required' and he resigned on 31 December 1878. Two replacement candidates were considered. One Harris aged 30 of London who asked £600, rising to £900/annum and one Sharrock aged 25 from Hamiltons Windsor Iron Works near Liverpool who 'had fitted himself for the position he seeks in every particular' who asked £300/annum and was appointed on 1 Jan. 1879.

P. D. Bennett was most dissatisfied with Sharrock, whom he found '...it absolutely impossible to inspire ... with the energy and administrative power which must be brought to bear to enable our engagements to be carried out.' Sharrock resigned in December 1879, and was replaced by James Evans who had been with the Horseley Company for very many years. He was most successful but died suddenly in November 1880. Highly emotive and complimentary eulogies were recorded – his loss considered '...almost irreparable'. W. Jacob from the Hamilton Iron Works was appointed until Christmas.

Considering the shop floor, the moulders' hours were increased in February 1878 to those of the other departments. Three apprentices were taken on in the Pattern Shop for a period of seven years starting at five shillings a week and finishing at 12 shillings. Having reduced the wages of fitters and turners at Spon Lane in 1879 the same was agreed at Tipton i.e. a reduction of two shillings a week to 32 shillings. The labourers were given the option of longer hours or a wage reduction and opted to work 57 instead of 54 hours. By August 1881 the moulders were agitating as James Watt & Co., who had reduced their wages had now raised them again. In 1885 the moulders' wages were again reduced by 2 shillings, which they accepted.

There were some general apprentices and the indentures of T. W. Piggott were approved in March 1880. This man, one suspects to be a member of the Piggott family of Thomas Piggott and Sons of Birmingham of whom much later.

The widow (or daughter in law) of the former partner Tiernay, applied for apprenticeship for her son and was offered this at premium of £250 with no salary until 21 years old. This she was unable to accept but '...in consideration of the late Mr. Tiernay's connection with the former Company' it was offered at 100 guineas, but again not accepted.

In August 1885 Harry S. Bennett was appointed Deputy Manager. A major blow occurred at the end of November 1885, when the Chairman Peter D. Bennett then aged 60, was killed in an accident. He had been invited on the 28 November to a Mayoral Luncheon at the Council House, Birmingham, at the visit of the Prince of Wales (later King Edward VII). The Prince had opened the Jaffray Hospital and the new Art Gallery and when he was about to drive away Bennett and several others went out on to the portico to obtain a better view. A player from the orchestra also went out, and stumbling, reached out suddenly for Bennett, who was unbalanced and fell through glass to the ground fifty feet below. It was reported that although his injuries were not severe '...the shock was so great that he died in twenty minutes'

In other activities Bennett had been Chairman of the West Bromwich Commissioners and of the Free Library Committee, Secretary of the District Hospital and a Staffordshire Magistrate sitting at West Bromwich and Tipton. He was Chairman of the Sandwell Park Colliery Co., and inspired the trial sinking to 400 feet. He was a member of both the Institutions of Civil and Mechanical Engineers and a Director of the Birmingham Joint Stock Bank. A special Board meeting was held on 1 December and a letter of condolence sent to his wife. The first twenty years of the new Horseley Works was therefore to end in tragedy.

CHAPTER 2
1885-1905

JOSEPH S. KEEP

Following the death of Peter Bennett, Joseph S. Keep became Chairman of the Company and Harry S. Bennett the General Manager. J. S. Keep had an office at 11 Broad St. Birmingham where meetings were occasionally held. James T. Daly offered himself as a Director and after consideration was accepted, joining the Board on 29 April 1886 when G. F. Muntz tendered his resignation due to ill health. The Mortgagees of the works were James T. Daly, William Dempsey, Chas. William Dempsey and Charles Holcroft each in the total sum of £20,000. Towards the end of 1888 the mortgagees each received half of their mortgage reducing the total liability of each to £10,000. The Director's fees were increased in total by £200 – £100/Annum permanently to the Chairman and £100 to J. T. Daly.

The proposals for the railway in the Tucuman Region of the Argentine Republic were approved and significant work was to come to Horseley. The Board Minute Books do not mention matters over which no Board action is required and the order for the major viaduct on the Antofagasta Railway, Bolivia was not directly mentioned although other contracts including 19 sheds for the Central Argentine Railway were. In April 1889 articles appeared in 'The Engineer' on the design and construction of the Bolivia Viaduct and on 1 May, Horseley ordered 25 copies of the work '...constructed and erected by this company'. The author has one of these copies.

Much work was obtained for India – 2 contracts in 1886 for the Indian Midland Railway for bridgework and 2 goods sheds for the Great Indian Peninsula Railway at Bombay, value £3824. In 1887 an order for 98 Bridges for the Indian Midland Railway was valued at almost £19,000 with some bridges of 150 ft. span. The Peninsula Railway ordered £7,524. 1s. 9p. of cast iron piles and some 50 bridges valued over £13,000 with spans up to 100 ft. Work also continued for the gas companies with gas holders at Wrexham, Oxford and Dartford. At Dartford it was reported that this was '...a very good piece of work. Curiously enough the flow of the tide is noticeable here – it percolates underneath the foundations of the tank although it has to flow $1^1/_2$ miles.'

The work on the Rochester and Charing Cross Bridges appears to have gone well and both were complete by 1888. A letter was sent to John Cochrane to express '... our sense of the able manner in which you have performed your portion of the work'. At about the same time the order was taken for the Osney Bridge over the River Isis for the Oxford Local Board, a handsome bridge which remains today. Bridges were also built for Japan, the Bengal and Nagpur Railway in India, and a swing bridge over the River Dee. An order for Lawley Street Warehouse involved 3000 tons of plates, 1000 tons of angles and 1300 tons of cast iron. Two jetties were ordered for Table Bay at £11/ton-about 6000 tons- total value £76,000 in August 1890, and in September an order for one of the piers at Port Elizabeth was received.

SPON LANE WORKS

Problems continued over the sale of this property. In June 1887, A. Kenrick & Sons were asked £10 year rent for use of the large fitting shop for the storage of their patterns. At the same time it was agreed that the seven large cranes should be broken up. A year later the property was offered to the Patent Copper Tube and Wire Co. for £5,000 but this fell through and the building's insurance was dropped to a sum of £1,650. In September 1888 John J. Bowater of West Bromwich offered to rent a portion at £30/annum which was agreed. Kenricks would not agree to a fixed rental for the pattern storage of £50/annum and were instructed to remove them. Felons damaged the property in May 1889 and the Superintendent of the local police was stated '...to have the matter in hand'.

Horseley then set about the purchase of the ground rent of the property for which £900 was offered initially, then raised to £1,200 which was refused. Eventually in January 1890 G. and W. E. Downing, Malsters, of Spon Lane agreed to purchase all except that rented to Bowater at £5,000, conditional on the purchase of the leasehold from the Commissioners of Queen Anne's Bounty which was finally accepted at £1,600. The documents were finally sealed on 30 May 1890. There remained nine small cottages, the total rent being £2/week.

WORKS DEVELOPMENTS

In March 1885 the men in the Foundry were required to adopt piece work and refused. They were given 14 days' notice and the Foundry closed. Three weeks later it re-opened with non-union men and doing without Simcox the Foreman. In May the Foundry was reported to be working well.

There appears to have been no official regulations covering the testing of boilers or chains but in October 1886 the Foundry crane chains were tested at J. Wright & Co., Tipton and a month later new ones were ordered. In December a new drilling machine was being fixed and a new foundry ladle with a patent lip was tried and found to be '...a great improvement – sounder work with less metal'. What was described as Westwood's (Foundry Foreman) method of moulding was also used with success.

In August 1887 Page, the Works Manager, suggested '...that we should utilize the trucks from our siding for testing the bridges – this would necessitate laying down fresh points from the siding and continuing the rail gauge track to the position of the bridges to be tested'. This was accepted as a good idea '...as moving of the of material about the yard is a serious item especially now we have so many bridges in course of construction – moreover the test of loaded trucks is the most practical'. This proposal was agreed and actioned.

In October 1887 the works boilers were tested hydraulically up '...to a test pressure to be specified by Mr. Mould' who would appear to have been, in effect, Chief Engineer and probably in charge of the Drawing Office. A year later it was agreed that the boilers should be tested every six months and in April 1890 it was agreed that the boilers on the travelling cranes and other steam cranes should be tested. Some months later two new vertical boilers were ordered from Davy Paxman & Co., of Colchester at £76. 10s. each less $2\frac{1}{2}$% followed by two more in May 1892 and another in September.

Discussions were held on Allen's Patent Portable Rivetting Machine made by De Bergue and Co., Manchester, but not then ordered. Meanwhile delays were reported in the Boiler Shop due to a number of wooden teeth being broken on the toothed wheel. A demonstra-

WORKS PLAN OF 1892

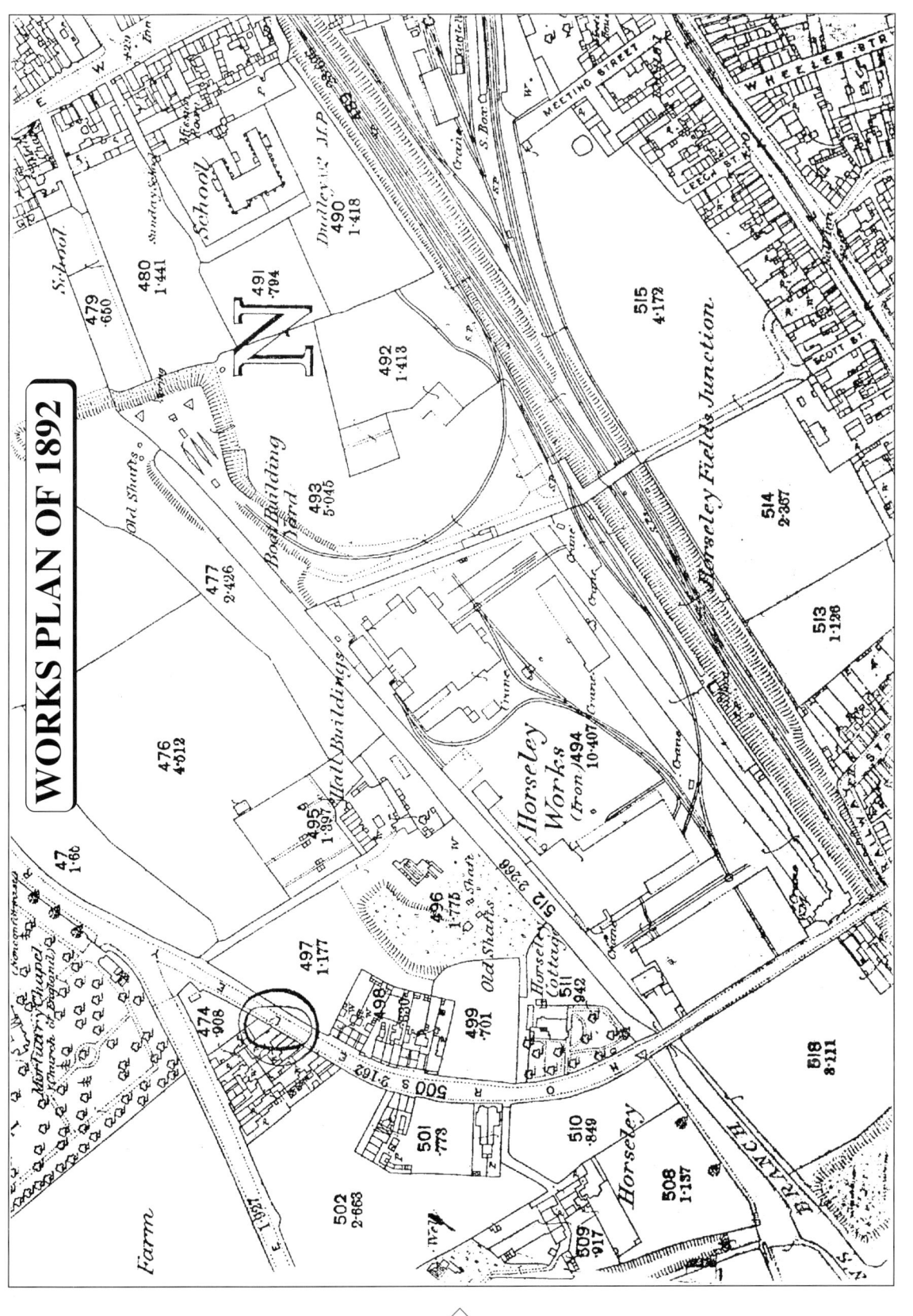

tion at Joseph Evans & Co., at Wolverhampton of a 'Lucigen Light' proved successful and over a period a series of eight were installed.

A fire engine was purchased for the works in 1888 and later the question of supplying the Fire Brigade with helmets was raised – a matter left with the Chairman !. Later there was discussion over fire protection and as Horseley had '…a fire manual engine' there was concern over the water supply. It was proposed '…to lay down a 6 inch main from the canal to the corner of the Pattern Shop and this 6 inch main to connect with the two tanks of the Fitting and Boiler shops. The tanks hold about 12,000 gallons each and would each supply a pump using 60 gallons per minute for 3 hours.' When this had been completed '…there seems plenty of power in the pumps to throw the water on the roof of the Pattern Shop'. In June 1891 J. S. Keep urged that '…the Fire Engine must be had out and into use or everything will be spoilt'.

Other items of new equipment were ordered for the works. The boiler shop cranes were altered in July 1888, a shearing machine from Jessop & Son, Leicester at £125, a drilling machine at £60, Craig & Donald flattening rolls at £105 less 5% were ordered. Prices for a new horizontal double drilling machine were obtained but it was decided to make it at Tipton for £140. A rebuilt 16 spindle multi-drill was later reported to be at work drilling flanges. A decision to operate the overhead cranes in the Boiler Shop by steam was taken and a system of rope gearing installed.

When the Rt. Hon. W. E. Gladstone passed through Great Bridge on 8 Nov. 1888 the men were granted leave from 11.30 a.m. until 2.0 p.m. to witness the event.

J. S. Keep was most upset by '…a sad accident to a lad (loss of right hand) on the new saw', and he determined '…The Co. must try and find a place for this lad. J. S. Keep will see to his being taught writing etc. so soon as he can leave hospital'. A sum of £5 was given to his mother.

In August 1889 there was a need to substantially repair the 5 ton cupola (next to Stonehewers) and also to experiment with Greiner & Erpfs system of upper blast but this was not considered sufficiently successful and removed.

In August 1889 one of Allen's Pneumatic Rivetters was ordered with a receiver and compressor at £300 and much attention was given to rivetting. An oil furnace for rivet heating known as a Lyles Furnace costing £20 was set up with which '…we should materially quicken the work'.

Comparisons were made with hand and machine rivetting:-
    Taking a gang of 2 men and 3 boys:-
    Cook's stationary rivetter   Days work   43 yards.
    Berry's portable
      hydraulic rivetter   "   "   43 yards.
    With a gang of 3 men and 3 boys
    For stationary rivetter   "   "   50 yards.

We shall have to look closely into machine rivetting and only employ hand rivetting where machine cannot be used.

Note. The machines do 60 yards. We shall be able to compare this with Allen's pneumatic rivetter'- This rivetter was later stated '…to be helping us well'. Further machines were ordered in July and August 1890.

Clearly the old form of cast iron girders were no longer made and a number of old moulding boxes previously used for this work were broken up. A new ram and glands fitted to the low pressure accumulator were working well '...and this will be a great saving in time. Our pump in connection with this accumulator is not sufficiently powerful and **causes delay** when the presses are all at work. We cannot with the present pump get the ram up fast enough'.

Six days later J. T. Daly was at Elliots metal works to inspect '...a No. 6 – $2\frac{1}{2}$ inch plunger vertical pump with frame and girders fixed on a C.I. tank. This is for sale'. It was bought for £100 and when set up reported '...as a credit to Mr. Page in the way he has arranged the connections'.

General Manager H. S. Bennett suffered poor health and was away in September 1889 and again in February 1890 when it was considered doubtful if he would return before six months. In November 1890 he was again ill and expected to be away some time.

In December it was decided not to replace the 24 inch cylinder on the Boiler Shop engine but to advertise for an engine '...in a newspaper issued in Bolton or district'. A rivet making machine was purchased from Samuel Platt, Wednesbury at £100, a new hydraulic press at £700 and a screwing machine from Kendall & Gent of Salford at £122.

A major order was received from the Admiralty for 113 lengths of cylinder of ten, eight and seven feet diameter. The ends had to be machined and drilled and the delivery was very short. Great efforts were needed to complete these on time. Problems occurred in the manufacture of sashes which had bosses and so it was decided to make a small cupola specially for these bosses.

In April 1890 matters of health were in review. Firstly the Company joined 'The Provident Surgical Appliance Society' for £5.5s.0d. and then considered '...an ambulance for ourselves as the one is now stationed at the Police Office'. The matter was brought to a head on 5 May when a man '...named John Bright was seriously hurt putting a Band on while machinery was in motion: his arm broken in two places – this man was obliged to remain an hour or more while the Dr. was being found: he was then taken to the Guest Hospital in the Drs. 4 wheel. This decides me to have an ambulance at cost of £10.10s.0d. so that we may take the poor fellows at once to the Hospital'.

A situation occurred in October 1890 with which those involved today will sympathize. Four 60 ft. spans for the Indian States Bridges were trial erected, which the inspector refused to accept – '...as the longitudinal rail bearers do not absolutely butt – iron to iron – on the cross girder. Unofficially, C. W. Dempsey has inspected the bridges and in his opinion they are **practically perfect** and he cannot understand the rejection which to a practical engineer is absurd'.

Having decided to make a compressor for the rivetting machine themselves, it was reported in February 1891 that '...we have now got our "blower" to work which takes the place of the "Compressor Engine" – it is a great success and does credit to all concerned – with engine running 44 Revs. 1'-6" stroke, 9" cylinder we maintain easily 56 lbs press of air in the receiver, steam pressure being 48 lbs in the boiler'.

In March 1891 the rise of James Dunn began. He was Foreman Fitter and he was appointed as General Foreman under the direction of the Works Manager, Page, whom he was later to replace.

Work on the Cape of Good Hope Jetty had progressed well. The inspecting engineer '...expressed his pleasure at the progress we have made with the work and said he had never seen a better class of work all round'.

WORKS PLAN OF 1902

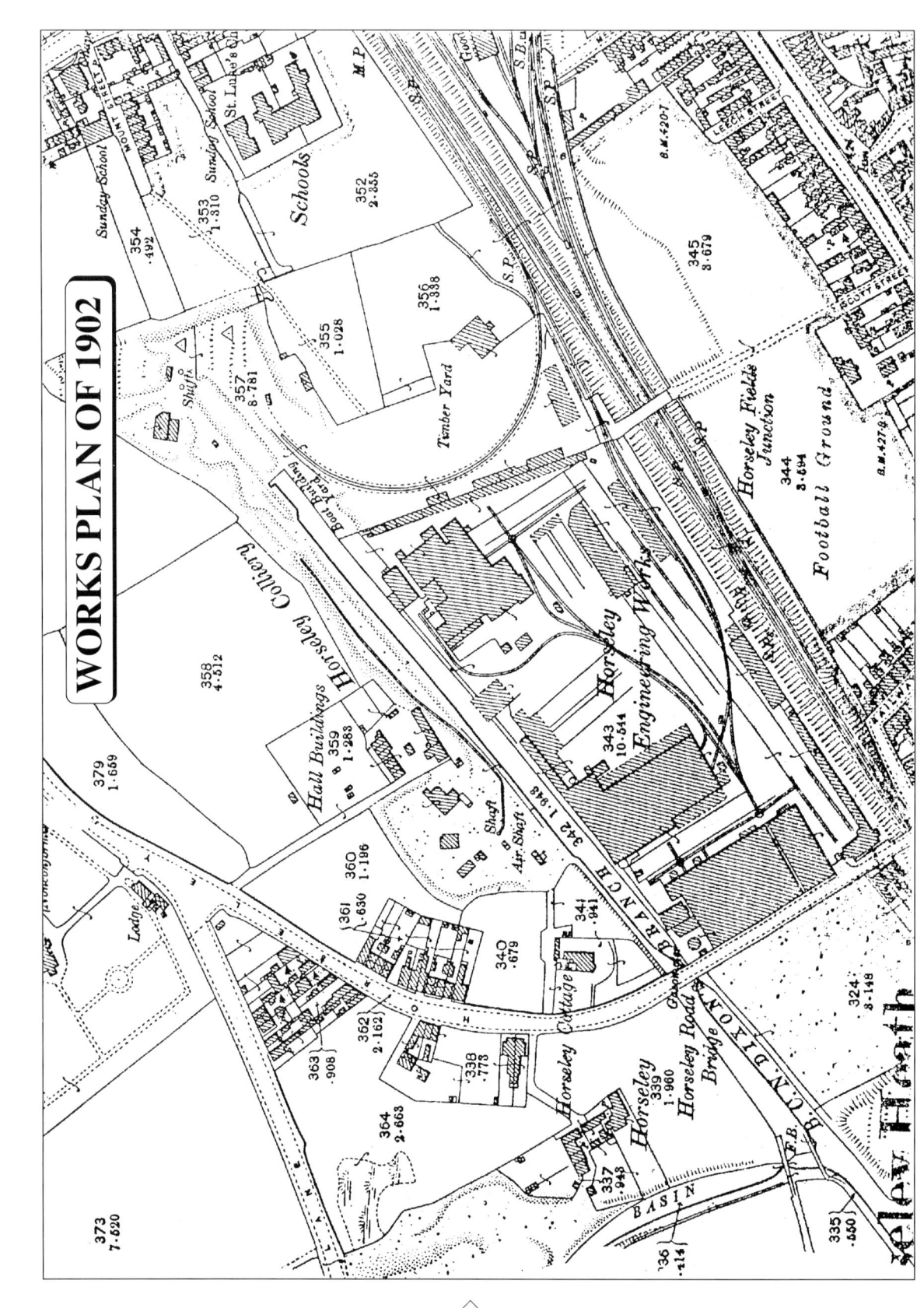

A list of all new plant purchased in 1890 includes:-

8 Radial Drills	£460.14s.11d.
1 Screwing machine	£130.9s.1d.
New Hydraulic Press	£1620.5s.2d.
1 Rivet Making machine (fixed)	£160.18s.9d.
Two Travellers for pneumatic rivetters	£192.10s.0d.
New Saw for hot iron	£82.18s.1d.

Shortly afterwards work in hand plus orders for both Blackwall Extension Work and the Beckton Retort Work were valued at £260,000 total. Some Beckton work was sub-let but with such a work load it is not surprising that many contracts were late and penalties were claimed.

At the suggestion of Page, Norton the Foreman of the Smith's Shop was given a rise from £3.0s.0d. to £3.5s.0d. Also a grant as the previous year of £25 was made towards the mens holiday trip when they had hired a special train. However '...they are to go on Saturday 18 July and to return and be at work 22 July (all of them) without fail or this grant will not again be given".

There were two mens' funds – an Accident and a Sick Fund. This latter on July 1891 was '...indebted to the Company about £5 due to the recent influenza epidemic'. The arrangements for the Sick Fund were:-

1st Class men pay 4d per week entitles 8/- for 13 weeks and 6/- for 13 weeks.
2nd Class men pay 3d per week entitles 6/- for 13 weeks and 4/6d for 13 weeks.
3 c boys pay 2d per week entitles 4/- for 13 weeks and 3/- for 13 weeks.
At man's death- family become entitled to £5.
Wife's death- man became entitled to £3.
Some 40 men were reported away with influenza in January 1892.

In June 1892 what was called 'ordinary dinners' were considered. They had been provided from September 1890 at 6d per head and started "...for the convenience of our clerks etc". The '...average number of dinners per week was 75 at a cost of 7.43d each dinner or at a cost to the company of about 9/- per week'. J. S. Keep later stated '...the dinner account must be amended' !.

The first reference to electric welding occurs in July 1892 when a deputation visited Lloyds tube works '... to see pipes flanged by the electrical weld process'. Significantly the Horseley Foundry had closed a month before due to lack of orders due to unremunerative prices.

Having installed a 12 hp gas engine in 1890 in the Boiler Shop, in July 1891 it was decided to purchase a new gas engine of 16 HP from Crossley Bros. at £400 plus £130 for pulleys and a house. These were the first steps in a change of power in which J. T. Daly was most interested. Suppliers of gas were considered and Tipton Gas agreed. Three years later a 40 hp Gas engine from Messrs. Tangye was ordered together with a Dowson Gas Plant the whole to cost £1,300. J. T. Daly lectured his fellow directors on the economic benefits of gas engines on 29 Jan 1895, and the next month a new 50hp gas engine was ordered. At the same time the rivet furnaces were to be changed from coal to oil. In October 1895 an old engine from the Fitting Shop was put on sale at £50.

On a more domestic note having had problems over '...certain Tradesmans accounts' Mrs. S. Evans, the housekeeper was given four weeks wages and dismissed.

The premium for pupils was reduced to £200 in 1888. Tom Percy Wood, son of Edward Wood, Contractor of Derby and John William Barker, son of John Barker, Civil Engineer of London were admitted in 1890. Barren who had his indentures endorsed in 1890 was transferred to the London Office at £100 per year. In 1894 Cecil D. Inman and Frederick Newton Macartney were admitted followed by Arthur E. Mould in 1895. Inman who completed his pupilage in March 1897 was given 25 shillings a week and Macartney 20 shillings a week.

Short weight in the delivery of pig iron by boat having been discovered, the pig weigher was discharged and two chains were slung across the entrance to the wharf and padlocked to keep boats out when the works were closed. A hut was placed on the wharf for the new pig weigher.

Problems occurred at high level in January 1891 when a special Board meeting was held to consider '…the matter of Mr. Bennett's private correspondence'. The Board '…unanimously condemned the mode of conducting the private correspondence – first with regard to its egotistical manner in dealing with the business of the Company and secondly the personal reflections made on the Directors'. Although Bennett apologised he was at first suspended and then had up before the Board and his apology and regrets accepted. London Office Manager, Batting was also criticized on his method of conducting business by private correspondence and also that from time to time some of this had been destroyed. In his apology he regretted carrying on a private correspondence with Bennett. Batting survived but fully detailed new rules for the operation of the company were prepared and the office of General Manager discontinued and the term 'Manager' substituted. J. T. Daly became Managing Director and responsible for all the company activities; with Bennett as Manager with restrictions on his activities.

Bennett continued to make his monthly reports to the Board but they cease in January 1893 and are replaced by those from J. T. Daly. It appears that Bennett had become ill again – so ill that it was decided in April 1893 to dispense with his services as an official of the Company, but in view of his past services he was to be awarded an allowance of £200/annum. However some three years later Bennett had recovered and '…his health re-established and that he is now able to follow his usual avocation'. It was then decided to terminate his allowance !.

Following this time six new pillar radial drilling machines at £50 each were purchased and a straightening machine at £110 together with a new planing machine from Smith Brothers & Co., of Glasgow at £651 less $2\frac{1}{2}$%.

In January 1892 the 53 hour week – a reduction of 1 hour was introduced – weekdays being $9\frac{1}{2}$ hours and Saturday $5\frac{1}{2}$. The working day was 6 a.m. to 5 p.m. with $\frac{1}{2}$ hour for breakfast and 1 hour for lunch. The labourers had been used to working an extra $\frac{1}{2}$ hour in order to clear up, but this was discontinued.

The weekly wages bill in 1891 and 1892 was compared as follows:-

	1891	1892
Pattern Makers	18 – £22.6s.10p.	23 – £24.15s.2p.
Smiths	43 – 48.17s.2p.	50 – 63.7s.4p.
Fitters	70 – 90.6s.11p.	74 – 87.13s.5p.
Moulders	83 – 120.2s.7p.	113 – 128.6s.9p.
Labourers	103 – 91.19s.5p.	98 – 85.9s.2p.
Boiler Makers	332 – 332.13s.1p.	372 – 334.13s.4p.
	649 – £706.6s.0p.	730 -£726.13s.4p.
		+171 Outworkers.
		=901 – Wages £999.19.7p.

There is a note below this summary that in 1892 some 60 to 65 men were away sick so that the calculation '...is not a safe guide'.

In July 1893 there was a revision to the duties of the Secretary and the correspondence clerk. In June 1894 a change in the Articles of Association were agreed by which the Managing Director was not to be subject to retirement by rotation. His remuneration was increased to £400/annum plus his Directors fees.

Consideration was given to the relocation of the Pattern Store a new one being made in the old Boiler House. The old store was turned into a Sash shop and some £200 spent on tools.

In the first reference to publicity other than by advertisement in technical journals, which was carried out on a broad basis worldwide, the Board resolved in 1893 to '...order some lithographs of the bridges made by the company, also of the ventilating columns and to send them out to the corporations and others with the lithographs of lamp columns and mouthpieces'. At the same time the Foundry men were to be put on the same basis with regard to time as the other departments and they were to be issued with checks in the new year. The death of '.. Mr Dempsey', one of the Mortgagees was reported in October 1893.

In 1894 there was a move to institute a general reduction in wages which the men refused to accept with a result that it was resolved to get rid of '...the higher paid'. An indication of the monthly activity in the company during the period 1888-90 is reflected in the number of enquiries received which was around 60/70 of which some 40 would be tendered, some 6/7 accepted and 10 declined. Two interesting enquiries which did not turn into orders were for the Tower Bridge quoted in conjunction with Andrew Handyside & Co. & John Cochrane, and for the Liverpool Overhead Railway.

Amongst work which was obtained were columns and girders for Montevideo Water Works, tanks at Rio de Janeiro, a significant number of contracts at Beckton Gas Works, some £30,000 work on the Great Eastern Railway, £18,500 on the Daventry & Leamington Railway, Columbo Harbour Jetty at £17,545 and the roof of Liverpool St. Station, London.

Developments in the use of steel are indicated in May 1892 when work in hand for Sir Alexander Rendel was discussed. He confirmed his decisions by letter dated 22 July in which he stated that '...on no account' would he '...agree to material made by the Staffordshire Steel & Ingot (Iron) Co., being used in any girder work nor any basic Bessemer Steel by any maker being used....... I will only assent to even Basic Open Hearth for cross girders and for main girders in compression. The work on main girders in tension I require Acid Open Hearth.'

Although the Horseley Company did not carry on any mining activities they were surrounded by working pits and clearly these concerns were operating beneath the works in some areas. Concern having been expressed by March 1893 the Deeds were examined but it was found that Dixons Trustees had reserved full rights to work the adjoining mines '...without being accountable for any damage or injury either immediate or consequential.'

The position of works manager was never secure. In November 1896, Jacob Page was in difficulty. The earliest reference to him is in January 1888 when his salary was increased to £500/annum. He may have succeeded W. Jacob in 1881. However a confidential report concluded '...that there was a need for radical change .... scarcely a job is carried out at the prices given in .... we want more energy and activity in following up the work in the yard and more time given to it by our Works Manager ..... he should be here at 8 a.m. and

The Fitting Shop

sign the attendance book ... as it is now his time is nearer 9.30 a.m.' Accordingly Page was asked to resign. In his letter he stated he had had '...excessive worry for the last 12 months ... I must have some mental rest'. It was agreed he should be paid his salary for six months. Page was followed by his assistant J. Dunn from 1 March 1897 at £300/annum, and from 1898 this was raised to £350. His was to be a most successful and long tenure.

From 1895 the Board minutes become ever more brief but a number of aspects can be followed in some detail. Each month there was a report from the Managing Director and from Batting at London Office. Regrettably these do not survive, but some further information can be gleaned from the Directors' Day books. For example, those engaged in the yards included 33 painters, 21 on duties such as carters, iron unloaders and pig weighers and 38 labourers.

A patent welding machine on the Lamures system was purchased for £20, a new oil rivet making furnace was installed. A very severe gale occurred on a Sunday in March 1895 which ripped off the Smiths' Shop roof, demolished two chimneys and rendered a third unsafe and caused extensive damage to all the roofs. One inspector '...Casson was considered to be impractical, frivolous and vexatious' and was not to be allowed on the ground again! In January 1897 Messrs Piggott were urging Horseley to join the local Association of Employers. In the same week a Rowland Hill came to see J. T. Daly. The next month saw the draining of the canal arm so that access could be given to the Colliery opposite to the works. The water was said to be '...too foul even for an eel to live'.

In November 1895 it was decided to make no more Mortar Mills which had been a standard product. In an attempt to save money the tasks of painting, unloading and loading up were put on a piecework basis. Early in 1896 new plant was purchased – a pneumatic or hydraulic rivetting machine and a 5 Ton steam travelling crane – maximum total cost £500. This crane was later reported to be doing '... valuable work'.

Only those tenders which required 'sealing' by the Board are mentioned in their minutes, but significant work in the issue of tenders continued. During March 1896 – 105 enquiries were received, 79 tenders issued, 6 orders accepted and 21 declined. This was a record but usually some 50-70 enquiries were received each month.

The Foreman Moulder, Alfred Westwood designed and patented '...rollers for bridges'. It was agreed a pattern and model should be made. Horseley persuaded him to sell his patent and the product was then known as the 'Horseley Patent Bearing' and 1000 lithographs were printed for publicity. In 1899 the Board approved '... an arrangement securing Watts so called improvement on these bearings, the Patent which has been taken out in Watts name'.

The general trade level must have been high in 1896 as a number of platers left, some to join the Ashbury Railway Carriage & Iron Co., at Openshaw. Platers marked out the position of holes on the iron or steel prior to drilling and then assembled the members. These men left without giving proper notice or finishing their agreed work. However it was considered '...not politic to summon them for neglect of work'. The remaining men were offered an extra 2 shillings a week.

The working area was extended in 1897 when two additional races with light gantries were to be constructed on the '...Core Bar Ground' at a cost of £250. Evans who had been Foreman of the Fitting Shop left and was replaced by Mr. Sanders, at 52/6d per week for 6 weeks, then rising to 55/- per week. The Queen's Diamond Jubilee was celebrated by a holiday on the 22, 23 & 24th July 1897.

A new pupil James Douglas Murray was accepted in August 1896 but in July 1897 the premium for pupils was increased to 300 guineas. At the same time the rivetters asked for a rise of 2 shillings a week which was allowed. On the 28th of July a visit was received from members of the Institution of Mechanical Engineers but only three arrived. A few more came later who had been entertained to lunch by the Mayor of Wolverhampton!

New plant was again ordered. A shearing machine from Craig & Donald at £580 and an hydraulic press at £1196. 10s. 6d. This press required very large foundations. Regrettably a helper at one of the existing large presses got his head crushed by falling plates owing to the breakage of a chain.

Horses were in use for many duties in the works. One of the best which had cost £65 died suddenly. The old Foundry horse had to be destroyed as '...he was cast last night and nearly knocked himself to pieces – his eye was knocked out – awful suffering –'. On 3 December 1897 Chairman J. S. Keep reported '...I think it is great damage to our horses galloping up with the trucks of coke. Could the Jumbo do it? I shall some day want to buy a small Tank Loco, if I can do it for £200 or about.' Confirmation that this was bought comes from an accident when on 8 Feb 1898 William Carpenter was crushed between the buffers of some trucks. Although the inquest was 'Accidental Death' it was agreed that a whistle was to be put on the Loco and it was to be sounded '...all the time it was shunting and removing trucks.' There are however many later references to the purchase and use of horses.

An extra strip of land near the works railway siding was rented from the LNWR at £10/year and then consideration was given to the use of the land '...opposite to these works', on the opposite side of Horseley Road. Horseley offered an advance of rent from £7 to £10/year or to purchase at £100/acre. This offer was far too low and they finally agreed to pay £250/acre, the land was fenced for £200 in May 1898 and in July the transaction was complete – 2 Acres 3 Roods cost £687.10s.0d. Some two years later the question of a railway across the Horseley Road to this land was discussed but there is no evidence that it was constructed. Plant was put down on the land in 1905.

One aspect which engendered action was the Workers Compensation Act which came into force in 1898. Stated to be probably the first accident under the new Act occurred at Horseley at 3.00 a.m. on 30 June when puncher John Backhouse crushed his toes and one had to be removed. At first Horseley refused to pay what were considered the '...excessive rates quoted' by the insurance companies, but later accepted an offer from the Scottish Employers Liability and General Insurance Co., Ltd., at 11/6 per cent of the wages paid. In 1900 this was changed to 12/6 per cent of the wages paid and half the profits on the results of twelve months working. (Presumably of the scheme).

In 1901 the situation from 1898 was reviewed. There had been 92 accidents and 4 deaths. The total compensation paid out had been nearly £1,000 and the premiums £721.10s.11d. Scottish Employers tried to raise the premium to £3 per cent but Law Accident Association Ltd. required only 10/- per cent and were accepted.

One of the deaths is noted in the minutes. Foreman Avery was killed on 5 May 1898 and his wife allowed 10 shillings a week for 4 years. Ben Hill who had lost a leg at the hydraulic press was granted 10/- week from September 1897. He was later to be fitted with a peg leg at £2.2s.0d. to £3.3s.0d. or which Horseley agreed to pay if requested! In July 1898 Bowen, an apprentice in the Pattern Shop lost two fingers on the band saw. This was considered to be less disastrous as they were the two least used on his left hand! Men Southern & Grice were involved in an accident in January 1901.

Further new plant was purchased in 1898:– two lathes for £199.8s.0d., a pile turning lathe at £180 and a rivet making machine at £150, also a new steam travelling crane at £900. The author suspects this to be the heavy crane in the main race – later converted to electricity – which survived until the 1970s. Some parts of the crane were supplied by Horseley. Two new fires, a stamp and the necessary shafting were purchased at £300 for the Smiths' Shop. At the same time there is reference to a 'telephone message' so that the system must have been installed.

Items noted from the Day Book include a reference to the ties on the Nottingham Roof where welds should be avoided '...which are in steel very dangerous'.

In order to minimise disruption the holiday held on Tipton Wake was proposed to be merged into the August holiday. In July 1898 a record despatch of 1766 tons in the month was recorded. In November 24 engineering students visited the works and were entertained to '...tea and cake in the large room', and foreshadowing later events Bewlay & J. Spencer of Piggotts met J. T. Daly to discuss Buenos Aires work with which Arthur Lloyd of Piggotts later agreed to assist.

2 February 1899 there was a great snowstorm and the water later overflowed from the canal. When the urinals and W.Cs. next to the office were repaired they were found to be '...in very bad sanitary state and a wonder we have escaped typhoid'! Support was given to the Birmingham University Scheme in the sum of £500 but William Sharrock, secretary of the Boiler Makers Association was stated to be '...on the war path and demands 2/- per week'. Having laid new gas mains a remarkable reduction in usage from 229.000 cu. ft. to 92.000 cu. ft. was recorded.

In the first reference to Military Service the effect of the Boer War is felt when G. Miles the leading man on the hydraulic press was called to the reserve depot at Newcastle. As the Government allowance was small Horseley assisted his wife. The next man called was single so no action was taken.

In 1899 a strip of land – presumed to be on the edge of the land purchased on the opposite side of the road – was sold to the Birmingham Canal Co. In return they reduced the rent of the Wharf frontage from £10 to £2 /year. Problems with land sinkage due to mining, first mentioned in 1892 became more acute in 1899 and in 1900 consultation was held with S. Bailey the mining engineer. He visited the underground workings of Hayward & Co., at Dixon's Horseley Colliery and discussions were held on the effects and likely future effects. Hayward was paid £100 – one half of '...the cost of cogging the road in our lateral supports', – that is supporting the roof of the passage in the mine.

Reports from the mining engineer were read each month but are not detailed, but he referred to Nos. 4 & 5 pits. The cost of the repairs to the Foundry buildings including three roof trusses which slipped off their shoes and to the wharf was £1423. 7s. 8d. plus a fee of £100 to the mining engineer. In 1903 it was agreed that the Fitting Shop '...be tied and any other building if found necessary', that is tie rods inserted in the building.

An accident occurred to a painter, Harris on 28 May 1900 from which he was later to die. Later in the year Ed. Sockett suffered an accident whilst oiling the shafting in the Fitting Shop. '...the muscles of his arm were torn and mortification set in'.

Old primary power technology survived in May 1900 when a new 50 hp gas engine and a planing machine for the Boiler Shop at £1500 were authorised. The proposal for the 50 hp engine was rescinded in March 1901 and a Stockport Gas Engine of 125 Brake Horse Power ordered, the advantages of this being put by J. T. Daly. However in July there was a proposal for the installation of electrical plant '...in the new Planing Shop and the small Boiler Shop'. This was discussed with the Electric Construction Co., at Wolverhampton and by October it was agreed that they '...had enough information' and should proceed. This became scheme No. 1 and cost £1496 as the supply of one 25 bhp and one 15 bhp was to be deferred.

Later more power was thought to be needed and another 50 hp gas engine considered but deferred. In July 1902 electrical scheme No. 2 was agreed, including a dynamo at £475, switch board £32, cables £100, emergency gas engine and house, clutch, belt pulleys, etc £1600 – total £2207. Chairman J. S. Keep ceremoniously turned on the current to start the six throw pumps and shearers on 28 May 1902. Scheme No. 1 was complete in October 1902 and in April 1903 a further £2,000 was allocated to complete Scheme No. 2 and in September a further £3,000. By December 1904 all the work was completed including the lighting of the shops and a spare armature not originally decided upon. The total costs of converting the works to electricity had been £9,057.3s.4d.

Following the reduction of the pupils' premium to £200 in December 1900 one was engaged and also an apprentice at £20. The pupilage fee was reduced to 100 guineas in 1902. Following the erection of some New Sheds at £750 in 1899 a new boiler for the Foundry was purchased from H. & T. Danks and later some new tools for gas holder and other work at £1200.

The funeral of the late Queen Victoria took place on 2 February 1901. '...throughout the district this day was observed as one of mourning and respect for our late Queen and all business was suspended'.

Chairman J. S. Keep congratulated J. T. Daly on his continued efforts to get work and stated '...what a mercy it is he's young and healthy and not old and worn out man as I am'. In 1902 the railway siding had to be renewed, the Horseley share being £123. At the same time documents were sealed with the LNWR concerning their land leased for the Strong Room and the new Machine Shop.

The question of additional land and the effect of mining continued. In 1902, £200 an acre was offered to Stonehewer for his land as marked on a plan but Stonehewer deferred his decision. It is suspected that mines in the area were being worked out as in 1903 there were negotiations with Charles A. Clarke of W. J. Haywood & Co., with regard to the purchase of Parker's mines and surface land. F. W. Peacock of Dixon Amphlett & Bedford also wrote concerning the abandonment of their mines but Horseley reminded them of the agreement of 7 Nov. 1874 when the value had been specified at £625.

Parkers estate was purchased for £1500 but the offer of £400 for mines at No. 3 Rook pits on the N. W. boundary had been declined. The No. 5 pit having been abandoned the purchase from Dixon's at £625 of the Eye Pillar mines was completed. An offer of £500 was then made for the No. 3 pits on the N.W. boundary, which was finally raised to £600. The purchase of Parkers estate appears to have included Stonehewer's land and he was requested on a number of occasions to remove his timber. Further, he was reminded that Horseley now had an access via Scott Street. Dixon's turned down the offer of £600 for the No. 3 pits stated to cover 2 acres 1 rood 12 perches of land and 6 acres 2 roods 28 perches of mines. In July 1906 Dixon's offered to sell at £900 but Horseley declined and the matter was left until after the end of the period of this chapter.

J. T. Daly was a director and on the board of Littleton Colliery and frequently attended their meetings, The first truck of Littleton slack arrived at Horseley on 2 April 1902, Horseley having made and erected much plant at the colliery.

A record lift of $31\frac{1}{4}$ tons on a girder 110 foot long was recorded on 16 April 1902. It was 'lifted by the main gantry with wire rope falls onto 2 bogie trucks (Pollen A & B) and was to travel on the Great Western Railway to Newport. The lifting pole will be 16 inches square'.

On 2 June 1902 it is noted '...Peace was signed in Pretoria yesterday closing 32 months war in South Africa. A deputation of men applied for a half day holiday and the works closed at 1.00 p.m What should have been two days holiday on 26/27 June 1902 for the Coronation was postponed '...owing to the illness of the King, our men decided to work'.

Much of the girder work continued in the open on the races. What were referred to as 'covered races' i.e. workshops, were discussed in November 1903 and in January 1904 material was ordered for their construction. They were to be 150 feet long and 40 feet wide. J. T. Daly stressed the '...extreme importance of covered spaces' in May 1904 and in November £1500 was voted for foundations, stanchions and principals for an area marked yellow on a plan and for two electrical cranes for the two bays already completed marked red on the plan. It is considered that these bays were those which became known as the Tank Shop before their demolition in the 1940s.

Further land deals occurred. when Doughty who had a 'Hinge Works' offered to buy land adjacent to his works – part of the Parker Estate. This was offered to him at 1/- sq. yd. without mines or minerals and eventually agreed at a total of £150.

As a private company the Horseley shares were not quoted on the Stock Exchange. The matter was considered in 1903 but dropped, however there was agreement that the shares should be £1 value and not £20. New articles had been proposed by a shareholder Pritchard in 1903 and Articles 109 & 79 of these had to be changed in 1906 in order to obtain a Stock Market quotation.

The death of C. W. Dempsey is noted occurring on 8 September 1903 at 11.45 a.m., his funeral being attended in London by J. T. Daly on 11 September.

On a number of occasions Horseley were approached on behalf of charitable causes a number of which were refused. They did, however, give £25 annually towards the cost of the workmens' summer outing. £500 at £100 a year was given towards the new Birmingham University following a meeting addressed by Joseph Chamberlain. In December 1899 £10.10s.0d. was given to an appeal by the Agent General, Walter Peace, on behalf of the Natal Volunteers War Fund and in 1902, £10.10s.0d. to the Coronation Fund for Tipton. Magnanimity was shown to the wife of Edward Stanton who died in January 1902 after 35 years service as a Time Keeper or on other duties. She was given £10. Gratuitous re-vaccination was arranged for the men in 1902 administered by Dr. Underhill and printed notices were circulated.

Some of the contracts undertaken were noted in the Board Minutes and include a gas holder at Redditch, various bridges and foot bridges for the Gt. Eastern Railway, the swing bridge at Lowestoft, a number of bridges for the GWR and for the London Brighton & South Coast Railway, including a viaduct at Battersea valued over £30,000, work for the Gas Light & Coke Co., at Nine Elms & Bromley valued at £25,000 and at Beckton valued at over £25,000, the steelwork at Nottingham Station, Birmingham Corporation purifiers at Saltley valued £13,000, Denver Bridge on the River Ouse, the Tram Car Depot at Coventry Road, Birmingham.

Information on other contracts during the period is given in Company catalogues and include :–

Bridges

Great Central Railway, London & Loughborough	6,000 Tons 1895/6
London & Blackwell Railway	3,670 Tons 1891/6
Gt. Northern Railway. Leen Valley Extension	1,000 Tons 1895/6
Midland Railway. – Leicester & Kingston	1,000 Tons 1891/2
London & N. W. Rly. Leamington to Daventry	1,400 Tons 1893
London & N. W. Rly. Lawley Street	800 Tons 1895

Buildings

Palace Theatre – London	350 Tons 1889
London B. & S. C. Rly. Sheds, Battersea Park	2,140 Tons 1904/5
London & South Western Railway	650 Tons 1896

Station Work

Great Central Rly. London to Loughborough	4,000 Tons 1898
Midland Railway. Lawley Street	4,000 Tons 1894

Jetties

Dom Pedro – South Africa	600 Tons 1902

Chairman J. S. Keep suffered an illness in early 1904 and was much weakened afterwards. In August he wrote that on his visit he '...was glad to have the arm of one of the men' and on his next '...glad to have Dunn's arm'.

Another record is noted in October 1904 – '...the despatch of a girder 47 T. 6 cwt – the heaviest but not the longest'. In 1905 the '...chimney shaft opposite the large boiler shop was dropped by dynamite with 10 cartridges'. Later – Cartwright was injured by 2 plates falling on him and he died shortly afterwards.

The Jetty at Port Elizabeth, South Africa, 1897

In November, it is recorded Mould slipped on a banana skin and splintered his shoulder bone which caused him to be away for almost a month. At the end of the year the '...houses and gardens in Railway Street are creating a nuisance by turning their manure and pig wash into our land'.

Continued use of a locomotive engine is shown by an accident '... to the Shunter Job .... who's leg was crushed between a block of timber and the axle of a wagon'. He was taken to Dudley Guest Hospital by Horse Ambulance. Notification was received that the former Works Manager, Page had died after running to catch a train at Stoke.

J. S. Keep is first mentioned in 1877 and from 1885 the Board Meetings were regularly attended by the Directors – J. S. Keep in the chair, J. T. Daly, Charles Holcroft (who became Sir Charles in 1905), F. E. Muntz and S. Rogers and the Secretary T. Hughes. This was to change on 26 September 1906 when Joseph Keep wrote – '...From old age and other causes I feel quite unable to continue to be the Chairman of this Company longer than today. I beg most respectfully and sincerely to thank all my co-directors for their great kindness and consideration towards my failings'. The Board accepted this resignation with great regret and it was agreed that F. E. Muntz would succeed. So ended an era of steady progress and continued work and improvement.

J. S. Keep died on 13 April 1907, some seven months later, aged 87. He had lived at Westmere, Edgbaston Park Road, Birmingham. His father had been an Ironmonger at Newport Pagnell later setting up as Keep & Hinckley for whom J. S. Keep acted as traveller, and later joined his father as partner, the firm becoming Keep & Son. J. S. Keep had been associated with Sir John Jaffray and others in founding the Birmingham Joint Stock Bank, which later amalgamated with Lloyds when he became a Director. He had also been a Director of the Midland Wagon Co. and also Elliotts Metal Co. and had represented Birmingham Council on St. Mary's Ward from 1860 to 1863.

He was survived by two sons and five daughters. Amongst many at the funeral were F. E. Muntz and J. T. Daly, and amongst the floral tributes were those from both the Directors and the Officials of the Horseley Company.

CHAPTER 3
1906-1919

THE FIRST WORLD WAR

Frederick E. Muntz took up his duties as Chairman in November 1906 and shortly afterwards pneumatic rivetting was considered and the order for the two electric cranes in September confirmed. A compressor costing £500 was ordered for the rivetting machines. In a move to reduce production costs, the benefits of high speed drilling machines was investigated and it was agreed to make a trial '...of quickening the speed of the drilling machines in the different shops'. These experiments were successful and three high speed drills were purchased in December 1907.

In October 1907 the labour situation in the Foundry was considered to be unsatisfactory and it was decided to dismiss the Foundry Foreman, Westwood and the moulders on 6 November and re-open the Foundry on the 7th obviously with selected men from the old labour force. John Davis was the new Foreman.

There was a Steel Association which met in London but then a 'National Association for the help and protection of Fabricators', referred to as the B. & C. I. Association – possibly the 'Bridge & Construction Industry Association', was created. Its legality was discussed with Counsel and stated to be in order. A Works Committee was set-up with J. T. Daly as Chairman and Mould, Dunn, Hughes, Perks and Cherrington as members. They were to hold regular meetings.

In December 1907 the drillers threatened to strike, accepted an offer and then went on strike for which they were all instantly sacked, replacements then being taken on. In March 1908 there was a change in the working hours and confirmation of the ban on overtime. The new hours were 7-12; 1-5.30 and 7-12.30p.m Saturdays making 53 hours. A few weeks later Saturday was reduced to 7-12 with a total of $52^{1}/_{2}$ hours. The work situation continued to decline and in September '...having in view the continued depression in trade' it was decided to reduce all salaries of over £100/year by 20% and the Directors agreed to relinquish their fees. They also dispensed with the services of Mould by giving him £125- three months salary. He died in April 1909. Senior Foreman J. Screen became ill and his son took over with Onions, a plater as his assistant.

The possibility of new mortgage arrangements was considered and a loan of £1500 by Sir Charles Holcroft paid off. It became necessary to repay mortgage sums of £2500 each to exors of the late Sibella Benthall and C. W. Dempsey. This £5,000 was then mortgaged by Sir Charles Holcroft.

In April 1909 a Wilson Gas Generation Plant offered by the Horsehay Company was ordered at a total cost of £4,500. Gas engines of 89 and 40 hp were ordered with electrical generators at a total cost of £660 plus a house at £50. Gas heating was extended to many of the furnaces.

The Board meeting on 31 December 1909 was held at the Shrubbery, Kingswinford the home of Sir Charles Holcroft who was becoming ill. Shortly afterwards in January 1910

Rowland Hill of the Firs, Kidderminster was elected a Director and he attended for the first time on 29 April. Sir Charles Holcroft returned his Director's fee of £75 in view of his reduced attendance and in April 1911 he asked for permission to retire. It was agreed that his name would remain as a Director and that he would attend when he could. He attended the next meeting on 31 May, his last, and this meeting was, after the formal business, adjourned to Kingswinford.

Changing modes of transport are noted in November 1909 when J. T. Daly reported that he had motored to Littleton, then to Umberslade and back to Wednesbury. In 1910 the local M.P., Norton Griffiths, returned from Canada and J. T. Daly drove with him around the constituency in a coach and four.

In February 1910 gales caused further damage to the slated roofs and a brick wall by Stonehewer's was blown down. On 20 May 1910 the works closed for a day on the occasion of the funeral of King Edward VII. The work situation improved such that by May 1910 the salary reductions were rescinded and the Directors' fees paid from 31 March. The Managing Director, J. T. Daly's, salary was increased to £1,000/annum. and the new lease of London Office was sealed. Thomas Harrison who had acted as Storeman for 51 years retired in July and was voted the sum of £50.

The working hours, changed in 1908, were not satisfactory to the men and when a vote was held some 540 voted to return to the old hours with only 30 against. From 31 August work again started at 6.00 a.m. In October 1910 – 32 students from the Crystal Palace School of Engineering visited the Works. They were said to be '...closely associated with the Westminster Engineers'.

On 9 March 1911 '...two kinds of fire extinguishers were tried in the field opposite the Works, one the Sanzer bucket pump and hose, the other a cylinder of 3 gallons, filled with water and $2^1/_2$ lbs of bicarbonate of soda and $2^1/_2$ ozs. of sulphuric acid. These chemicals when united form the mixture which gives the pressure for throwing the mixture over the flame. Both methods were successful.'

In May 1911 a meeting was held with the Works Manager at Piggotts '...re pressing tank plates' and on 22 June a holiday for Coronation Day was held.

In 1912 a number of land and mining transactions took place. In February Stonehewer offered to sell their land and this was agreed for the sum of £4,000. They were informed of the terms on which the canal dock, the land on the other side of the railway and the use of the railway siding would be let to them. Their timber business included a boat building yard situated at the end of the Dixon's canal branch and a separate rail branch which ran from the same branch which fed Horseley.

Horseley then purchased the land and mines from Dixon's Trustees for £650 and in April a further purchase was made at £159.15s.0d., the total cost being £834.15s.0d. which account was sealed in July. The final cost of Stonehewer's land which included quantities of timber was £4,389.1s.2d.

G. Gadd and Co. also enquired about land for which they offered 1/- sq. yd. which Horseley declined and were then offered the lot for £1,000. A similar offer was made to a William Thomas. This was for land part of the Dixon's estate near No. 3 Pits, presumably part of that recently purchased. William Thomas purchased at 1/6d sq. yd. an area of 2a. 1r.12p., total cost £843.19s.6d.

Nationally there had been the first great coal strike which commenced in February and ran until April 1912 but Horseley had managed to work throughout. The men were grateful for this and sent a letter of thanks to the management for making appropriate arrangements. On 17 April they watched an eclipse of the sun at maximum at 12.10 and '...had a fine view'.

It was agreed that the offices be modified and the work was let to Mark Round & Sons of Dudley. Furniture and carpets were bought from Maple's in London for the new Board Room in which the first meeting was held on 1 November 1912.

Work increased and the London Office Manager Batting was encouraged by an award of 15/- per cent for any increase in sales over £150,000. This money was to allow him to engage assistants including his son(s) if he wished. Sir Charles Holcroft made a loan to the Company of £4,000 and for security he was given the deeds of Stonehewer's land.

The platers and their helpers in the works applied for an increase which was left for the Managing Director to agree. The Secretary's and Works Departments were to be kept quite separate and while the Secretary was to deal with finances the Assistant Manager was to be responsible for the Works Managers and Estimating.

The possibility of an electrical supply from Ocker Hill Power Station was given extended consideration and eventually agreed at £1,800 in March 1913, an extra £2,000 being added in February 1914 for extensions. The plant was tested at 4000 volts and most motors were being powered by the mains by February 1914. The first Private Branch Telephone Exchange was installed and the increase in work indicated by the returns for February 1913 – Enquiries 97. Tenders 55, Accepted 8, Declined 26. By April 1913 this had risen to a high of Enquiries 106, Tenders 56, Accepted 11, Declined 28.

A Royce crane was ordered for the Fitting Shop and a lathe for the "new Shop" and two 100 hp motors at £120. A rotary converter was ordered from Thomson-Houston.

In April 1913 came a first hint of labour problems as labourers in the Midlands were agitating for 23/- week minimum. The Patent Shaft and Axletree Company and Braithwaites had given it and Horseley appeared to have no option. However the employers created a Midland Federation of Employers '...to organise against undisciplined labour'. To support this they subscribed 1/- in every £100 wages paid. Trouble did arise and on 13 June it was noticed that an '...agitator was addressing the men outside the Works'. On 25 June a large crowd of demonstrators arrived outside the works and sent in four men but '...it was not known who they represented as they refused to give their names.' They were told that the firm was '...in the hands of the Midland Employers Federation. Our men went out as usual at 1 p.m. to dinner and although we had police protection the men were intimidated from returning to work at 2 p.m. At 2.30 p.m. we informed the Inspector of Police that we had no alternative but to close the works – the crowd then dispersed'.

The works remained closed and on each day from 28 June to 4 July, except Sunday, there were meetings at the Employers' Federation and Sir George Askwith attended 2, 3 & 4 July with the men's representatives. Finally, a conference was held in Birmingham, '...attended by employers from the Rolling Mills, Nuts & Bolts and General Engineering and representatives of the various unions. Agreement was reached at 10 p.m. giving the labourers in the Black Country 22/- with a shilling advance in 6 months time and 23/- for the Birmingham District'. On July 8 a notice was posted on the works gates '...Works will start at 6 a.m. tomorrow Wednesday 9 July'. The Works had been idle 14 days.

In October 1913 there was a display at Tipton of a 'Sirius Welding plant' but no comment on its effectiveness is made. Shortly afterwards there was a meeting of the organisation PROOF at London.

WORKS PLAN OF 1913

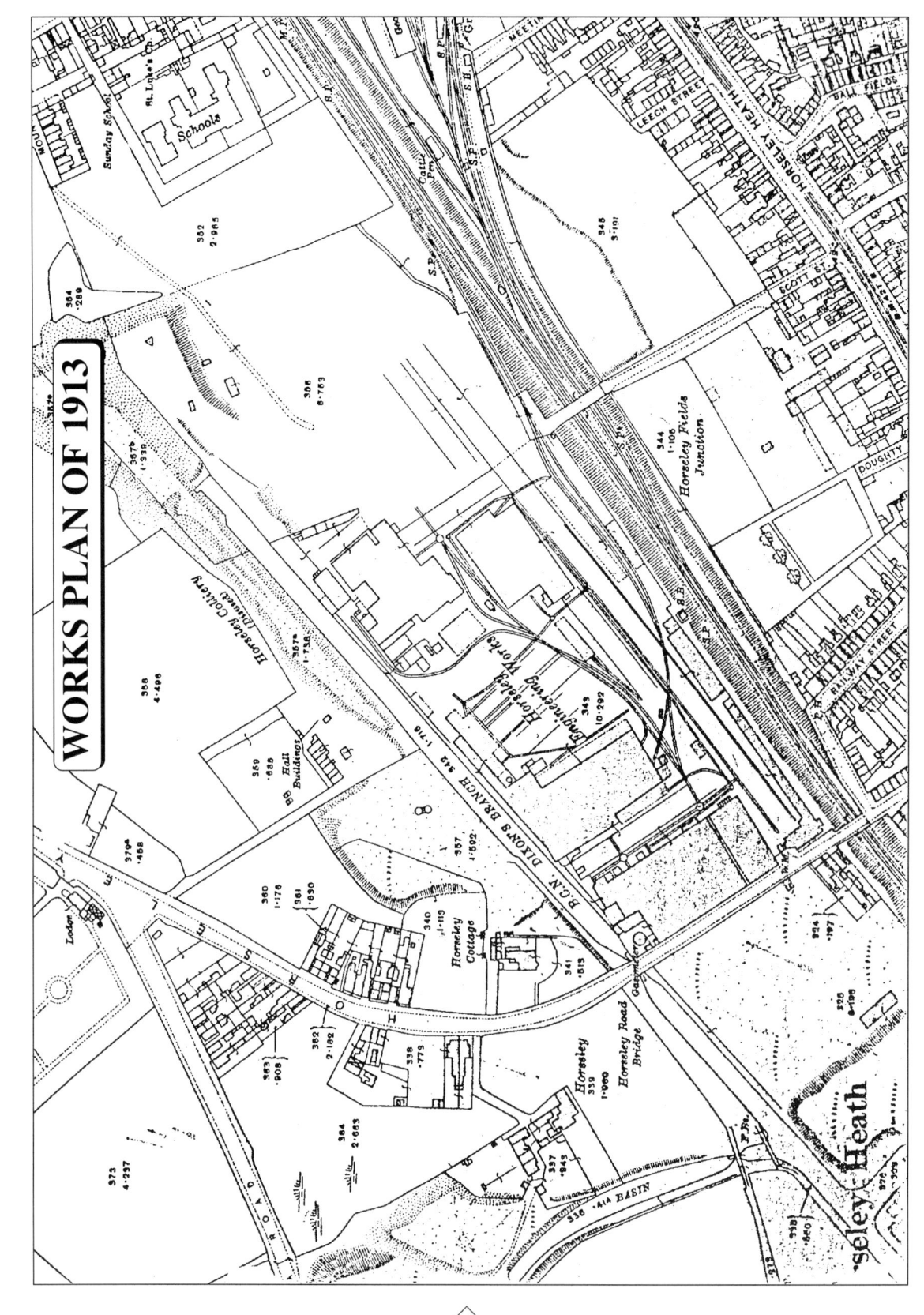

One of the major contracts at this time was for a number of cranes in London ordered by Cory's and the jibs were lifted by the 50 ton floating crane, Hercules. Another was the construction of an extension to Paddington Station by the erection of a new roof. This was achieved by the use of a movable stage beneath the main ribs. A further job was a swing bridge for the Port of London Authorities. In January 1914, J. T. Daly spent a 10 day holiday at Engleberg, Switzerland. Further problems arose when the platers and rivetters demanded an increase and threatened to leave if they were not met in seven days time. Having discussed the matter at a meeting of the Midland Employers' Federation an offer was made to Sharrock of the Boilermakers which after further discussion was accepted. Further troubles came on 23 June when the foundrymen '...downed tools and left' over alleged victimisation of two men. A deputation from the Friendly Society of Iron Founders came and the dispute ended on 29 June.

Stonehewer was slow to leave his old land and was given notice to quit in October 1913 but did not finally leave until July 1914. Further land on the opposite of Horseley Road was sold to the New English Glass Co. Advances in transport continued – when one Bulmer called it is noted – '...sent him in Motor Car to Earl Dudleys.'

No doubt the possibility of war was engaging many minds. The increase in enquiries and work has already been noted. The Board took significant steps in the purchase of new plant to meet the demand. In June 1914 the Managing Director prepared a list which was agreed as follows:-

Compressor & Motor

Approx. cost of Compressor	£250	
" " " Motor	£200	£450
(New Motor as spare)		

Pneumatic Rivetters

Four new frames @ 31.10.0. ea.   £126
2A – 30" x 19½"
2B – 24" x 28"
2 Frames A ready for work fitted with 12" cylinder.
2 Frames B not yet fitted up.
Three new frames 3'-0" deep x 2'9" width of jaw   £60
Patterns made. One cylinder cast.
Second cylinder being cast. Steelwork made
Rivetters to be completed by Sept. 8, 1914.   £200

Annex to Large Boiler Shop

No.4 High speed radial drills – new.   £640
New rails, Traveller, Traveller rails
and joists. Alterations to Shed and
Electric Lights.   £400
New Planing Machine for Fitting Shop.   £250
Already passed by the Board for Rotary
and wiring (27 Feb. 1914)   £2000

Total £4126

The Board Minutes make no direct reference to the commencement of the war and the reports continue much as before, but the Day Book has **'War declared against Germany'** heavily underlined. Soon men were called up and the Company agreed some funding for the wives and dependants and also the mens' contributions to the Prince of Wales National Relief Fund.

Changes in Directors took place in September 1914 when G. H. Holcroft of The Grange, Stourbridge became a director and Rowland Hill resigned. Some seven months later Samuel Rogers resigned due to ill health and Washington Van Wart Kell was appointed in his stead. The death of Rowland Hill was reported in January 1916.

Wage increases were discussed between the Midland Employers' Association and the various unions and in January 1915 all men were granted an extra 1/- week plus a further 1/- for those who had not received an increase since October 1911, and in addition there was a 5% advance on Piece Work Prices. The platers and rivetters asked for a further 2/- week but this was refused. Walter Perks was promoted from Assistant to Manager at a salary of £350 – an increase of £25/year. Wage demands continued and Horseley offered to agree the Birmingham area figure involving about an extra 1/- week and costing them about £2,000 on the year.

Clearly an unusual event as it is recorded – '…Mr. Daly motored to the works from Leamington'.

A new electric crane was ordered for the new machine shop to replace the hand crane and it was soon reported that 60 men were employed on Admiralty Mooring and Dragging Buoys. The Admiralty agents were the Bullivant Company and frequent meetings took place with them throughout the war.

On 6 May 1915 '…all the platers and leading hands had thrown down their tools and left work and had induced the machine and hand rivetters to go out with them in 'sympathy'. The mens action is inexcusable and we are taking the matter up with our Federation'. They returned to work on 10 May. The fitters were not satisfied and soon demanded an extra 3/- week and after negotiation agreement was reached. Sharrock of the Union later agreed there would '… be no more downing of tools without proper notice' Meetings took place under Sir G. Askwith and in December the award of 2/- per week plus 1/- per week after 27 October was confirmed.

It was decided to extend the races to the bottom of the works near the schools. Barber of the Royce Company advised that electric capstans were not suitable and a locomotive engine was needed. On 15 July 1915 a new locomotive 'Pioneer' arrived supplied by Manning Wardle & Co. and on 12 September it was reported '…our Loco 'Pioneer' steamed down to the boundary of the Horseley Co. extensions for the first time over the new Railway'.

In October 1915 the Company received a letter from the Ministry of Munitions informing them they were to be a Controlled Company and subject to the Munitions Act 1915. The possibility of attack by air was a concern and insurance against damage both for the buildings and out-door work was sought. A bridge for Compeigne, France was completed. Throughout the years there were frequent delays to work due to the effects of bad weather, snow and rain and consideration was given to the erection of cover, particularly for the rivetters.

On 31 January 1916 a Zeppelin raid occurred at Tipton, and on 1 February, J. T. Daly recorded – '… I regret to note that between 8 p.m. and midnight yesterday, the neighbour-

Trial erection in the yard of large span bridge for Chilian Railway

hood was visited by Zeppelins and much damage and loss of life – approx 15 deaths and many injuries occurred to Union Street, Tipton. I visited the site and the wreckage of houses and broken glass was in evidence.

From reports the Zeppelins appear to have passed through Nottingham, Derby, Burton, Lichfield, Wednesbury and Tipton arriving at the latter place about 8.30 p.m. and apparently they returned about midnight – what the Zeppelins were doing in this long interval I cannot understand. Most of the Works standing (idle) owing to the Raid'.

On February 7 Mr. Dunn, Works Manager, was sent '...to a Meeting at the Public Offices, Tipton to discuss the best means of reducing the lighting when the presence of Zeppelins are reported. Various suggestions were made and it is to be hoped that they take concrete form. A subscription list was opened for the sufferers of the Air Raid and I sent £10. 10s. 0d. on behalf of the Horseley Company.'

In February 1916 J. T. Daly made a hurried and dangerous visit to France. He left Southampton on 23 February to Le Havre en route to Rouen, by S. S. Normannia, where he interviewed the Port Engineers on an enquiry for cranes which the Cory Company proposed to erect at Rouen. He later visited Paris on the same matter and on 29 February was at Le Havre waiting orders to cross the Channel – a French Mine Sweeper the 'Au Revoir' had been torpedoed outside the harbour. On 1st March the S. S. Vera left without lights and arrived safely back at Southampton.

At Tipton the foremen had asked for an advance and were given 5/- week costing the Company £91 per year (i.e. seven foremen).

A further Board change took place in April 1916 when Sir Charles Holcroft who had been a Director for 41 years retired. His colleagues wished him health and strength for his remaining years. He died on 11 March 1917 aged 86 unmarried and was buried in Brierley Hill Cemetery. He is recorded as having taken a leading part in establishing Birmingham University. S. H. H. Henn, his nephew, replaced him as a Director.

A Midland holiday departure appears to have started at Easter 1916 when the usual hours were worked on Good Friday and Saturday morning with Monday and Tuesday holiday.

Having taken down a shed from 'the field' and re-erected it in the extensions, the Chairman queried whether it could be used by women workers as it '...would be very convenient as to providing conveniences for the sex in proximity to their work'.

On 22 May 1916 the Daylight Saving Act came into force and '...the men started work for the first time under the Act, and the Works Manager reports that the attendance was not good as 67 men were absent, approx 15% short' (i.e. Total 450 approx). At the beginning of June the Government stopped all export work and the Whit Monday holiday was postponed in all firms working on munitions and Tuesday 8 August was considered a suitable date.

War work continued and '...an excess profit of some £6,000' caused difficulty. In July 1916 the position of General Manager was created and Walter Perks appointed. He lived at Clent, and he was to deal with all technical matters, purchases of steel, iron, coal, coke, pig iron, stores and materials of every description, and to be under the supervision of the Managing Director.

Roof at Becton Gas Works, 1890

An application was made on behalf of the Engineering Trades for a 25% advance on day work. A few days later the staff applied for an increase and were given a 5% bonus on salaries.

A month later the name of the Company was changed to 'The Horseley Bridge & Engineering Company Ltd., as '...it would be more explanatory to our business friends'. Due to illness Bowen of London Office retired after 26 years service and was awarded £225 – a year's salary. One Smith was appointed at £200 year. The level of work was such that the arrangement with Batting at London had to be cancelled '...and the amount overpaid be also cancelled'.

In October 1916 another claim was made – 5/- week for day workers and 25% on piece work and this was followed by the Foremen asking for 20% on salaries and later '...the officials made application for an increase'.

A requirement for additional lathes was met by the purchase of some 12 at £1500. The General Staff asked for an increase of 10% 'during wartime'. This was agreed to be paid as a bonus with 5% payment immediately, and Perks's salary increased from £400 to £500/yr. A list of those concerned is given below. The Managing Director's salary was increased by 50% to £1,500/year, this having been agreed by the Ministry.

10% War Time Advance – January 1917

J. Cherrington	Cashier	Kidson	Draughtsman
J. Troath	Contract Clerk	T. H. Allen	Order Dept.
W. Ellis	Prime Cost Clerk	T. Humpage	Clerk
W. E. Evans	Invoice Clerk	E. Fenton	Wages Clerk
T. Cherrington	Draughtsman	J. Bushell	" "
J. S. Leach	"	N. Lofthouse	" "
K. R. Allen	"	H. Easthope	Junior Clerk
E. Evans	"	E. Lovesey	Typist
G. Page	"	M. Perks	"
H. Massey	"	Evans	Junior D.O.
C. Fearn	"	L. Dunn	D.O.
Birch	"		

On 20 January 1917 J. T. Daly attended a meeting in Birmingham '...when Neville Chamberlain addressed our first meeting as Director General of National Service. In February 1917 it was decided to purchase £10,000 of New War Loan issued at 95% (1929-1947) of which £9,000 was to be borrowed from the bank and the remaining £500 from current funds. There was a scheme for the workmen to take up this loan and £1600 was purchased for them '...when payment of their instalments is completed'.

In severe low temperatures the gas went out in the Engine Rooms during the night and the water froze breaking the back end of the cylinder on the 140 hp engine and the back end and cylinder on two 120 hp engines.

An indication of the war effort is given by orders received in March 1917 – for mine sinkers £88,200 and for barriers £16,477. Further quotations were given – £51,660 to the War Office and £72,000 for sheds and steel buildings. The mine sinkers were '...rectilineal vessels 2'-6" x 2'-6" and attached to these vessels is a spherical vessel containing the mine explosive'. The work was anticipated to employ '...200 women before we have finished'.

All this work required new facilities and in July £2,100 was authorised for new sheds and some £2,300 for the cost of a set of hydraulic pumps, motor driven. An accumulator was purchased for these sheds together with a tank and connections of total cost £2,250.

A gratuity of £50 was presented to one Harper who volunteered for military service in September 1914 and in October 1917 the cashier John Cherrington retired after 66 years service and he was awarded £2 week pension and a gold watch with a suitable inscription.

The Deeds of the Company were produced and checked against a list. These are some 32 in number and date back to 1732. Only the date and the type of document is listed and so it is not possible to ascertain to what they refer. The purchase of the land in 1864 is not included as presumably these documents would be held by the bank or the mortgagees.

A copy of a letter received from the Agent General of New South Wales is reported in the minutes and has been copied on to Horseley letter paper. This is interesting in that it contains three vignettes – the swing bridge over the Dee near Chester, bridge over the River Itchen, Southampton and the River Loa Bridge, Bolivia. The letter paper was originally that of the Horseley Co., Ltd., and has been overprinted in red with the new style. The telephone system was installed and the lines were numbers 107 and 108. London Office was at 11 Victoria Street.

The Drawing Office and General Staff asked for a further $12\frac{1}{2}\%$ increase in November 1917 which was stated to be allowed by the Ministry of Munitions. This was granted in March 1918.

Compressed air machine rivetting in the yard

Kingston Bridge for L. & S. W. Rly over River Thames, 1907

C. S. Riddell was appointed in January 1918 having been recommended as a suitable man to organise the mine sinker work. He was from Head Wrightson and given a salary of £400/year, plus bonus of £1/week.

There were great problems and delays on the mine sinkers contract and many complaints were made by the Admiralty with a threat to take away part of the order. The causes were stated to be two fold, '...the suppliers of the various parts are to blame for sending in imperfect parts, but nothing can excuse the bad workmanship of the Horseley Co., especially with regard to the drums and the whole trouble has arisen through the Works Manager not accepting the advice of the Admiralty and their agents.'

Sharrock of the Boilermakers' Union requested a further wage increase which was refused. The Horseley system was to be changed by increasing the number of template makers and providing the platers with all the templates they needed. However on 8 January 1918 a letter was received on behalf of 13 leading platers, 23 platers and markers-off threatening to leave in 6 days time, signed N. H. Jukes, who spoke for them all. Later '... an understanding' was arrived at. The Government had agreed a $12\frac{1}{2}$% and 5/- advance.

J. T. Daly was still not satisfied with progress on the mine sinkers, particularly with the Foreman Fitter, Sanders and stated '...that from time to time I have urged our Works Manager to make a change and now I am insisting'. The work improved and the quality was considered satisfactory but Sanders resigned as of 1 March 1918 after 50 years service.

The 5% War Loan Bonds were sold in March 1918 and replaced by 4% War Loan. Further, some 1243 War Savings Certificates of 15/6d. each were purchased on behalf of the workmen and they were to purchase at 4d. per week for each certificate with 12 certificates as a maximum for each man.

In March 1918 there was a meeting of the Midland Auxiliary Shipbuilding Committee with a view to the building of Standard Ships in the Midlands. Horseley built parts of N1 and N type ships.

In April 1918 Works Manager James Dunn offered his resignation which was accepted '...with great regret'. He had served for 21 years as Works Manager and had 51 years service with the Company. It was stated that '...there seems little doubt that the conditions of the new work and general pressure have been beyond his powers. The interview was a painful one !' C. S. Riddell was appointed in his stead. K. Allen was appointed to take charge of the Drawing Office, Leach having been dismissed.

What appeared to have been harsh decisions, both probably due to age and therefore could have been more kindly dealt with, were alleviated somewhat, when the Board agreed to give James Dunn £500 and Leach £300. A house, 40 Hallewell Rd, Rotton Park, B'ham 16 was purchased in July and was to be let at £30/annum. Its occupant was to be new works manager, C. J. Riddell.

Another death occurred in the works when a rivetter – Webb – fell from a crane and was killed instantly. In another change Morris, the Weigh Clerk was placed in charge of all yard labourers and horse drivers. In June 1918 both Perks and Batting were awarded 10% wage increases. In July J. Davis, Foreman of the Foundry tendered his resignation and 12 girls were discharged for breaking the rules.

The danger of fire resulted in the installation of a 3" water main and the fire insurance cover being increased 50% in August 1918. Some 40 canal men were engaged for a week in clearing mud, debris, coal and pig iron from the canal.

On 5 November 1918 Tipton held a "Gun Week" and J. T. Daly with Doughty and others met the procession. He reported that '...within the first hour £21,500 of War Loan was taken up and one McConeke (?) added a like amount'.

The end of the Great War came with no mention in the Board minutes but J. T. Daly in the Day Book wrote on 11 November 1918 '...This is an important day not only to the Horseley Bridge & Engineering Co., Ltd., but undoubtedly of the greatest importance to the whole of the civilised world as today the Central Powers, consisting of German & Austrian representatives in accordance with their request met the allies, as represented by Great Britain and her Dominions, France, America and Italy to discuss Armistice Terms. These terms the Central Powers accepted and consequently a cessation of hostilities on all Fronts. In Great Britain this was notified to the various industrial centres by hooters and ringing of Works Bells at about 10.45 a.m. The men and women immediately ceased work but before leaving the gates the Managing Director (James T. Daly) addressed a few words to the men and women and told them the Works would re-open on Wednesday 13 inst. at the usual time'!.

So few turned up that the works shut at 10.30 a.m.! A '...fair start' was made on 14 November. Significantly at their meeting on 29 November 1918 it is recorded that the working hours are to be reduced from 53 to 47 per week. They also decided to extend the Girder Shop forward by five trusses '...bringing the shop and travelling crane over the rails – so that material can be lifted from the trucks into the shop and the men will be protected from the weather at the rails and shears.'

It is recorded that during the war '...practically the whole energies of the company were devoted to the manufacture of buoys for the channel barrage, steel barriers for Scapa Flow, mines and mine sinkers, booms and paravanes (towed by ships to clear mines) steelwork

Chapter 3 – 1906-1919

for standard fabricated ships, kites (underwater), cranes, gantries and transporter bridges (75 ft. and 120 ft. spans)'.

However the Board minutes refer also to bridges for the L. B. & S. C. Railway, G. W. R., Great Indian Peninsula Rly. Co., Aqueduct for Outwell, Birmingham Corporation Gas Works purifiers, lift bridges, and other orders.

In November 1918 the purchase'...of the required Loco & tools at £800' was authorised, presumably a replacement for 'Pioneer'. ('Demolished 1928'.) The sum allocated was increased to £1500 on 29 August 1919. This locomotive was purchased from the Ministry of Munitions Board, London and was called 'River'. It is believed to have been a Manning Wardle & Co. engine and was used until 1933 when it was sold for £201-17-0.

It has been recorded in mid 1916 that Bowen of London Office had retired due to ill health. However he seems to have continued in work until November 1918 when his retirement is confirmed and his successor named again as Smith, but this time with a salary of £250/annum.

Another Association – the 'Central Bridge Building Association' was formed in December 1918 and it was agreed that two directors could attend the meetings. A 'Midland Structural Association' was also formed. By January 1919 Sydney Henn is first referred to as Sir Sydney Henn.

The new works manager, C. S. Riddell had his salary increased to £500/annum. plus a bonus and signed a new agreement with the Company. In March the gable end of the

Extension to Paddington Staion for the G. W. R., 1913

Boiler Shop had to be made safe – presumably the continued effects of earlier mining work on the boundary.

The Admiralty advised that they were cancelling two-thirds of the ship work which caused alarm as it was understood this would continue for 2 to 5 years after the war. Financial matters were raised in March 1919. The Company turnover was over £200,000 which was much in excess of the liquid assets which caused a considerable bank overdraft. It was agreed to pay off £10,000 of mortgage, call up the unpaid 2/6d per share and offer the shareholders the remaining £10,500 of uncalled capital. Finally the advisability of raising £50,000 in debentures was to be considered and the bank was instructed to sell the War Loan Bonds.

A night shift was started with Jukes as Foreman and these men were allowed time and a quarter. The front extension of the Boiler Shop was completed during the Whitsun 1919 holiday '...and we shall now take the canal end in hand'.

In July a resume of authorised expenditure on works development was attached to the minutes:-

Boiler Shop Extension 'A'	£4,000
Boiler Shop Extension 'B'	6,000
New tools & Loco (see above)	800
Shaping machine, pulleys etc.	300
Weighbridge	1000
Crane	1500
Foundry Hoist.	600
Alterations to road, new railway Rails, Sleepers etc.	1500
Alterations to Offices.	500
	£16200

'Peace Day' was held on 19 July and a general holiday observed. The Directors' fees were increased by 50% as from 1 April 1919 in July 1919. There was also reference to the offer of some six acres of land at 2/6d yd. but '...the right of way over Scott Street to be preserved'. When the Works re-opened on 7 August 1919 it was against the background of the funeral of Arthur Jones, the leading plater and all his colleagues attended the funeral.

During the period of this chapter there is reference in Company catalogues of other important work not mentioned in the Board Minutes:-

Jetties for Penang	5,000 Tons	1908
Jetties for Freetown	600 Tons	1906
Piers for India Office		1909
Richmond Bridge over Thames for L.S.W. Rly		1907
Kingston Bridge over Thames for L.S.W. Rly		1908
Paddington Station Extension – G.W. Rly.	1,000 Tons	1913

The meeting of August 1919 was significant as the last at which Thomas Hughes attended as Secretary, he having to retire '...due to advancing age'. He had acted for 35 years and was awarded £4 week pension and a gold watch was presented to him on behalf of the Directors and Staff.

This watershed is an appropriate point at which to conclude this chapter. Minute number 5007 was the last to be numbered- a new era was to begin.

CHAPTER 4
1919-1928

THE POST WAR YEARS AND THOMAS PIGGOTT

The Board Meeting of September 30, 1919 had J. W. Baillie as Secretary, a man who was to serve for many years, rise to Managing Director, and be remembered by many living today. He stamped his style immediately by writing more detailed minutes and by reporting each item without a minute number. Each resolution was identified by the word **Resolved** underlined in red.

The repayment of the £10,000 mortgage was actioned and the re-conveyance of the deeds requested, £10.291.13s.1d. being paid to the Exors. of Sir Charles Holcroft, a sum which included interest. There still remained some unaccepted shares and the legality of issuing them to the Company's Officials was considered.

The works gas was to be supplied by The South Staffordshire Mond Gas (Power & Heating) Co., and the London firm of Solicitors to the Company was changed to Johnson, Ekin & Keeling of 36 Waterloo Street, Birmingham.

Due to the national strikes by both the railwaymen and the foundrymen it was considered probable that the works would have to close on 14 October, 1919. However, the railway strike finished on 6 October but the foundrymen continued until at least the end of November. A national coal strike began on 18 October.

On 31 October it is recorded that the General Manager, W. Perks attended the Board Meeting and he continued so to do afterwards. Sir Sydney Henn was ill and asked for six months leave of absence, which was granted, and later was allowed a further two months. The representative of the Works on the Joint Committee was H. Collins.

On 11 November '...This being the first Anniversary of the Armistice, the King appealed to his people for a minutes silence – the men assembled in the yard and the Managing Director gave them a short address previous to the two minutes silence at 11 a.m.'

Two further accidents occurred – a boy crushed his arm and in the Fitting Shop a man's clothing caught in the drill spindle.

The new Secretary was instructed to enter into a Fidelity Bond for £1,000 and in view of the enhanced value of the company property it was resolved to increase the insurance to £120,000.

J. W. Baillie was already making his presence felt and submitted a report on the secretarial and office re-organisation which was approved.

Members of staff had requested some of the remaining shares and the following were allotted:-

C. S. Riddell	750
Mrs. A. M. Baillie	50
D. Perks	25
Frank Perks	25

a.) Works frontage modified. *b.)* Fitting Shop. *c.)* Structural Girder Shop

The remaining 387 were divided between the directors as follows:-

J. T. Daly	96
W. V. W. Kell	97
Sir Sidney Henn	97
G. H. Holcroft	97

In January 1920 it was agreed that the 5/– week bonus being paid as a special war bonus be merged into normal pay and also that the foremen should be given a further extra 5/- week. Some staff in the Drawing Office and General Offices would be given further increases based on merit.

The death of retired director Samuel Rogers was reported and the directors placed on record '...their appreciation of his extremely valuable services to the Company'. At the same time they noted the excellent military record of W. Shakespeare. A subscription list had been opened and it was agreed that the Chairman would make the presentation to him in due course.

J. W. Baillie's services were obviously appreciated and a house – Arthog, Foley Road, Streetly was purchased for £1250 and let to him for £65 per annum. The men who had returned from the war were to be entertained and a sum of £25 was voted towards the cost.

The ends of the two bays of the girder shop before extension. The large shears originally steam-driven can be seen at the end of the right-hand bay

Left: Stuctural machine shop, No. 2 Bay showing plate edge planing machines

Below: A view of the main bay in the foundry

Bottom: Erection race No. 3 (main race)

The Work of the Past.

▢ ▫ ▢

Of the work we have done in all the many parts of the world, our existing records do not extend much beyond the seventies, but the following, which is only an abridged list, testifies that we have more than a fair record for the last fifty years.

BRIDGES.

We have constructed bridges for all the Railway Companies in England, among them being :—

Great Central Railway, London and Loughborough	6,000 tons	(1895/6)
The Railway necessitated over 100 new bridges, including two very large ones at Braunston Gate and Aylestone Road, Leicester.		
London and Blackwell Railway	3,670 tons	(1891/2)
Bishopsgate Street Widening for the Great Eastern Railway Company	3,000 tons	(1888/9)
Beckton Viaduct, for Gas Light & Coke Company	1,500 tons	(1891/2)
Hackney Down Widening for Great Eastern Railway	2,550 tons	(1893/4)
Kingston Bridge for London & South Western Rly. over the R. Thames		(1908)
Richmond Bridge for L. & S.W.R. over the R. Thames		(1907)
Galton Bridge over the Birmingham Canal at Smethwick, Staffs		(1829)
Charing Cross Bridge over the Thames		(1884/5)
Ordsal Lane Railway Widening	2,000 tons	(1884)
Leen Valley Extension for Great Northern Railway	1,000 tons	(1895/6)
Leicester and Kingston, for Midland Railway	1,000 tons	(1891/2)
Bow and Stratford Widening for Great Eastern Railway	640 tons	(1891)
Skinner Street, for Great Eastern Railway	535 tons	(1892)
Worship Street and Mint Street, Great Eastern Railway	800 tons	(1891/2)
Leamington to Daventry, for London & North Western Railway Co.	1,400 tons	(1893)
Lawley Street Widening for London & North Western Railway Co.	800 tons	(1895)
Manningtree Viaduct for Great Eastern Railway Co.	650 tons	
Dore to Sheffield Widening	500 tons	(1902)
Coal Storage Viaduct for Beckton	500 tons	(1894)
Aynho to Ashenden for Great Western Railway.		
New Line, Earlswood, for London, Brighton & South Coast Railway.		

Earlier work listed in a 1922 advertising booklet. Continued on pages 90/91.

A major change in Company finance was envisaged in February 1920 after discussions with the British Foreign Colonial Corporation Ltd. who agreed to take up either 100,000 or 150,000 of new shares at 19/- each if they should be authorised. It was eventually agreed that 200,000 new shares would be issued, half taken up by the B.F.C.C. Ltd., thus raising the total capital to £350,000. Special meetings were held and formal approval obtained. By March 1920, £12,500 had been received from B.F.C.C. Ltd., and the final £82,500 was expected shortly. Eventually the Birmingham Stock Exchange quoted these shares.

In addition, we have made Swing Bridges for—

Lowestoft Harbour; Littlehampton; Hawarden, over the River Dee, near Chester, 140ft. clear span; and others for Port of London Authority; besides Bridges for Rochester and Southampton.

Abroad, our Bridges are scattered over all parts of the Globe, and are far too numerous to specify in detail. They include, however—

Viaduct for Bolivia, 800 feet long, 310 feet high; Bridges for Indian State Railway, 200 feet, 100 feet, and down to 12 feet span; also Bridges for British North Borneo Railway, Great Indian Peninsula Railway Co., South Indian Railway, Assam-Bengal Railway, Queensland Government, South African Union, Nigeria, Gold Coast, Africa Railway (South America), South America, and Japan.

ROOFWORK AND STEEL BUILDINGS.

Folkestone Station, South Eastern Railway Co.		
Goods Warehouse, Huddersfield	4,000 tons	(1884)
Leicester Station, Great Central Railway Co.	400 tons	(1898)
Coal Depot and Bridge, Great Eastern Railway, Cable Street	1,590 tons	(1892)
Purifier House, Beckton	4,000 tons	(1890)
Palace Theatre, London	350 tons	(1889)
Sheds for Battersea Park, London, Brighton & South Coast Railway	2,140 tons	(1904/5)
Rugby Station, London & North Western Railway Co....		(1883)
Waterloo Road Front, London & South Western Railway	650 tons	(1896)
Nottingham Station, Great Central Railway Co.	2,000 tons	(1898/9)
Paddington Station, Great Western Railway Co.	1,000 tons	(1913)

Stationwork for Great Central Railway, London to Loughborough, 4,000 tons (1898); Warehouses at Monument Lane, London & North Western Railway, 700 tons (1884), and Lawley Street, Midland Railway, 4,000 tons (1894); Purifier House, Beckton, 1,500 tons (1889); Purifier House, Beckton, 1,600 tons (1893); Retort House, Beckton, 2,850 tons (1894); Leadenhall Market (1882); Warehouses, Stores, etc., for Buenos Ayres & Pacific Railway Co.; Colombo; East London; Central Argentine Railway; Great Indian Peninsula Railway Co.; Assam-Bengal Railway; Mexico; Hong-Kong; South African Railways.

Clearly this placed the Company in a better financial position and they first paid off the Bank overdraft. Some £30,000 was invested in 3 month Treasury Bills and £10,000 in the Bank Deposit Account, the balance being retained in current account.

The salaries of the principal officials were considered:-

General Manager W. Perks. Increase from £700 to £800 plus £100 bonus.
Secretary J. W. Baillie. Increase from £450 to £600 plus £100 bonus.
Works Manager C. S. Riddell. Increase £600 to £750 plus £100 bonus.
London Agent H. L. Batting. Increase £600 to £800 plus £100 bonus.

Jukes was appointed assistant Works Manager at £350/annum.

JETTIES, WHARVES, DOCK AND HARBOUR WORKS.

Railway Pier for Ryde, London, Brighton & South Coast Railway	1,500 tons	(1878)
Harwich Landing Pier for Great Eastern Railway	8,000 tons	(1879/80)
Three Piers at Port Elizabeth, South Africa	5,000 tons	(1897)
Jetty for Dom Pedro, South Africa	6,000 tons	(1902)
Wharf for Port Harcourt	5,200 tons	(1920)
Jetties for Penang	5,000 tons	(1905/8)

Railway and Landing Pier for Portsmouth (1876); Three Piers at Table Bay; Jetty for Apapa (1910); Wharf for Iddo, 2,000 tons (1920); Jetties for Freetown, 600 tons (1906); Piers for India Office (1909); and Jetties for Secondi, Chittagong, Swettenham; Piers, British North Borneo; Floating Dock, Portsmouth.

GAS WORKS PLANT.

We have constructed Gas Plant for all the leading Gas Companies in the world, some particular items being—

Gasholders and Tanks for Buenos Ayres Gas Co. and the Belgrano Gas Co. (all fixed by us); Purifiers and Purifier House at Kensal Green, for Gas Light & Coke Co., 2,000 tons (1891); 4/4 Lift Gasholders for Manchester Corporation, 4,000 tons (1878); Gasholders for Westminster Gas Light & Coke Co., 1,600 tons (1884), Croydon, Newcastle, Warwick, Birmingham; The Danish Gas Co., Odenso (1885), Frederiksberg (1886), Veil (1886); and numerous holders for the Imperial Continental Gas Association. Also Oil Storage Tanks for Argentine Naval Commission and Asiatic Petroleum Company; Gas, Light and Coke Co., and others.

MISCELLANEOUS.

As is to be expected, with facilities such as ours, a host of structures is constantly being made for all sorts of services. The following are examples :—

Crane structures of all descriptions, including 7 Coaling Cranes, 118ft. 6in. high for dock work (Royal Albert Dock), capacity, 2,000 tons coal per hour; Sheet Piling, Hodbarrow; Steel Riveted Water Pipes, Sydney Water Supply; Coal Tips for Nigeria, West Africa; Ropeways, Dorado, South America; Lighthouse Towers; C.I. Piles and Bridge Cylinders for all parts of the world; Steel Culverts, Antofagasta Railway; Buoys for Admiralty; Pit Head Frames for Colliery work.

The foregoing is merely a record of work accomplished—it can give no indication of the many intricate and troublesome engineering problems we have overcome.

It was necessary to make changes in the Articles of Association of the Company and these were agreed at special meetings in 1920. A house was purchased for Riddell at Edgbaston in 1920.

The Managing Director reported that he considered a change in the layout of the Foundry to be essential and was asked to make proposals, but it was agreed that the preparation of the longitudinal girders be proceeded with. The Foremen requested an increase of £2 per week in April 1920 and the Managing Director was asked to negotiate with them.

A view down the main race with hands leaving work. Upper left is the Template Shop and below the Carpenters' Shop and Stores

Trade was again buoyant as reflected by the enquiries received in April 1920 –

Enquiries	100
Tenders	41
Accepted	16
Declined	5

As usual the Company made a donation towards the workmens' annual outing, this year of £60 and uniquely as part of the annual dividend £100 was allowed to be divided amongst the staff. The Foremen, no doubt aware of the buoyant situation sought an increase. Gay was given 10/- week and the others refused, but it was indicated that a percentage bonus scheme would be considered and such a scheme was later agreed.

J. T. Daly was again concerned with power supplies and recommended a scheme to separate the lighting system from the power at a cost of £5,500. To assist with the cost it was decided that as they had an excessive amount of iron scrap for the Foundry some 1500 tons would be sold. A month later another 700 tons was sold.

In addition some 35 items of old plant were sold to J. Cashmore.

These included :-
>
> Planing Machine-Embleton & Co.
> Slotting Machine-Sharp Roberts & Co.
> Cutting off Machine-R. Roberts & Co.
> Various drills and lathes & punching machines.
> Wilsons power gas plant by Horsehay Co.
> National gas engines.
> Steam travelling crane.
> The total received was £2,297.8s.7d.

In September 1920 Len Harper was appointed as outside sales representative at £350 annum. He was to remain local for only some twelve months before he was transferred to the London Office where he was to serve with distinction for very many years to come. In 1927 his salary had increased to £600/annum.

In October in response to a letter from A. J. James, his son L. H. James was admitted a pupil without premium. (Would this be a member of the present Engineers, R. T. James & Partners?) Perhaps in response to the problems of the 1920s some consideration was given to insurance against loss due to riots or civil commotion.

A major boost to the order book occurred when news arrived that Horseley's offer for the jetty at Port Harcourt, Nigeria had been accepted for the sum of £289,000. This was at the meeting on 29 October 1920 which sadly was the last to be chaired by F. E. Muntz who died at Umberslade, Tanworth in Arden on 25 November 1920 aged 75, having been Chairman for fourteen years.

He had been educated at Corpus Christie College, Cambridge, called to the Bar at Lincolns Inn in 1873. He became High Sheriff of Warwickshire in 1902, Honorary Major of the late 3rd Battalion of the Devonshire Regiment, Lord of the Manor of Tanworth in Arden and had contested the Rugby Division of Warwickshire in 1899. The Board of Directors' meeting the day after his death expressed their profound sympathy with his widow and family.

J. T. Daly took the chair at the October and December 1920 meetings before he was formally elected Chairman in January 1921. At the same meeting Walter Perks was elected a Director.

On 11 November 1920 the men again stood for two minutes silence on the second anniversary of the Armistice. This practice continued each year and a bugler sounded both the 'Last Post' and 'Reveille'.

Work was becoming more difficult and it was agreed that a cost variation clause in Tenders could be dropped pending a satisfactory number of orders on the books. An increase was allowed for the General Office & Drawing Office Staff and new staff Dining arrangements were approved. The question of subscribing to the funds of the University of Birmingham was considered but deferred.

At the end of 1920 there were problems at Ocker Hill Power Station said to have been due to the lack of spares during the war. It was two days before current was restored. The final meeting of the Midland Auxiliary Ships Committee was held on 20 January 1921.

J. T. Daly's proposals for changes in the power system were approved in February 1921 when an A. C. distribution system was agreed at £2692 but later deferred. The proposals on power were later re-considered and an offer from the British Thomson-Houston Co., Ltd. accepted for a rotary converter and transformer at a cost of £3,300. A new motor for the pumps at £350 was purchased, but a scheme to extend the works railway system was postponed.

Significantly the overdraft facility at the Bank was raised to £100,000 and no further expenditure exceeding £25 was to be made on maintenance without sanction of the Management Committee. This Committee first met on 14 March 1921 and comprised J. T. Daly, W. Perks, J. W. Baillie and C. S. Riddell. Its function was to discuss '…any item which on consideration may be of benefit in the working of the company.'

The Company Cashier and former Prime Cost Clerk, W. Ellis was reported to be ill and he was allowed full salary for a month after which it would drop to half salary. There was an outside contract with the Gas Light & Coke Co., at Beckton which needed a new portable rivetting machine at £1,000 and this was ordered.

On 1 April 1920 it is noted that a 'colliers strike' had begun and on 14 April the '…Triple Alliance consisting of miners, railway men and transport workers have issued a notice to the effect that all men in these Associations are to cease work at 10 p.m. Friday 15th: this matter is serious and will dislocate all trades and appointments involving travelling are cancelled'. However on 16 April the railway and transport men decided to continue work and not to support the miners but the railways were curtailed due to the lack of coal and this strike continued through May.

The Company had been using Lloyds Bank at Birmingham and this having involved various delays, better facilities were sought or the account would be transferred to the local branch. This transfer took place in December 1921 and amongst other requirements it was stipulated that all accounts must be signed by two Directors and countersigned by the Secretary.

In view of the state of trade in 1921 no general salary increases were allowed, However discretionary bonus could be awarded to W. Perks and to C. S. Riddell and J. W. Baillie was awarded £100 bonus.

The need for further office extensions was agreed and a piece of land on the railway embankment was to be rented and an extension built. Another problem was envisaged, that of a rating increase following a Local Authority Survey. Horseley joined the 'Manufacturers Association' with the object of contesting the matter, if necessary.

In July there is the first reference to a 'staff trip' and on the evening of the 6 July a cricket match, Staff versus Works, was held at grounds opposite the Hawthorns and it is noted – 'Staff won.'

Instructions were given to proceed with the laying of cables for the new 500kw rotary converter and transformer. The War Memorial in Tipton Park was unveiled by the Marquis of Cambridge, the then Earl of Dartmouth, on 24 August and J. T. Daly attended the luncheon afterwards.

In September 1921 three items of expenditure were agreed:- repairs to the coping on the main building at £100, experimental work on 'Motor Disc Wheels' at £120 and the purchase of the first company car, an Angus Sanderson at £355.

Concrete construction was increasing and Horseley decided to broaden their activities by taking up 500 – £1 shares in a company proposed by the Association – 'PROOF' to undertake 'ferro-concrete work'. In the works the need for a water supply from the canal was agreed with the Birmingham Canal Navigations.

Due to the economic recession it was noted that the cost of living had decreased and it was resolved to decrease the salaries of the foremen and staff officials by 10% and those of female staff by 5% as from 1 Jan. 1922. However the Managing Director Mr. J. T. Daly, was awarded a 33% increase back dated to April 1921 – an increase from £1500 to £2000!! J. W. Baillie's salary was to be £750/year to 31.3.1922, £800 to 1923 and £850 to 1924.

For the purposes of advertising it was agreed to spend up to £250 on a new trade catalogue which would also be a souvenir of the building of the 'Aaron Manby' in 1821. This was to be entitled 'A Century of Progress' a 24 page A4 booklet which gave a detailed company history, lists of earlier contracts and included many photographs of the works and of contracts, a number of copies having survived (see pages 86-92).

The first reference to electric welding is made in December 1921 when the Managing Director outlined his proposals for the purchase of a plant. It was agreed to consider this further at a later meeting but no further comment is recorded.

In spite of the difficult trading conditions the company, due to the share issue, had surplus capital and it was arranged that Sir Sydney Henn should consult Sir John Fergusson for advice. The next month it was reported that £70,000 had been invested in $5^1/_2$% Treasury Bonds.

In January 1922, J.T. Daly recommended the purchase of a moulding machine for tank and purifier plates and £1,000 was allocated subject to a favourable report on a visit to Newton Chambers & Co., of Sheffield. He also reported on his proposals to convert the old Mine Sinker shop for light construction purposes and this was agreed at £2,000 for conversion and tooling.

Leonard Railton was appointed as agent for South Wales under '...conditions similar to those contained in his agreement with the Lilleshall Co.' He survived only to December 1922 when he was given three months notice.

In spite of the trading conditions it was anticipated that there would be a cash surplus of £50,000 in March and this was to be invested on the advice of the Bank Manager.

In March 1922 further labour problems occurred, when there was a lock out of members of the A.E.U. which continued through April, May and into June. At the same time '...arising out of the depression in trade the policy to be adopted in the case of the staff officials and foremen' was considered. It was agreed that for the time being no dismissals or reduction in salaries should be made. Orders were extremely difficult to obtain and very low prices were being quoted '...The Secretary pointed out that to close the Works entirely would cost approximately £20,000 per annum and that to quote below present prices would involve the Company in a greater loss owing to the fact that the Factory on cost could not be recovered'. It was considered that '...to close the works voluntarily would be a very serious matter and it was decided that the greater loss must be accepted for the time being'.

It was also agreed that the tenders for large contracts should be '...prepared on a basis of 30% of Productive Wages to cover a portion of the Company's on cost charges'.

A new patent was applied for in connection with Horseley Patent Flooring – Wadsworth Patent. In May 1922 a further significant balance of some £63,000 at the bank was reported and £30,000 invested in $5^1/_2$% Treasury Bonds. During this month large foundations were being prepared for the new moulding machine – some 14 ft. square and 12'-6" deep. Below this depth lay some 20 ft. of water and running sand and specialist advice was sought to complete the foundations. New postal rates of $1^1/_2$d for letters and 1d for cards were introduced but telephone rates were reduced.

C. J. Riddell the Works Manager resigned his position on 31 July 1922 to take a position with Rubery Owen. This was accepted with regret. Pullan Mitchell from Braithwaites was appointed Chief Engineer and Works Manager in his stead with a salary of £650 rising to £700 and £750 in the following years. Jukes was Works Superintendent.

J. W. Baillie's progress continued and he was appointed Secretary and Chief Accountant. In contrast only £20 was granted for the summer outing and the office extensions were postponed. The extensions based on plans by Cherrington & Stainton were however approved in June 1922 and a further sum of £800 allocated.

In September 1922 Sir Sydney Henn who was often on Government business asked for four months leave which was granted. He had just been elected Conservative M.P. for Blackburn and noted as '...being Horseley's first M.P.'. P. Mitchell proposed that apprentices should be employed in the Drawing Office subject to indentures and this was agreed, they being paid from 10/- to 20/- a week.

There was a need to reconstruct the Hydraulic Shop '...as walls and columns are out of plumb to a dangerous degree' and this was agreed, £3,000 was allocated and a further £130 for a contactor for the accumulator. A grinding machine was also purchased at £390. Regrettably David Fryer was killed whilst erecting the roof of the new shop.

In October 1922 serious consideration was given to the commercial position of the Company as reported by the Secretary. '...After discussion it was agreed that steps must be taken to employ the Company's surplus capital and to increase output and turnover; and to achieve this object it was considered advisable for the Company to undertake general contracting work such as the erection of brick abutments and approaches, the preparation of foundations and any work which could conveniently run in conjunction with the company's legitimate business'.

The following month further consideration was given and Sir Sydney Henn '...expressed the view that in view of the difficult geographical position of the company the question of amalgamation with a firm engaged in a similar trade on the coast should be given attention'. The creation of a selling organisation had been agreed and in January 1923 the Secretary confirmed this was in place and functioning.

Various repairs in the works were authorised:-

Repairs to Fitting Shop Roof approx	£300
New Blower approx	£300
New Starter & Switches for Cranes approx	£170
Switch gear for large shears	£35
Reconstruction of Housing Machine	£120
Sectional Driving in Girder Shop	£280
Sectional Driving in Pattern Shop	£440
Total	£1645

Problems of obtaining orders still continued, and '...owing to the continuance of keen competition it was still necessary to estimate for work on a very low basis of Oncost charges....Not only was the Company not recovering Indirect Oncost charges but that at present selling prices were insufficient to cover actual outgoings in the form of Material, Wages and Factory Charges the result being that the cost of production greatly exceeded the contract prices received and that in addition to the standing charges amounting to not less than £20,000/annum there was a loss on Factory oncost amounting to a considerable sum'. However it was agreed to follow the present procedure and obtain as much new work as possible '...in order to lower the standing charges and keep the works going'.

In the first direct reference to the 'Welfare Scheme' a sum of £100 was to be expended on a pavilion for the Sports Club to be sited adjacent to the bowling green and tennis courts. Although this is not otherwise noted it is understood the Sports field was created on the land on the opposite side of the railway. A further sum of £200 was allocated in May 1923 for the completion of the drainage and painting at the Club House.

In February 1923 consumers are reported as protesting over the costs of electric current, protests which resulted in a price reduction by the Power Company which it was estimated would save Horseley some £600/annum. The following month a contract for supply was signed with the Midland Electric Corporation for Power Distribution Ltd..

An agency agreement with J. B. Barnes for the north west coast having terminated he was offered a further period of six months.

Reconstruction work had proceeded on the new Light Construction Shop but the Chief Engineer reported that some further £3,000 would be needed to complete it and also to build a new store for the light sections which would be used. The matter was deferred until there was a prospect of greater demand. The Repair Shop was transferred to a site adjoining the Fitting Shop at a cost of £200.

In October 1923 J. T. Daly's health became a problem and he was granted a month's leave to recover. He came back and immediately became as involved as before.

Interesting contracts obtained during 1923 included the steelwork for a new pavilion on Eastbourne Pier, Treorchy Bridge for the Rhondda Council and the steelwork for a new Fish Market at Preston. Orders for two swing bridges were obtained from the London & N.E. Railway, one at St. Olaves and one at Beccles.

There were problems in the works over travelling cranes two of which were considered to be in a dangerous condition and needed reconstruction whilst the machinery in three others was obsolete. It was agreed that work should be carried out. The cranes were again considered in May 1924. Although work had been commenced on two of the cranes and £977 spent the serious condition of a number gave continued concern. The present wooden structures were to be replaced by steel and the electrical drives modernised.

A total sum of £3300 was allocated as under:-

1. New 20 Ton electric winches for cranes Nos. 2 & 5 — £840.0.0.
2. Dismantling old wooden structures and rebuilding in steel. Crane Nos. 9 & 10 — £640.0.0.
3. Dismantling old wooden structures & rebuilding in steel. Crane No. 5 — £300.0.0.
4. Dismantling existing vertical & cross shafts for long travel of crane Nos. 2, 4, 5, 9 & 10 & fitting double motor drives — £1300.0.0.
5. Dismantling existing vertical and cross shafts for long travel of crane No. 3 and fitting double motor drive. — £300.0.0.

Total £3380.0.0.
Deduct estimated value of scrap £80.0.0
Net estimate cost £3300.0.0.

The Secretary had considered the cost of production and stated that the average oncost should be quoted at not less than 60% on Direct Wages.

Near the end of 1923 it was proposed that '...owing to the amount of local work now being undertaken a light lorry would be found extremely useful'. A 30 cwt vehicle was purchased in January 1924.

At the same time the retirement of H. L. Batting of London Office who was over 70 years old and had served for over 42 years was considered. Since '...he had carried out his duties efficiently and with complete satisfaction' he was awarded a pension of £500/annum and the thanks and best wishes of the directors conveyed to him together with the presentation of a gold watch.

The replacement was to be Leonard Harper at £450/annum plus £50 expenses who was allowed an assistant, one Kettle. Further the sum of £100 was allowed for the redecoration and lighting by electricity of the London Office. In one of those actions which so sadden the historian '...the Secretary was authorised to destroy all old books and documents in the London Office which in his opinion are valueless'!

The gas industry was still most important to the Company and they decided to become members of a Gas Trade Association called 'Unity'. Further a £50 subscription was voted towards the installation of a Gas Exhibition at the 1924 British Empire Exhibition at Wembley Park. A year later a request for support for the 1925 Wembley event was turned down.

By March 1924 problems had been encountered with the Eastbourne Pier contract which also included widening the pier. This was due to '...bad weather and other unfortunate happenings' and the Pier Company threatened to claim the full penalty of £25/week. One problem related to a pile fracture where the metal was only $1/2$ inch thick and not $1^{1}/_{2}$ inches, due to the core moving, stated to be due to the '...gross negligence of the Foundry Foreman in sending the castings away without inspection'.

Protracted negotiations over excess profits and Income Tax were resolved. A sum of £1200 was agreed but could be allowed as a special writing down allowance. Further some £2500 rebate on Income Tax was allowed.

In May 1924 the Managing Director made proposals concerning the use of horses for cartage purposes in the works. A Fordson Tractor was to be demonstrated and if found satisfactory purchased at £200. By September the tractor having proved successful a second was purchased and '...as a result it has been possible to dispose of all the horses' A third tractor was authorised in March 1925.

Reference to the sale of horses occur in the accounts for 1924:-

1 Horse (dead) £5, 1 Horse Chestnut £10 & 1 Horse Bay £10.

In 1925 another horse and harness was sold for £10, together with pony harness and old harnesses. It was reported in 1956 that an old servant Payton had died aged 86 and that he had formally been in charge of the eleven horses which were used in the works.

In September 1924 the Fitting Shop Foreman Gay was replaced by Harrison, an old employee of the Company. A Ford 1 Ton Lorry was purchased and a year later was involved in an accident but no one was hurt. A visit was received from C. S. Riddell the former Works Manager who was then an agent for foreign steel.

Problems with the state of the trade continued and the policy of the Company in regard '...to undertaking erection work abroad and also mixed contracts wherein other trades are concerned' was discussed and decided that '...it would probably be necessary to run greater commercial risks than heretofore and any such enquiries should be seriously considered'.

For some while there had been proposals to complete the railway in the works to provide a circular route and this was eventually agreed in October 1924 at £385. Tipton Council wished to purchase land adjacent to the school at Great Bridge and in due course some 1120 sq. yards was sold for £125 with the Council agreeing to erect a suitable strong fence.

There was concern over mounting Drawing Office costs due to the increasing number of designs which had to be made in order to obtain work. A girder for Horbury Bridge was recorded as weighing 48 tons and was sent by the L.M.S..

In January 1925 the Chief Engineer discussed his proposal to construct cast iron houses, and it was agreed he should prepare a complete housing scheme. This turned out to be a difficult proposition. It was first reported that there was difficulty '...in getting down to a price which would compete with houses built of other materials'. In March the problems still remained but '...the question was being seriously tackled', and it was agreed the experimental work should continue. However in April it was agreed to drop the scheme and discontinue all work.

The broader engineering base was again considered and J. W. Baillie suggested that the Company should undertake Civil Engineering but the Chairman considered it '...too great a risk'.

Concern was expressed when it was discovered that the steel mills in the north were selling steel locally at 10/- ton cheaper than to the midland companies. Later the Rolling Mills Association agreed to sell at the same price to all firms south of a line from Leeds to Manchester.

In furtherance of proposals to widen the Company base discussions were held with Thomas Peacock, Managing Director of Guest, Keen & Nettlefolds Ltd. with a view to entering an agreement. GKN reported that the matter would be considered by J. Lysaght Ltd. of Bristol but later stated that they did not wish to pursue the matter.

Although it was confidently believed that an order valued at £110,000 would be received for an extension to the wharf at Port Harcourt, staff reorganisation was considered essential. Accordingly Tom Cherrington of the Drawing Office (58 years service) and John Troath of the General Office (47 years service) were retired and Chief Draughtsman Ken Allen relieved of his duties due to his health and made a senior draughtsman at a lower salary. John D. Vaughan was appointed Chief Draughtsman. In addition H. Harris was dismissed and replaced by a girl for Wages Office duties. Pensions were considered for Cherrington & Troath and solicitors were asked whether these could be awarded without sanction at a General Meeting. They were later awarded £2/week. John Troath who had asked for an increase in his pension in January 1926 died on 4 March 1927 and his son wrote that his widow was '...in straitened circumstances'. His pension was paid until the end of the month and a gratuity of £25 awarded.

The property rating was proposed to be raised to £3250 but eventually a figure of £3000 was agreed. The seriousness of the situation is reflected in the trading figures. A loss of over £25,717 was reported in 1923/4 and the 1924/5 figures show a further loss of over £4257, however the usual grant of £60 towards the works outing was agreed. The working hours were increased from 47 to 50 with a wage increase of 5/- week.

An interesting enquiry was received from the Air Ministry for an Airship Hanger at Karachi to involve '...some thousands of tons of steel'. An order in hand for pipes for Pauling & Co., required the sum of £500 to be expended on a runway, electric blocks and a punching machine for the Hydraulic Shop. A second motor car was purchased, an

Austin 12 HP at £180 (second hand-new price C£475.) The Drawing Office was further extended at a cost of £80 to which was later added £120 to provide accommodation for inspectors.

When the case of one of the Company's old servants, aged 77, was considered it was agreed that the whole policy of awarding pensions was to be reviewed, particularly in view of recent legislation. The case of this man, Earp, was considered in November 1925 when he was then 78 and had been employed for 48 years and lost an arm in a works accident. He was awarded 5/- a week pension. However when Noah Fellows who had served 47 years asked for consideration he was refused.

In the works the hydraulic flooring press was improved but a new hydraulic forging press was ordered at £600.

The effect of the National Insurance Act was that employees away ill were to '...suffer deduction from their salaries of the amount of benefit received by them'. However no increase in the price of the Staff Canteen meals was to be made.

An order was received from the Southern Railway for six bridges on the Boat Train Route 1A for £18,946.14.4d. However during site work on the Beecles Swing Bridge a 50 Ton girder fell into the river. Further work was obtained in early 1926, Lift Bridges for Nechells Power Station and steelwork for the L.M.S. in the Horbury & Wakefield widening at Thornes Lane.

Still fighting for work it was agreed the oncost could be reduced from 60 to 50% for large contracts. A profit was declared for 1925/6 of some £10-£12,000 but when reserves for Income Tax and depreciation were made only some £6,000 could be carried forward and no dividend allowed.

A large enquiry for the supply and erection of complete locomotive shops in New Zealand was received, involving some '...thousands of tons of steel' but the standing of the site contractor was a matter of concern. Sir Sydney Henn applied for another period of 6 months absence to commence in August 1926. An agent was appointed for the South African Union and a proposal for one in India deferred.

In May 1926 the situation '...arising out of the position created by the recent General Strike (May 1-12) and the illegality of the action taken by the men in withdrawing their labour without giving the customary seven days notice, it was the opinion of the Board that the legal position should be explained to the Works Committee, and the Secretary was instructed to prepare a statement dealing with the men's responsibility in the matter, a copy of which should be handed to each member of the Committee'.

J. T. Daly's health gave further problems. He was at home in Leamington from 26 to 31 January 1926 and on 21 February, he '...was obliged to give up work due to illness' and did not resume again until 26 May.

The miners continued their strike after the General Strike and the matter is referred to in July when it was reported '...that owing to the continuation of the Miners' strike and the consequent inability to obtain steel, it had been necessary to close the works – excepting the Pattern Shop and Foundry'. As the strike continued and the works remained closed much repair and maintenance was carried out and the laying down of the circular railway progressed. As the seven months dispute moved towards its end in November, the Managing Director discussed '...the position arising out of the coal dispute'. Just before Christmas some 94 men asked for a £1 loan which was to be repaid at 5/- week when the men were at work. They returned on 29 December.

Chapter 4 – 1919-1928

At this time a number of major contracts were out to tender, including swing bridges for the Port of London Authority at over £41,000 and for Wireless Masts by Henleys Telegraph Co., valued at over £300,000.

Looking to expand production the Light Construction Shop was again considered, and the need for such work to be in a separate department appreciated. An increase in capacity amounting to 80 tons/week was envisaged and £5023 was to be spent on the project.

At the same time other capital was authorised:-

Extension to Travelling Gantry in Girder Shop annexe and new electric travelling block	£150
New overhead travelling crane for Hydraulic Shop	£560
Moulding Machine for Standardising C.I. Tank Plates	£675
New Oxygen Cutting Machine	£120
Total	**£1505**

The company Structural Steelcrete Ltd. offered a sub-licence to Horseley to manufacture steelwork under "Ritchie" patents and the offer was accepted for a fee of £150.

The Swing bridge quotation was successful and the order for two bridges at West India Docks for the P.L.A. received. The comfort of the staff was increased when the central heating system was extended throughout '...in order to obviate the use of coal, gas and electricity'. The work was placed with Parker, Winder and Achurch at £265.

The foundry systems were considered to be outdated and some £7250 needed to enable it to compete for tank and purifier plates. This was deferred and in April it was reported that a major order for Birmingham had been lost. In September 1927 the Foundry was reported closed due to lack of orders. The Engineering Employers Federation decided to resist a demand by the Engineering Unions for an advance in wages.

In mid 1927 a number of major orders were obtained including Crane Runways for Derby Locomotive Works, Bridge No. 90 for the Southern Railway at St. Mary Cray and a rolling lift bridge for Tilbury Docks Improvements at £21,978. A contract value £55,500 was obtained for the Buenos Aires and Great Southern Railway and in order to expedite approval of drawings an office was set up in Finsbury Circus – London, next to the Engineer's Office where six draughtsmen were employed. Regrettably at the same time Chief Engineer P. Mitchell resigned to take up a position at Dorman Long, Middlesborough on 18 August 1927.

August 1927 signalled a bout of capital expenditure:-

Extensions of Light Construction Shop	£400
Straightening Rolls & Motor	£350
Pneumatic Rivetters	£65
5 Ton Steam Derrick Crane	£285
Ending Machine	£500
4 High Speed Drills	£1100
10 Ton Electric Crane	£800
Foundations	£500
Total	**£4000**

The staff changes following Mitchell's resignation were agreed but not detailed. However, F. D. Perks was appointed as Assistant Secretary. Miss Perks's salary was increased to that of Miss Lovesey – £130/year. A month later Thomas H. Allen, the Company Buyer with 49 years service died. His salary was paid for the month and he was stated to have been '...a good and faithful servant'.

Momentous changes were foreshadowed in November 1927 when it was recorded that Sir Sydney Henn and Sir George Holcroft had interviewed T. Horton (of Thomas Piggott & Co.,) at Birmingham to discuss '...certain aspects of the Company's affairs'. Horton's response was cool – he had no definite views of any amalgamation but stressed the use of the most up to date machinery. '...Mr Horton is connected with a great many firms but not carrying on business in the Bridge & Constructional trades similar to the Horseley Company'.

There was also discussion on the setting up of a 'selling organisation' which was later created '...in accordance with the Secretary's proposals at a cost of £1000 per annum'.

W. V. W. Kell who had last attended a board meeting in May 1927 died on 27 December. At the January 1928 Board meeting it is recorded that '...those present rose as a mark of respect'. In the same month the death of long serving Secretary, Thomas Hughes occurred and his pension was paid to the end of the month.

The Government Pension Scheme (Pensions Act 1925) is first referred to during the same month when it was reported that W. Ellis, Cashier was ill and unable to continue. He was awarded '...a pension of £84.10s. for 5 years ending 31 January 1933 and £78 annum for a further 5 years ending 31 January 1938. At the expiration of this period the pension to be considered and adjusted according to the amount to be received under the Government Scheme of old age pension'.

Further discussions were held with Piggotts in January 1928 when J. T. Daly as Chairman was requested '...to interview Mr. Barker', but in February he reported that in company with J. W. Baillie, Secretary, they had had an interview with T. Horton of Piggotts '...on the subject of fusion'. He stated that Barker & Dyson had '...shown the different processes of steel welded and rivetted pipes and also the Boiler Tube Works across the Dudley Road and made my visit a very interesting one'.

The matter was now of serious importance and Sir George Holcroft and Sir Sydney Henn were appointed to continue discussions. Events moved quickly and at the next meeting with Piggotts it was proposed by them that Horseley should purchase the whole of their share capital of £52,240 on terms to be arranged and subject to certain conditions. By April 1928 the Horseley Board agreed unanimously that the recommendations of Sir George Holcroft and Sir Sydney Henn '...be accepted in their entirety'. The Secretary was instructed to '...inform T. Horton and ask him to lay the position before Messrs Piggotts Board for an early settlement'.

Meanwhile at Tipton a further major order had been received for another rolling lift bridge, this at Manchester Road, Millwall, again for the P.L.A. and Sir R. McAlpine & Co.. Two cranes for erection purposes at £1570 total and an air compressor plant at £474 were purchased. Orders were also taken for steelwork for Charing Cross Station Booking Hall, a purifier for Stourbridge Borough and cast iron troughing for the City of Bradford. A little later a swing bridge for the GWR at East Bute Dock was ordered.

In May 1928 it was reported that some difficulties had arisen over the buy out of Piggotts. One of their major shareholders T. Lloyd had failed to agree. He asked that Horseley should lend T. Piggott & Sons the sum of £30,000 in order that they could pay off a loan due to him and Horseley agreed to this request, but although a draft agreement had been prepared and accepted by Horseley for the purchase of all Piggotts 3684 shares, Piggotts were not ready to sign the agreement by 17 May. However Sir George Holcroft & Sir Sydney Henn were authorised to accept or reject any changes which might be proposed and if they agreed to sign and seal the document.

There were also draft agreements with the Managing Directors of Piggotts, T. P. Barker and A. Dyson and with J. W. Baillie. Sir Sydney Henn was authorised to accept or reject changes and if acceptable sign them on behalf of Horseley.

Other major changes occurred. Walter Perks stated that he was prepared to resign his office of General Manager as of 28 June 1928 and would not seek re-election as a Director. The Chairman J. T. Daly intimated that '...owing to advancing years he felt it necessary to retire from active participation in the management of the business and that he desired to vacate his position as Managing Director from 29 June 1928 and as Chairman forthwith.

These two resignations were accepted and J. T. Daly vacated the chair. He had joined the Board in 1886 and hence had served for 42 years, a remarkable record. It was then proposed and accepted that Sir Sydney Henn should become Chairman and he then occupied the chair.

The terms of retirement of Daly and Perks were then considered. They were to receive full salaries up to March 1929 and thereafter pensions of £750 and £600 respectively. New directors were elected to join Sir Sydney and Sir George. They were T. P. Barker, A. Dyson, T. W. Horton, Henry Bewlay, T. O. Lloyd and J. W. Baillie. On 7 June 1928 the seal of the Horseley Company having been affixed to the agreement with Thomas Piggott & Sons Ltd., counterpart was produced and signed. The last Day Book entry of the Chairman is on 6 June 1928 and is poignantly incomplete – '...James T. Daly attended to current ......'.

The Secretary reported that he had the names of Piggott's shareholders who had agreed to sell and he had prepared a list showing the number of shares and the cash consideration they would receive from Horseley. Later five thousand Piggott's £10 shares were exchanged for fifty thousand £1 Horseley shares. Horseley then owning three fourths of the shares in Thomas Piggott the restriction on the shares retained by Piggott's directors was waived.

The £30,000 agreed loan was made, the new directors formally voted in and a letter was circulated to each employee of Horseley informing them of the changes in administration. T. P. Barker and A. Dyson became Managing Directors and J. W. Baillie, Assistant Managing Director and Secretary.

And so the old order changed and the long single history of the Horseley Company ended with notices in the Birmingham Post and the Gazette on Saturday 9 June 1928.

CHAPTER 5

1928-1932

THE FUSION

The agreement with Thomas Piggott & Co., Ltd., complete and the new directors in place, further decisions in connection with the fusion were made in June 1928. A great deal of work was to be involved in dealing with the shares and a Transfer Committee comprising H. Bewlay, T. O. Lloyd and J. W. Baillie was created to deal with the matter and they reported on their work at succeeding Board Meetings. Sir Sydney Henn was appointed to represent Horseley at any meeting with Piggott's and Thomas W. Horton was appointed Deputy Chairman.

At the same meeting the death on 25 June of long serving London Office man, H. L. Batting, was reported. Mrs. Batting's daughter had written to state that her mother was destitute but it was decided that his pension should cease and no further grant could be made. He had previously been granted a substantial pension.

Further amalgamations were considered but none proceeded with. One was with John Butler & Co., Ltd., of Leeds, another Teeside Bridge & Engineering and also South Durham Steel & Iron Co.. Sir Sydney Henn was again required to go abroad on Government business for six months, this time to Argentina but he did not leave until December 1929. Horseley & Piggott's were admitted to the Dry Gas Association, paying £250 and also purchasing 500-£1 shares.

As the two companies were amalgamated, in September 1928 the directors, Barker, Dyson & Baillie reported on a scheme to combine the staff of the two organisations at one central location. They had taken a fourteen year lease at £700/annum of 85, Lionel Street, Birmingham. It had '...an excellent elevation and contains an entrance hall, five private offices, two rooms 130 ft x 33 ft for the staff'. It was estimated that an annual saving of at least £2500 would accrue but they recognised that there would be problems in re-organising the staff. Such disorganisation was reported in January 1929 but '...this has now been accomplished'. Later it was reported that '...the staff appear to be quite satisfied with their new environment'. This became the company Registered Office, and they also decided to have a combined Staff Dinner at the year end. The Horseley rates were also reduced by £800 to £2200.

Thomas Piggott & Co., Ltd., had a Reserve Fund and they decided to capitalise £33,110 of it by giving as a bonus to their shareholders, five £10 ordinary shares for each eight shares they held, and also to issue 189-£10 shares for cash.

The meeting of 4 January 1929 was held at Lionel Street and the Chairman referred '...in sympathetic terms to the loss the Board had sustained by the death of Mr. James T. Daly and those present rose as a mark of respect'.

Two men were killed in an accident on the Leicester site and a man seriously injured in the Tipton Works.

The possibility of complete fusion with Thomas Piggott & Co., Ltd., was discussed, and the Chairman asked that the Directors give the matter careful consideration. With the change in the Registered Office, the Lloyds Bank accounts were transferred back to Birmingham at the Colmore Row address and the signed authority for this transfer is fixed in the Board Minute Book. It was later changed to the Temple Row branch.

Arising from discussions with the executors of W. Stonehewer who would not accept an offer of 10/- a share it was discovered that no official certificate had been issued for these 600 shares. It was considered that some or all the shares might need to be re-numbered.

Work was still difficult to obtain but a rise in steel and pig iron prices being anticipated some 10,000 tons of steel and 1500 tons of pig iron was forward ordered. Site work needed a new crane and a 10 ton steam derrick was ordered from Wm. Morgan & Co., at £1035.

The Tipton Foundry, slack for long periods, was ordered to do the work of Thomas Piggott's foundry at Spring Hill. The foreman from Spring Hill was moved to Tipton and the Tipton foreman dismissed.

The national electricity grid was being extended and large orders for transmission line towers were being quoted. A. Dyson reported on discussions with the Pirelli Co. and in May 1929 an order was received for some 7,500 tons of steelwork for the Central England Electricity Scheme, from Milliken Bros. & Blaw Knox Limited at £14-10s-0d per ton and some £5,000 of plant was agreed to be ordered for the work. In August orders were anticipated from Pirelli and a further £6,000 of capital authorised. New motor lorries were also to be ordered as required. A year later in April 1930 another order for 7000 tons was received for which another £1500 of plant was authorised. Thus the transmission tower steelwork facility was created – work which would continue for very many years ahead.

Some improvement in trade having occurred, a dividend of 5% was declared in June 1929 and an order for the swing bridge at Folkestone obtained at £15,765. A lease for 5, Victoria Street, London was agreed.

The boom in 'Picture Houses' proved advantageous and over half a dozen orders were obtained for their steelwork frames.

In October 1929 Sir George Holcroft resigned his position on the Board, a decision accepted with regret but no reason for the action is recorded. In November the company applied to join the British Steelwork Association. At the same time discussions were held over what was then called 'Lamellen Construction'. Models and drawings were considered and it was agreed that negotiations should continue. A month later the rights for the British Empire excluding Canada had been obtained but it was not until 9 May 1930 that the formal documents were signed.

These were with the Junkers & Zollbau Syndikat of Berlin and in particular with Kaloriferwerk Hugo Junkers. Horseley bought 5000 – £1 shares and Baillie & Dyson were to be directors of the Lamella Construction Co., (British Proprietary) Ltd. This Lamella pressed blade arch construction was to be used extensively for clear span roofs and for aircraft hangers. Problems occurred which will be discussed in due course. An ice rink in Leicester was under consideration and the use of Lamella was proposed. Horseley were asked to donate £1500 to the company in return for the order. This was not accepted and the first erected was an aeroplane hanger at Heston for Henleys (1928) Ltd. for £1500 with parts supplied from Germany.

It is strange that no reference until January 1930 is made in the Board minutes to the supply of gas lamp columns, when an order from Belfast is noted, to be followed by two from Liverpool. Orders for 60 for Coventry and 10 for Tipton of 'Type 10' are noted in the Managing Directors' report for July 1928 and they must have been in production for many years. An undated catalogue of designs exists from which a large variety of patterns can be seen and it is known that many towns and cities were supplied.

The traditional Works summer outing seems to have ceased but annual staff dinners were held and that on 4 Feb. 1930 was supported in the sum of £30.

Orders were received for a landing stage at Neyland and for Ammonia Stills at Belfast. It was agreed that A. Dyson should visit the USA '...for investigation purposes', and he sailed in May 1930 by the CARMANIA. He was to consider American methods of tower production and galvanising, said to be more economic than U.K. methods. New orders for towers were in mild steel which had to be galvanized instead of 'copper steel' as heretofore.

An annex to the Light Construction Shop was constructed for £300 and a new notching machine was ordered at £150. Consideration was given to the purchase of a galvanising plant for the Tipton Works but A. Dyson advised against it and subsequently all galvanising was sub-let – quantities over the years of many hundreds of thousands of tons of steel principally to Messrs. Frost and Sons.

With continued low trade the Directors agreed to accept no fees for the six months to 31 March 1930. A heavy snow storm in March caused the collapse of an annex to the Girder Shop which would have cost £1,000 to rebuild, but it was decided to demolish it. It was considered that '...generally speaking the outlook is brighter –' and a small profit of £4157 was made and carried forward to 1931. The directors accepted half fees for the year. The Humphreys & Glasgow Co. offered Horseley accommodation at their London Office, 6 Carlisle Place. It was agreed that if the Westminster Chambers Association would cancel the leases of 5 & 11 Victoria Street they would accept and the move took place in October 1930. Sir Sydney Henn was again on his travels between 27 June & November when he visited Tanganyika Territory.

Another 5 ton steam loco crane was purchased for £425 second-hand for use on site and an order received for the renewal of Bute West Dock Lock Swing Bridge at Cardiff. Other orders for railway work were obtained including bridge 1479 for the LNWR and reconstruction at Tinsley & Meadow Hall, Sheffield for the LNER. Regrettably an accident occurred during the building of the Folkestone Swing Bridge when George Kett was killed. His wife was awarded a pension of 15/- week subject to reconsideration.

The bank was anxious for a debenture to cover the overdraft but were informed that '...certain negotiations were proceeding which might affect the Company's financial position.' Unfortunately T. P. Barker was ill and his specialist Leonard Parsons advised some four months rest and he did not return until March 1931. The negotiations over rationalisation had continued and A. Dyson was appointed to replace T. P. Barker. It was also agreed that an expert in works re-organisation would be appointed to offer professional advice.

There had been problems with the castings for the repair of Newhaven Bridge and the Southern Railway had claimed penalties. Horseley agreed to guarantee the bridge for four years in settlement.

The continuing depression caused further problems, prices were tending to fall even lower and in spite '...of very unremunerative prices it had not been possible to secure any substantial contracts'. It was agreed to lower quotations even further '...in order that the Tipton works may be kept employed' and also to reduce hours by not working on Saturdays.

At the same time staff reductions were made and the pension of retired officials reduced. However an appeal by the Birmingham Hospital Centre was supported by a sum of £125 spread over seven years.

The final steam locomotive to be purchased was supplied by Bagnalls of Stafford, Works number 2540 of 1931 and was named 'J. T. Daly', in memory of the man who had played such an important role in the history of the Company. She was an 0-4-0 tank engine with 12"x 18" cylinders costing £1200 and was used until she was given into preservation in 1969 when she was replaced by a diesel 0-4-0 .' J. T. Daly' is now on the island of Jersey and it is rather sad that she should be so far away, although she can still be seen in steam.

In January 1931 the works were so short that they decided to work on only three days per week- Monday, Tuesday and Wednesday. '...It is difficult to see any silver lining in the depressing cloud that hangs over us'.

Piggotts had joint interests in Cardiff as Guest, Keen & Piggotts where pipes were produced, Earlier discussions with South Durham were concluded and the Cardiff works were to be developed.

The complete merger of Horseley & Piggotts, for some time under detailed discussion was considered to be essential, and a decision was made to conclude this as soon as possible. A. Dyson & J. W. Baillie were to prepare the schemes. A month later T. W. Horton made proposals on behalf of Piggotts and their Debenture & Preference Shareholders approached to obtain their agreement. Eventually in May 1931 it was agreed to submit the merger proposals to a firm of London Accountants – Deloitte, Plender, Griffiths & Co.. It was to be a further eighteen months before the merger was concluded.

In June 1931 A. Dyson & J. W. Baillie visited competing firms in Glasgow and although not detailed this must surely have included Sir William Arroll. It was noted that a '... recent agreement entered into between the Federated Employers and the Engineering Trades Unions affects our Employees to the extent of reducing piece-work and overtime rates — should reduce our costs'.

In July T. P. Barker resigned as Managing Director of Horseley and Chairman and Managing Director of Piggotts, no doubt as a result of his health. He revoked his agreements with the companies and was awarded a pension of £1500 per annum as from July 1931. This pension was paid 50% by Piggotts and 50% by Horseley. At the same time H. Richards an employee of Horseley for 55 years requested financial assistance, a request left with the Managing Directors to agree.

In July 1931 a small profit of £864. 3s. 6d. was made and this was to be carried forward with the previous surplus. In view of the resignation of T. P. Barker, J. W. Baillie was appointed Joint Managing Director of Horseley and pending the appointment of a Secretary he was also to maintain that role and to have no salary increase. His appointment came at a time '...of unprecedented depression in trade' and salaries had to be reduced as follows:-

    Salaries less than £52 annum   – no change
    "   between £52 & £156 annum   – 5% reduction
    "   exceeding £156   – 10% "

Any anomalies were to be dealt with by the Directors.

Some railway orders were received including steelwork at Hammersmith Station, reconstruction of Hammersmith Rail Bridge, a footbridge at Acton Town and also an order for steel dolphins (mooring buoys) at Pembroke, but overall trade continued to be very slack and in December 1931 some nine members of combined staff were put under notice but old servants were to be retained where possible. The list of pensioners was considered and the Managing Directors '...were to deal with as they think fit'.

The sales organisation and publicity departments were allocated £1,500 for the year 1932, but work was extremely difficult to obtain. It was the unanimous opinion of the Board that it was '...essential in the interests of the business and the Company's employee's that a continuity of orders must be obtained'. Accordingly they were to quote on materials plus labour only and also to look for work similar to that carried out by Thomas Piggott & Co..

In February 1932 the condition of trade was considered '...to be desperate' and the works was practically empty but for the transmission line tower work. The Directors' fees were to be halved for the year April 1932 to 1933. In order to reduce their overdraft a £15,000 loan had been made to Piggotts increasing the total to £30,000. The Birmingham Hospital Scheme was reported stopped and further payments were suspended.

Consideration was given to the manufacture of glass lined tanks but it was decided not to spend the £3000 needed for the special plant required. In June 1932 a loss of £11,424.12s.4d. was declared and deducted from the sum carried forward leaving only £2,244.6s.10d to carry forward. The Managing Directors were required to '...carry out a drastic staff reorganisation either by dismissals or salary reductions..... to effect a substantial curtailment of expenditure'. As a result they pensioned Arthur Page ($48^{1}/_{2}$ years service) and Ernest Evans (51 years service) at 15/- a week and thanked them for their '...loyal & faithful service'. They also placed on record their '...appreciation of the sacrifices made by the staff to assist the Company during the present difficult trading conditions'.

The bank reported that they could not meet the cheques drawn on Piggotts and Horseley paid a further £5,000 into their account. The merger considered essential, it was decided to make an offer to the Preference Shareholders of Thomas Piggott & Co., including:–
Each holder of the 5229 – £10 – 5% Piggotts shares to receive ten £1 -5% Cumulative Preference Shares in Horseley. This issue to be part of a £100,000 share issue and those who accepted would receive 5% dividend per annum from 1 April 1933. Piggotts debenture holders were to agree to convert to Horseley Debentures.

Meantime Piggotts were in increasing financial difficulty and Horseley had to transfer a further £7,500 to them, increasing the total loan to £42,500. In July 1932 T. O. Lloyd resigned his seat on the Board and was succeeded by Henry D. Lloyd of the Old Vicarage, Stretton, near Warrington.

All Piggotts Preference & Debenture holders having agreed to the terms it was possible to proceed with the merger scheme immediately and so on 29 November 1932 the special resolutions were put to the Board as outlined in the offer together with others necessary and it was decided to put them to an extraordinary general meeting to be held on 30 December 1932,when they were agreed.

And so the two old companies became fully merged.

CHAPTER 6
1932-1939

HORSELEY BRIDGE & THOMAS PIGGOTT LTD

Before the merger Thomas Piggott & Co., Ltd. had at least three locations where they carried out their fabrication work. The oldest was the freehold land at Spring Hill, Birmingham where they had been based for so many years, a site alongside the canal and although near to the railway, with no connection. Nearby was the Hooper Street site, which contained both leasehold and freehold land and for which they had a lease agreement, and which had rail access. This works concentrated on pipes and furnaces. In South Wales, at Cardiff, they had a pipe production plant styled Guest, Keen & Piggotts.

Quite fortuitously the Board Minutes following the merger are recorded in a new book, still styled 'The Horseley Bridge & Engineering Company Limited' No. 6 and the form of the reports continues as before with the new directors attending. They were Sir Sydney H. H. Henn, Chairman, T. W. Horton, Vice Chairman, H. Bewlay, H. D. Lloyd, A. Dyson & J. W. Baillie (Secretary). The Assistant Secretary was F. G. Holly and the Accountant, F. D. Perks.

Financially Horseley had invested £82,000 in Piggotts and loaned them a further £40,200 and clearly Piggotts had encountered problems due to the severe recession. Affairs of both companies were now considered by the Board and decisions made affecting all relevant matters. The Transfer Committee was busy with all matters concerning shares and continued to report at each meeting.

There were still matters of finance to be resolved, and problems over the legality of a plan to exchange Piggotts Debentures for those for Horseley occurred. There were also 600- £10 Ordinary Piggott Shares still not owned by Horseley. The owners were to be offered £5 each in cash and this was agreed, in particular by T. O. Lloyd and T. P. Barker who each owned 100 such shares. The matter of the Managing Director's fees was also not settled and this involved a number of discussions, it eventually being agreed that they would each receive £2,000 per annum plus commission on profits, the agreement with A. Dyson to be until the end of his current agreement, when it would be replaced and that for J. W. Baillie for three years. These agreements were continued at the relevant intervals. By February 1932 the matter of the shares had been finalised and the owners of the Debentures had their shares exchanged. There were 271 Debentures of £100 each and one of £72,900 which was issued to Lloyds Bank, Temple Row West, Birmingham, this latter to cover the overdraft facilities.

Much attention was paid to the commercial policy of the new company and an agreement with Barrages Automatiques S.A. concerning the manufacture of Automatic River Control Gates was made. Further an arrangement was reached with J. P. O'Callahan over the establishment of a department for the manufacture of Water Softening Plants at a cost of about £5,000 for '...the first year or so'. Discussions were also held concerning the manufacture of rotary filters and thickeners. A new man was to be engaged at London

Office to persue chemical & industrial plant.

However, schemes for the manufacture of concrete lined pipes and also the manufacture of pressed steel tank plates in France were not accepted. A proposal by a C. Helsby to set up a special department to deal with welded structures was considered '...but whilst it was recognised that serious developments were taking place in the direction of substituting welding for rivetting it was not felt that this Company is in a position at present to expend the sum of around £3,000 required to install the necessary plant' This was a very large sum and it would be interesting to know what was being considered.

Schemes to reduce costs were soon considered. Firstly the office at Lionel Street was closed and the Registered Office moved to Tipton with its personnel. This including re-decoration at Tipton which was to cost £500.

Since Piggotts were in voluntary liquidation it was observed that no formal accounts need be submitted to the Registrar of Joint Stock Companies. There is no doubt that trade was very depressed and that '...excessive price cutting was now prevalent'. It was decided to close down the Spring Hill Works as the first steps in a major reorganisation plan. This site was of 20,776 square yards and was initially to be offered for sale at £1 sq. yd. with six months possession to the Birmingham Estates Department. A figure of 15/- sq. yd. was eventually agreed. At this time Hooper St. Works was to be retained in work and also the freehold lands retained.

Plant considered to be appropriate was moved from Spring Hill to Hooper St. or to Tipton. Moves to Hooper St. were to cost £2,900 and the complete scheme no more than £12,500. There were old cottages in Dudley Road known as Willoughby Cottages said to need some £300 in essential repairs. It was agreed to apply for a clearance order or to spend a maximum of £310.

Transmission line tower

Chapter 6 – 1932-1939

In May 1933 the order for the 900 ft high radio masts at Droitwich for £2775 was received. These were stated to be '...80 feet higher than Rugby'. Shortly afterwards an order to repair Colwyn Bay Pier at £2425 was obtained. Interestingly it was reported that of eleven quotations for the reconstruction of a bridge on the Southern Railway, Horseley were the only Company to offer a welded solution which had been requested.

The Assistant Secretary F. G. Holly resigned as of 30 June 1933 and was replaced by F. D. Perks at a salary of £500 per annum.

Proposals to spend £1250 on an artesian well at Hooper St. and to install a waste heat boiler were deferred. However the Managing Directors considered that '...the outlook generally is brighter'.

The name of the new company was given much thought and on 1 January 1934 the style 'Horseley Bridge & Thomas Piggott Ltd.'. was adopted, it having been agreed that '...it would be a great mistake to drop the name of Thomas Piggott' As reaction to the problems of cost cutting a number of trade associations were set up or re-formed to control prices. One of these was the Marine Furnace Association which was under discussion in May 1933. Another was the Pressed Steel Tank Association which was formed as of 1 July 1933. Whilst the furnace situation was under discussion it was stated that prices were '...being forced down to a ridiculous level'.

On the domestic front two men retired and were granted 5/- week pensions; they were John Brannan with 54 years service and T. Lawrence with 34 years service. J. T. Woodward with 43 years service was reported as '...broken down in health' and was awarded £2/ week for six months.

Dry gas holders had been developed in Germany and were known as Klonne Type. They had a 'piston' which floated on the gas and moved inside the holder. One of these was constructed at Port Talbot and consideration was given to insuring it during erection. A. Dyson went to Dortmund, Germany to learn of further developments in their design. A

A hangar for Sea Planes at Las Palmas in Lamella construction, 135 feet span, 135 foot long, 1933

600 foot long Lamella hangar building for the Austin Motor Company, 180 feet span, 500 feet long, 1936

contract with Lancashire County Council for a lift bridge at Litherland was considered and objection taken to the condition which specified unlimited liability for damages for non completion.

The Company made a loss of some £530 for the year ending July 1933 which when deducted from the reserve left £1313.11s.9d. to be carried forward.

An approach was received from Braithwaite and Co., concerning closer collaboration in the manufacture and sale of pressed steel tank plates which was at first considered to be beneficial but later the proposals were not accepted. By March 1934 it was reported that '...the new Pressed Steel Tank department will commence next week, at Tipton'. Significant work was obtained for water softening and treatment plant both for the railways and for public baths.

The works at Cardiff – Guest Keen & Piggotts were given consideration and a suggestion made that a new works on the coast should be built which would enable them to break away from the agreement with Guest Keen & Nettlefolds.

However in January 1934 notification was received from Guest, Keen & Baldwins Ltd. that they would require the Cardiff Works by 30 June 1934. Horseley called on them to honour the agreement of 29 January 1925 by which, they were in these circumstances, to find alternative accommodation and transfer the plant. A. Dyson visited Guest, Keen & Baldwins and returned with most important proposals. They would pay Guest, Keen & Piggotts £15,000 as the purchase price of the pipe plant at East Moors Works, Cardiff and for the cancellation of the 1925 agreement. Horseley would have the option to buy the plant at 20/- ton plus 30/- ton for dismantling and loading on trucks. In return Horseley Bridge & Thomas Piggott Ltd. would agree to purchase all plate for pipes from Guest, Keen & Baldwin. Guest, Keen & Nettlefolds, the other party to the 1925 agreement were to be urged to accept these terms.

As a result, it was agreed to build a new works at Tipton, and all suitable plant would be transferred to it from Hooper St. & Cardiff. This works would be built on the sports ground on the Great Bridge side of the railway line and would have rail access. This proposal of April 1934 threw the original re-organisation plans into disarray. '...In consequence of the Sports Ground being taken over for the Pipe Works, there is now no means of providing any social life for the men, and the Sports Club is being wound up. It has been explained to the men that this question cannot be considered until prosperity returns'

Certain additional expenditure had previously been agreed including:-

New glazing, sheeting, purlins and foundations for Welding Shop	£603
Second hand set of pumps	£150
New sewer and latrines	£450
Shanks planing machine	£1200
Additional welding sets	£320
Tanks for storage of water for testing purposes on top of rivetting tower	£150
Additional pipes for sewage	£100
Spot welding machine	£80
Tractor	£150
New Compressor	£400

In January 1934 the contract for the sale of the land at Spring Hill was sealed as was the contract for the sale of a small piece of land at Walsall.

The Water Treatment Department was strengthened by the purchase of a patent from R. Hoggins of the Birmingham Corporation Baths Department concerning water purification. Trade in general, however, continued to be very difficult and a gas holder quoted on a basis of materials and labour only was lost to Clayton Son & Co., Ltd.

Domestically, Len Harper at London Office was given an increase of £50 year and W. Onions, a Foreman of 44 years service, was retired and given £100 lump sum. Sir Sydney Henn was required to be in South America from January to April 1934 and was granted leave of absence. The house at Streetly occupied by J. W. Baillie was reported to fall vacant and was offered for sale at £800. Further pensions of 5/- week were awarded to:-

George Capewell	aged 67	46 years service
G. Kent	aged 72	40 " "
Wm. Workman	aged 68	53 " "

and in 1934 George Harrison aged 67 and J. Benfield aged 71 years, both retired Foremen with 54 years service were awarded 10/- week pension.

Two portable electric welding sets were ordered at £60 total and a garage was built in Horseley Road at £250 and £200 was spent on new works offices.

In May 1934 A. Dyson presented the Managing Director's plans for the new Pipe Works at Tipton. It was agreed '...That a committee consisting of Messrs. A. Dyson, J. W. Baillie and H. D. Lloyd be appointed to prepare a scheme for building a new Pipe Works at Tipton at a cost not exceeding £20,000 excluding the sum to be received from Guest, Keen & Baldwins upon liquidation of Guest Keen & Piggotts'. They were to proceed immediately with that part of the works required for the pipe screwing plant which was to be transferred from Spring Hill.

The sum authorized was soon considered to be insufficient and one of £40,000 more appropriate. There was a building at the Coventry Ordnance works which might be suitable for transfer but this purchase later fell through and the original plans were resumed

Works frontage following office modifications

with authorisation to spend £33,055. The large new works was constructed with a two bay Lamella roof structure.

Arising from the liquidation of Guest, Keen & Piggotts some 500 -£1 ordinary shares and 500- 6% £1 Preference shares were purchased in Bituminous Pipe Linings Ltd. at a cost of about £250.

By June 1934 Spring Hill Works was cleared and handed over for demolition for completion by July 1934. The financial problems continued and a loss of £2,186.10s.6d. was reported in June 1934 for the preceding year, resulting in a carry forward loss of £872,18s.9d.

Reports were made in September 1934 on the various trade associations. The Marine Furnace Association was still not re-formed, but the Large Tube Association was fully agreed and a quota scheme proposed for the gas-holder trade. The Structural Association had accepted the principle of minimum prices for structural steelwork. It was necessary to establish a credit of £3,200 in favour of the Large Tube Association and this was renewed each year.

Later it was reported that the five corrugated furnace makers in the country had formed a selling company under the style of 'The Boiler Furnace Co Ltd.' based in Glasgow. The five makers were:-

Broomside Boiler Works Limited.
Deighton Flue & Tube Co Limited.
Horseley Bridge & Thomas Piggott Ltd.
John Marshall & Co Ltd.
John Thompson Ltd.

In September 1934 an unfortunate chapter was commenced with the National Coke and Oil Company who planned to build at least five plants and give the work to Horseley. A. Dyson & J. W. Baillie bought shares privately, and then offered them to Horseley but they were declined. When two plants were ordered Horseley agreed to buy the shares but problems of payment for the work arose and eventually it was necessary to go to the Courts to get settlement.

The scheme was to obtain 'motor spirit' from coal. A plant at Cannock had obtained 16 gallons per ton of coal but figures of 50/70 gallons per ton were considered obtainable by the promoter, one Mitford.

Further consideration was given to pensions and a number of old Piggotts servants had lost their jobs when Spring Hill closed. They were awarded 5/- week and an old Horseley workman, F. Tooby the same sum.

Two further Klonne 'Dry Gas Holders' were erected, both for Guest Keen and Baldwins at Cardiff and they were insured during construction against explosion. The contract value was £50,000.

A Lamella bus garage roof in Belfast, 800 feet span, 225 feet long, built 1931

Work proceeded on the construction of the new Pipe Works and a waste heat boiler was purchased from Humphreys and Glasgow. In order to cope with increased site work three compressors were bought at £1,200 and the directors authorised to buy new transport vehicles at a cost of £780.

Land at the rear of Doughty House, some 5833 square yards in area including a cottage, were purchased for £1,250 this being adjacent to the new Pipe Works. Nationally there was celebration on the occasion of the Jubilee of King George V. and Queen Mary and the Company decided to make an ex gratia payment for the holiday '...at the least possible cost to the Company'!. This would appear to be the first time that men were paid for a holiday.

In April 1935 an order was received for a swing bridge at Exeter, value £18,000. A report had been commissioned from F. H. Holland on works organisation and this was adopted in May 1935 and authority given to engage additional staff to operate the scheme. By July 1935 for the first time in many years the Directors were able to report "all departments of the works are fully employed".

The structure of the new Pipe Works having progressed plans were made to move to it plant and buildings from Hooper Street and Horseley Works.

These were:-

Move flanging and finishing presses.	£750
Move sundry plant for grinding, pickling etc.	£250
Taking down 600ft. of buildings and re-erecting at Tipton, providing new roof and side sheeting	£1750
Move set of pumps and motor	£350
Move large steam hammer	£250
Move welding machine and provide new room	£500
Move air compressor and provide new motor	£150
Move four cranes	£400
Move screwing lathes from Main Works	£500
	£4900
Less residual value of motors, scrap machinery etc. at Hooper Street	£3000

Nett £1900

Hooper Street could then be closed as soon as possible except for the Furnace Plant which was to remain pro tem..

As late as June 1935 agreements between the Employers Federation and the Engineering Joint Trades Movement had increased the War Bonus which were stated to increase company costs by £40 week as from 13 May 1935 and a further £40 week from 15 July 1935. At the same time a staff pension scheme was proposed prepared by the Prudential Assurance Co., Ltd., and left for further consideration.

The Structural Superintendent W. H. Jukes retired after 43 years service and was presented with a gold watch and a letter of appreciation.

A minor improvement in trade having occurred it was possible to carry forward a credit of £230.16s.8d in June 1935. There was a capital loss suspense account which amounted to £171,912.8s.3d. and in order to write off this sum the capital of the company was reduced by halving the value of the 300,000 ordinary shares from £1 to 10/-. At the same time a further 300,000- 10/- shares would be issued. This action left £21,912 .8s 3d. as a capital loss and this sum was transferred from the Reserve Fund reducing this to £28,087.11s.9d.

In view of the difficult financial position work on plant transfer from Hooper Street was deferred. However a new cupola for the Foundry at £300 and alterations to an existing crane for the Pipe Works at £250 were authorised, together with a new copier for the Drawing Office at £155. By November 1935 the new Pipe Works was reported to be in full production.

Towards the end of 1935 it is possible to detect an increase in trade. An account was opened at Lloyds, Victoria Street for the London Manager and the Marine Furnace Association was agreed to commence from 1 January 1936. Harry Green was appointed Midland Representative with a remunerartion of $2^1/_2\%$ on all business in structural steelwork with an office at Lombard House, Birmingham and was soon asking for two more rooms. S. Wright was appointed manager of the Chemical and Industrial Plant Department. The tender for a new swing bridge at Upton on Severn had proved the lowest but above the County Surveyor's estimate. Proposals were made to reduce the costs.

H. Hobden offered to act as reporting agent in China and was granted £100/year towards his expenses. The Chairman, Sir Sydney Henn was granted leave of absence from November 1935 until March 1936 for a visit to Africa. By December 1935 it was possible to report that Hooper Street Works was closed apart from the manufacture of furnaces and that some electrical plant had been sold for £600. The Marine Furnace Association had opened an office in Glasgow and would distribute all orders in an agreed manner. Competition was arising from electric welding of pipes and the various types of automatic welding machines available were to be considered.

At the year end the pensions were agreed to be continued and staff salary increases agreed. F. D. Perks was required to act as Registrar and granted £50 per annum increase and the sum granted for the staff dinner increased to £20. H. D. Lloyd was granted three months leave of absence for a visit to Africa.

Although the new Pipe works was in production it was not fully completed and a building at Hooper St. 150 foot long was to be added together with lathes from the Welding & Fitting Shops, at a cost of £1,000. Two sets of rolls were also transferred at a cost of £750.

The first indication of the gathering war clouds occurred in January 1936 when an enquiry for 22 Lamella hangers was received from the Air Ministry valued at £513,000. This became an order at an increased value of £689,784 and £6,000 was authorised to purchase all the new plant needed.

In the Pipe Works various explosions had occurred in the gas and air mains and A. Dyson reported on these and also requested that another pipe welding machine be transferred from Hooper St, at a cost of £500.

Another 2 million cu. ft. Klonne Gas-holder was ordered to be built at the Ford Motor Co., Dagenham for £36,500 and Fords requested that it be of welded construction. A. Dyson visited the States to study the 'Stacey' methods of welding. He reported favourably and the work of building the first welded holder of this type in the country went

Constuction of Patent Lamella roof showing minimum temporary support needed

ahead. By June 1936 with the Pipe Works in full production Mr. Dyson submitted a report and it was agreed that further capital expenditure could be increased at the discretion of the Managing Directors. Two items were involved, the removal of the large rolls from Hooper St. at £750 and the purchase of a new automatic pipe welding machine at £1,000. This machine was presumably an electric welding machine intended to supersede the old forge or 'roller welding' equipment of the type transferred from Cardiff and Hooper St..

An order from Christy Brothers was for an hydro-electric scheme in Devon and was welcomed '...as the first contract of this nature carried out by the Company'. Further they tendered for a pressed steel tank 180 ft x 60 ft x 16 ft deep, 1,000,000 gallons capacity which would be the '...largest Piggott Tank ever made'.

The accounts to June 1936 showed another small profit and £25,028. 8s. 11d. was carried forward. An agreement was reached with the bank to allow the overdraft to rise up to £140,000. A cold saw for the Girder Shop at £900 was authorised together with a new crane for the Welding Bay at the Pipe Works at £1,000 and another pipe welding machine from Hooper Street at £500.

Following correspondence from several old workpeople who had ceased work it was agreed that they should be granted pensions at the discretion of the Managing Directors.

Sir Sydney Henn who chaired the Board Meeting on 13 October 1936, died suddenly and a special meeting was held on 27 October at which the sad event was reported. He had been associated with the Company for 20 years and had suffered a fall in which he broke a thigh and double pneumonia had set in. He was aged 74 and had been born in Manchester, the son of Canon John Henn. He spent thirty years in Chile for Duncan, Fox & Co., South American merchants. On the outbreak of war he joined the staff of the Surveyor- General of Supply at the War Office and in 1919 was transferred to the Ministry of Munitions until 1921. From 1922 until 1929 he was Unionist M.P. for Blackburn, being knighted in 1918 for his public services.

T. W. Horton was elected Chairman, pro tem. Shortly afterwards the proposals to issue the £150,000 of new shares was actioned, the issue being underwritten by Tighe & Horton for a commission of 1/-per share. Of these shares 134,028 were taken up and some 51.999 others applied for of which only 15.972 could be sold to complete the issue. £7,500 was paid as the underwriters' commission.

Twenty guineas was given to the Tipton Council for Social Services, and an order received from the G.W.R. for £8,000 for a swing bridge at Barry Docks.

In January 1937, A. Dyson visited Rangoon in connection with a large tender for 27,000 tons of 58 inch concrete lined pipes which was valued at £660,000. The minutes do not record whether this was successful.

On 11 March 1937 the Right Hon. the Earl of Dudley was elected Director and Chairman of the Company and immediately took the chair of the meeting. He was allotted 250 – 5% Preference Shares, at par. During the meeting the matter of the wages of employees joining the Territorial Army and on the occasion of the public holiday for the Coronation were agreed.

Further capital plant was agreed – an automatic welding plant at £1,000 (apparently the second) and a Pels Folding Press for the Air Ministry contract – £3,500. Interestingly the company accounts from the end of 1937 include items concerning the costs of 'electrode making', both for materials and wages.

It was decided finally to close down Hooper St. and transfer the Furnace Plant to Tipton. Discussions with both the lessors and the railway company resulted in a payment of £2,500 being agreed to surrender the lease and to be relieved of all liabilities, except for some railway fencing.

In May 1937 it was reported that an order for steelwork for the new headquarters of Imperial Airways Ltd. in Buckingham Palace Road, London would require 1,000 tons of steel. In the same period a number of orders from Cadburys for steel framed buildings were received. Reference was also made to a dispute between one of the electric welders and the Welding Superintendant when all the men had walked out. They returned the next day.

At Tipton it was agreed to re-organise the Girder Shop at a cost of £1,000. The gas industry Trade Association was the F. C. Construction Co., Ltd., and Horseley had previously invested in 1000 shares of this company. They distributed some of their funds in shares in June 1937 and issued 554 – £1 shares to H. B. & T. P. at 17/6d each.

Problems continued to occur over the deliveries of steel from the mills and this frequently delayed production. On Sunday 5 September 1937, a special board meeting was held at Witley Court, the residence of Lord Dudley and was attended by only two other directors, T. W. Horton and J. W. Baillie. The meeting was to agree the year's accounts and for the first time for many years a substantial profit had been achieved, totalling £56,796. 3s.7d. From this a 10% dividend on the ordinary shares (less 5/- in the £1. Income Tax) was paid and the dividend of 5% paid on the Preference Shares.

In addition the expenses of the recent capital issue of £7,628. 4s. 8d. were written off, £2,000 was set aside to '...Inaugurate a fund for the benefit of the staff of the company,' £21,912. 8s. 3d. was taken to reserve leaving a balance to carry forward of £6,408. 13s. 3d. It was later agreed that a bonus be paid to the staff in total no more than £1,100, the first occasion on which this occurred.

A very large order for the Air Ministry was obtained in September 1937 which involved about 5,000 tons of steel at St. Athen for – four 'C' Type Hangars and sundry workshop buildings. The value was £135,000. The order for the new bridge at Upton on Severn was finally obtained in November 1937 with value £30,207. Preparations for possible war continued with work on Lamella Hangars and for nine Drill Halls in Cornwall. It was stated that the Government Departments would require a total of 300,000 tons of steel in 1938. Many commercial firms were reported '...as refraining from placing orders pending an improvement in the International situation'.

A proposal to set up a staff Group Pension Scheme was agreed in principle. The Prudential Assurance Co., Ltd., had provided a quotation but a second was obtained from the Phoenix Assurance Co., which was accepted and put into operation on 1 April 1938. It was to cost the company some £1,675 per annum.

New modern offices were considered for Tipton and plans were to be proposed by Bye, Simms & Gifford. After considering the possibility of modifying the existing offices the new building was approved in February 1938.

Domestically it was agreed to pay £7. 10s. 0d lump sum to the widow of A. Robinson an employee killed in a road accident. A gold watch valued at £10. 10s. 0d. was purchased and presented to W. Screen, Foreman of the Light Construction Shop who had completed 51 years continuous service. A 5/- week pension was granted to G. Randall, Repair Shop, invalided by a serious illness.

Further union agreements concerning holiday pay had been accepted and an account was opened with Lloyds Bank known as 'The Horseley-Piggott Employees Holiday Accumulations Fund' for this purpose.

Re-siting of the corrugating furnace equipment continued to give problems and the outside bay of the new Pipe Works, originally allocated was stated to be '...fully occupied with electrically welded pipe work and the power presses for 'Lamella' and roof sheets.' It was agreed that a building from Hooper St. be re-erected at the end of the Repair Shop at a cost of £1,000.

T. W. Horton who had attended the meeting of 10 January 1938 died suddenly and this was reported on 21 February, the '...Directors deploring the death of their colleague' and recorded their appreciation of his services as a director over a period of 10 years.

A number of other matters were reported at the same meeting:- J. W. Baillie referred to a booklet on the new Pension Scheme, the sum of £26. 5s. 0d. was subscribed '...to the fund organised by a number of Tipton Industrialists for the purchase of the Regalia for the Tipton Council upon it being granted the status of a Borough'; £10. 10s. 0d. was donated to both the Society of British Gas Industries and the British Gas Federation; £400 was agreed for an horizontal drill and £820 for a cold saw. A month later a quotation was submitted for the reconstruction of the Menai Bridge, but this was unsuccessful.

The pensions of two old servants J. Clark and G. H. Harris of 5/- week had ceased on 31 December 1937 but were renewed and the Managing Directors were authorised to make similar grants to '...old servants in necessitous cases'.

In March 1938 it was noted that the Large Tube Association was to be continued for a further five years. Tenders and plans for the new offices, those in use until closure, were agreed and the work placed with Maddocks & Walford of Birmingham at £8,527. 10s. 0d.

The Lincoln automatic welding plant purchased from Buck & Hickman '...had been rejected as inefficient' and replaced by four transformer hand welding sets at no extra cost. The type of this equipment is not known.

Some further expenditure was authorised:– a new 5 Ton Loco Crane at £800; £2. 2s. 0d. to the Tipton Council for Social Service; £250 for a stand at the Building Exhibition, Olympia, and the completion of an extension to the Pipe Works with 'Lamella' roofwork at £2,000.

In May 1938 J. W. Baillie was able to announce that all statutory requirements of the Companies Act had been fulfilled and the liquidation of Thomas Piggott & Co., completed. A new director was appointed, Lieutenant Commander Colin Buist, M.V.O., R.N..

The Water Purification Department which had progressed well was to be set up as a separate company and they became Horseley-Piggott (Water Engineers) Ltd., with a capital of £5000 with loan facilities up to £2,500. J. W. Baillie & A. Dyson were to be directors and F. D. Perks as Secretary but with no fees.

There was a desire to increase the status of the London Office Manager Len Harper and he was created Official Director – London Director at £850 per annum plus £150 expenses.

A very serious problem over defalcations of the accounts was reported in September 1938 and F. D. Perks was summarily dismissed. Some £1100 had been traced from 1 January 1936 '...but they had in a small way been going on for some time prior to that date'. Criminal proceedings were considered '...but in view of Mr. Perk's long service and his family connections with the company' they were not taken. A. E. P. Turner was appointed Accountant and Registrar at £500 per annum.

The Boiler Furnace Co., had appealed for one or two manufacturers to cease production for a period in view of a fall in demand. Such manufacturers would be compensated at £12. 10s. 0d. for each furnace lost from their quota. This suited H. B. & T. P. as they were still moving the plant from Hooper St. and they agreed to assist for three months, later extended to six.

A contract for a Scherzer lift bridge for the London County Council was obtained in March 1938 at a value of £49,000. The financial year to June 1938 was successful and a balance of £64,481 was achieved resulting in a dividend of 10% less income tax of 5/6d in the pound on ordinary shares and the final dividend of $2^1/_2$% on the Preference shares. £40,000 was transferred to reserve leaving a carry forward of £7,199. A staff bonus of £1,100 was awarded.

In July 1938 a detailed report was made to the Directors on the various hangars being built for the Air Ministry. This was signed by J. D. Vaughan. A manufacturer of a cleaning agent known as 'Grymoff' had a works and offices in Scott St., adjacent to the Pipe Works and they came on to the market at £2,200 and were offered to Horseley.

It will have become clear that A. Dyson, as the engineering half of the joint Managing Directors, had an interest in the rapidly expanding use of welding, and that H. B. & T. P. were now significant users of the process. As a result he was invited to join the Board of the 'Arc Manufacturing Co.,' who produced '...welding apparatus and electrodes'. He later became President of the Institute of Welding.

Although the Staff Pension Scheme was in being no such scheme yet existed for the workmen and they had to rely on a gesture by the Company. Three such grants were made in November 1938

J. W. Bourne	51 years service	6/6d per week
J. Mountford	53 " "	6/6d " "
W. W. Robinson	41 " "	5/- " "

In July 1938 the Managing Directors calculated that the order intake for 1937/8 at £958,858 was the highest in the Company history except for 1935/6 when half a million pounds was included for the Air Ministry Hangars. Sadly they also reported the death of a 14 year old rivet heater who was crushed by a travelling crane.

A week's Holiday with pay had been granted to the work people which they '...had much appreciated'. They also noted the cost of £2,336 and the loss of $3^1/_2$ days output!

In September 1938 Mr Dyson reported on a visit to Gelsenkirchen, Germany where he had seen the erection of a 21 million cu. ft. Klonne holder and he detailed the production and erection methods. This was to be the largest in the world – diameter 262 ft, height 446 ft., total steel 5,000 tons.

Towards the end of 1938 A. Dyson was able to report that Hooper St. Works had been fully dis-mantled and all the required buildings and plant moved to Tipton so that the agreed sum of release, £2,500 was paid to the lessors. There remained the freehold land and property which should be sold, but the old Willoughby Cottages were scheduled for demolition and it was not until September 1939 that this land was sold to the Catholic Schools at 10/- sq. yd. and another area at 15/- sq. yd.

Towards the end of 1938 the crisis had seriously affected trade and by early 1939 the war clouds were becoming ever darker and a number of matters in preparation occurred. A large order for pipes from the Admiralty was obtained and as these required to be pickled, such a plant was installed at £2,000.

Arrangements were made with British Electric Ray Ltd., to manufacture A.R.P. Shelters '...and a large demand is anticipated' and agreement made to exhibit at the B.I.F. However great problems occurred in attempts at manufacture and when it became clear that only a part licence was offered the matter was dropped. Another proposal to manufacture underground car parks was not taken up.

With the issue by the Government of the Civil Defence Bill it became necessary to provide air raid shelters in the works and to take suitable fire precautions. The air raid shelters and other precautions were to cost £6,000. Large orders for 'dovetail sheeting' no doubt for air raid shelters were being received and a new folding machine to cope with the work was bought for £2,000.

Men joined the Territorial Army and it was agreed that similar arrangements to those of other companies would be followed. On domestic matters A. Dyson proposed that the Company should obtain the equipment to be able to undertake Lloyds Class 1 welding. Only Babcock & Wilcox, John Thompson Ltd., and one other were then approved. The matter was postponed but a few months later he raised the matter again and requested it should be '...given serious consideration as the Company's prestige was involved'. The plant, X-Ray equipment and buildings would cost £20,000 but an X-Ray set might be bought for £2,000. The matter was again deferred and did not evolve until 1942. The manufacture of boiler furnaces was re-commenced following the moratorium.

A pension of 7/6 a week for twelve months was paid to the widow of F. Jukes who had '... died as a result of injuries believed to have been caused by his work and not covered by insurance'. Miss A. Stanton with 52 years service was awarded 10/- week pension. A house, 7, Horseley Road, next to the Company garage became vacant and was purchased for £460 whilst a house 40, Hallewell Road, Edgbaston until recently occupied by one of the company's servants (F. D. Perks ?) was sold for £400.

The new offices were expected to be ready by February 1939 and whilst they were being built a temporary Drawing Office had been created in a wooden building in Horseley Road and this was later turned into a staff canteen at a cost of £500. Weather conditions during early 1939 were reported to have been 'appalling' and delayed work including the Upton-on-Severn Bridge where the banks were under water. Another tragedy occured when a man was killed in the Pipe works. An order for a one million cubic foot conventional, but welded gas-holder, was obtained for Tipton Gas. This was the first such holder to be built by Horseley.

The year to June 1939 was again profitable and a balance of £59,979 was recorded from which a dividend of $12^1/_2$% less 5/6 tax was paid, £10,000 to reserve, £10,000 for A.R.P. expenditure and £5,000 for the staff pension scheme, leaving £13,618 to carry forward.

Capital expenditure was agreed as follows:-

    Ransomes & Rapier Mobile Crane £1250
    Circular Saw   400
    Band Saw   250
    Shears   800

In August 1939 J. W. Baillie who was on holiday became ill and had to undergo an operation which required several weeks of absence. A. E. P. Turner was appointed Assistant Secretary pro tem. and so with the new offices completed, the works very busy and profitable and with air raid shelters and other precautions in place and work in hand for the Admiralty including the making of mines, war was declared on 3 September 1939.

Rolling Lift Bridge, Port of London Authority – West India Dock

CHAPTER 7
1939-1945

THE SECOND WORLD WAR YEARS

A letter was received from Lord Dudley, confirming that he had been appointed by Royal Warrant as Regional Commissioner and he would not be able to attend any more Board Meetings. These duties were obviously not as time consuming as he feared as he did later attend many of the meetings.

Many instructions were received at Tipton concerning '...obscuration and camouflage' and every effort was made to comply, and an expenditure of £6,000 was authorised. The company was placed on the 'Associated Firms' List' by the Admiralty and an order for 2,000 mines was received. The equipment needed for this work would cost £7,500 and the Admiralty were asked to share this.

The London Office was closed and some staff moved up to Tipton and a house 'Lansdowne', Horseley Road was purchased for £800 for their occupation. In addition air raid shelters were constructed and both a decontamination and first aid depot were built at a cost of £2,500. Further large orders were received for press work. A further folding press at £3,000 and a large power press at £4,000 were authorised but only a Wilkins & Mitchell power press at £8,000 was purchased.

A number of men joined the Territorials and the question of providing a supplement to their Army pay was considered. Each case was to be considered and the Managing Director's discretion used to 'alleviate hardship'. It was reported that the hydraulic pump equipment was obsolete and inadequate. A new set would cost £3,500.

In a first direct reference to the British Constructional Steelwork Association mention is made of an insurance scheme for the value of work in progress and steel stock. The cost would be half of one percent on selling value, in the case of Horseley, thought to be about £5,000 per annum. To cover these costs an addition to the maximum selling prices of structural steelwork was made.

Delivery of mines was required by the Admiralty to be increased from 150 to 500 per week, for which they would bear the costs of new plant for production. The value of this plant was placed at £15,000 and included:-

    1 Set Hydraulic Pumps and Accumulator.
    2 Boring Mills for necking over.
    2 Automatic Welding Heads.
    Sundry jigs and loose plant.
    Further capital was authorised for:-
    2 Hydraulic presses at £800 and £200.
    New temporary buildings on the crane race
      between the Girder Shop and Fitting Shop – £1,000.

The first reference to a major works reconstruction scheme is made on 17 Jan 1940 when A. Dyson's report was considered. This work was to be '...at some future date'.

There was heavy snow in early 1940 and this was responsible for two major problems of roof collapse both of Lamella construction. One was at Southampton on a garage for the Apex Motor Co., Ltd., and the other at Meteor Garage, Moseley, Birmingham. Responsibility was accepted and offers to rebuild made. Later investigation showed that these roofs were both of early light construction and shallow relative to their span. Some 10 years later there was a problem with another early roof but these three were the only ones in some 120 total to give problems and a large number of these Lamella roofs remain today in excellent condition including all the Air Ministry hangars.

In January 1940 the gas holder for water gas in the Pipe Works exploded due to the formation of ice which prevented the crown from descending creating a vacuum which pulled down the crown and when bracings penetrated the shell a spark caused the explosion.

For the mines contract, machinery was installed for making bands and rings at £4,800 which was to be charged to the contract. The total orders to February 1940 were for 16,500 mines.

The BCSA recommended a war bonus be paid from 19 February 1940 and this was agreed. Len Harper was appointed a Director at £1.000/annum plus £150 for expenses, but he was not to receive director's fees or commission.

Two erectors were killed during February 1940, one on the Daimler contract at Coventry and the other at Southampton. The Grymoff buildings next to the Pipe Works for which Horseley originally offered £2,200 were bought in July 1940 for £3,000 including fittings.

The Company were informed that they would be called upon by the Government to produce parts of standard ships. A works nurse was appointed and two War Savings Groups set up and £1,140 of certificates bought by the company on behalf of the groups. No holidays were being allowed.

In July 1940 the Secretary indicated the likely trading profit and the Chairman expressed his thanks to all for their '...initiative and hard work in adapting the plant so successfully to the requirements of the Government in the National Emergency'. The profit, in fact, was £52,634 which allowed $2\frac{1}{2}$% to be paid on the preference shares and $12\frac{1}{2}$% on the ordinary shares, with £10,000 retained for contingencies, £25,625 carried forward and £2,000 distributed as a staff bonus.

Work on pipe contracts was reported nearing completion and a view expressed that no more orders were likely until after the war. In order to find work for the Pipe Works consideration was given to the assembly of military tanks but the costs of conversion were considered to be too high.

The Factory Inspectors demanded that rest rooms for boys and youths be erected and canteen facilities were requested by the men. The costs were considered to be high and the matter deferred. A. Dyson considered the number of welding sets inadequate and his survey showing 47 welding points, he proposed 12 more. The sets had to run on DC as this was the main supply. New types of work were introduced, such as the manufacture of wheels for tanks. A young erector was killed on a contract at Wolverhampton.

The collapse of France is noted and this prevented the delivery of a number of furnaces to that Country. Problems arose over disposal of effluent from the acid pickling plant which was moved outside the Pipe Works and the damage to the roof sheets due to acid fumes was repaired.

Problems with air raids and labour difficulties caused the night shift on the mines to be closed down in December 1940. Nevertheless all requirements under the Civil Defence Acts had been provided and the works were reported to be '...adequately protected by the ARP personnel, Home Guard and Fire Watchers'. The Horseley platoon of the Home Guard numbered 160 men and they mounted nightly guard in the works. An order for 1,000 steel helmets was placed for the men to wear during air raids.

A new order for 1,000 lb. bombs was received from the Air Ministry, but by April 1941 the production of mines was cut by 50% by order of the Admiralty. The space saved was devoted to the manufacture of pontoons. There were problems over the supply of Mond gas said to be of low quality and pressure. Consideration was given to installing a pitch burning plant to heat the furnaces.

There developed '...considerable feeling in the works at the absence of Canteen facilities' and since the Admiralty had refused to assist with the costs, some £4,000 was authorised for the erection of the canteen and its equipment. By January 1941 the enemy had damaged many industrial buildings and plant and Horseley were engaged in repairs to gas holders at Coventry, Smethwick and Cardiff. The Foundry Dressing shop was to be used for Pressed Steel Tank production and a new dressing shop built for £1,500.

In March 1941 a further war bonus was paid and Len Harper's salary increased by £200. A. E. Dilley, Works Manager had his salary increased from £600 to £800 per annum plus £26 expenses. In April an accident to the old hydraulic accumulator occurred. It was in a bad condition and the pump man had to cut it in and out by hand. However he let it rise too far and the final safety chain broke so that it came out of its cylinder and fell over. The second accumulator was brought quickly into action. At about this time it was reported that the works engineer had left. This is understood to have been Bill Rose and he was succeeded by George Rowley.

In May 1941 it was reported that the Company was on the Ministry of Labour Protected List and scheduled under the Essential Work (General Provisions) Order 1941. As a further indication of the war time conditions it was agreed that a lavatory and cloakroom be provided for women workers at a cost of £565. It was intended to train women as welders as they were unable to obtain skilled men. Some 45 women were at work by October.

It became clear that many more than first believed would use the canteen facilities and this required a reconsideration of the proposals which concluded with agreement to provide a building for 500 people at a cost of £9,000. The building was constructed with a Lamella roof. The heavy work load had caused deterioration in the main works road and the railway tracks which had to be repaired at £2,500. In May 1941 it was reported that work was in hand for the shell plating of six standard ships and negotiations were in hand for an order for sections of tank landing craft.

The property, Doughty House, came on to the market and this was situated adjacent to the Pipe Works. A sum of £2,500 was to be offered and the sale was eventually concluded. It was later used by the fire-watchers. Overall war damage insurance was taken out at £225,000 for a cost of £3,375 for the year to September 1941.

An accident occurred during repairs to a gas holder at Cardiff Gas Works, built by Thomas Piggott in 1881, when the timber supporting the middle lift gave way and it collapsed settling on the inner lift. The men were at lunch and it appears no one was injured. In August 1941 an order for 300 small armoured plate bodies for 'Beaverette' tanks was obtained.

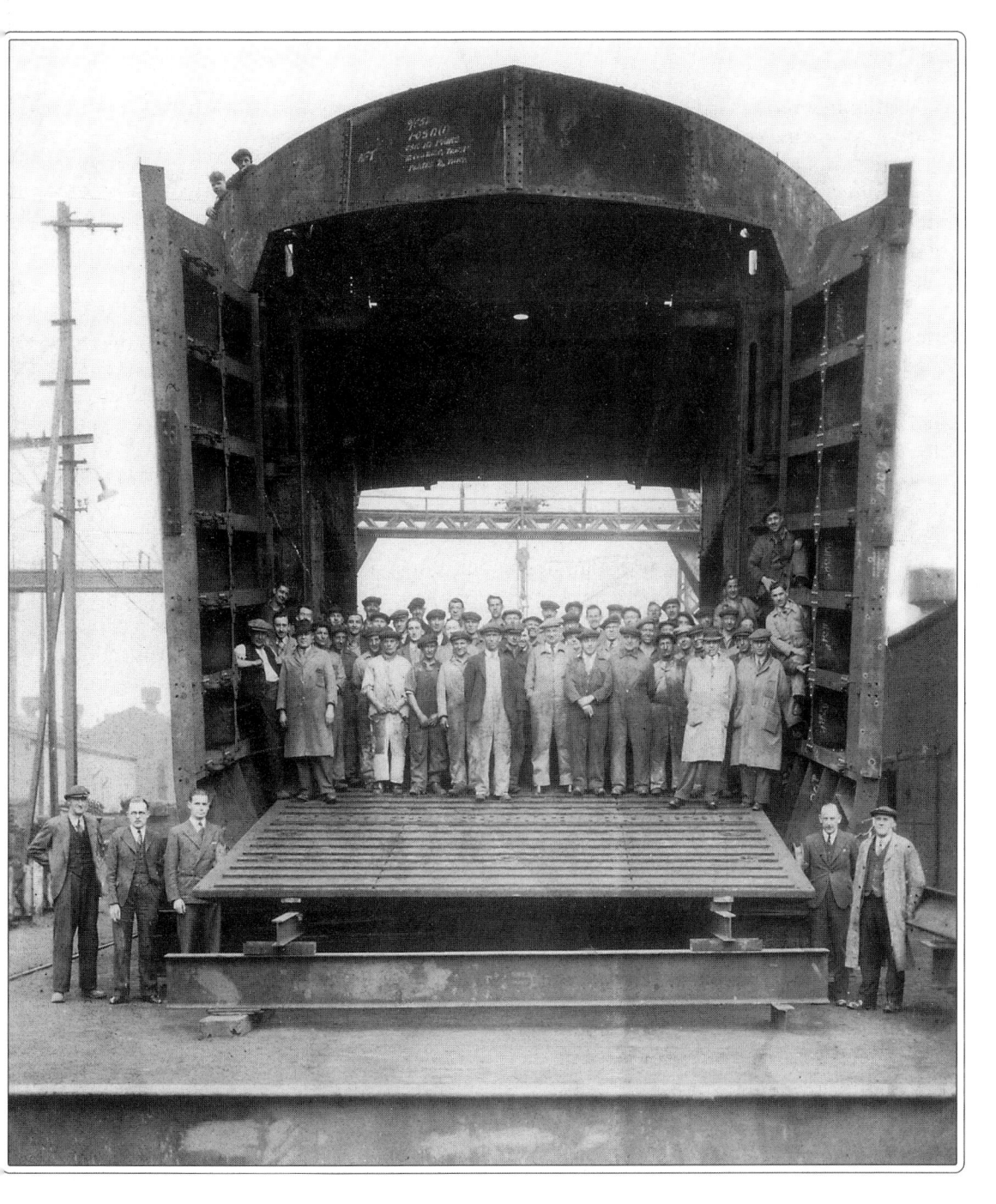

A section of a tank landing craft with all those involved, c1942. (Photo: H. Parton)

In September 1941 the profit was declared at £61,430 which allowed the final $2^1/_2$% to be paid on the preference shares, $12^1/_2$% on the ordinary shares, £10,000 to reserve and a balance of £36,698 to be carried forward. A sum of £1,900 was distributed as a staff and foremens' bonus.

The electrical power supply was stated to be in use to full capacity and concern was expressed over the situation of possible damage by enemy action. £1,350 was proposed to be spent on a linking cable to the Pipe Works Power House. In November 1941 an additional order for bombs of 4,000 lb. size was received and this required new plant which would cost £8,500.

At this point Board Minute Book No.6 is concluded and further information has to be obtained from other sources. Fortunately copies of the Managing Director's reports survive from 1928 to 1949 and these give much detail of interest, although it is not always possible to know whether the recommendations were accepted. These reports have been used to fill in some detail in Chapters 5 & 6.

One matter that these records do not show is that on 16 February 1942 one John S. Allen was accepted to serve an Articled Apprenticeship to Structural Engineering which was to last until 1946, following which he was to serve the company in various positions until 1988 and by consultancy until the Company closed formally on 18 May 1992, and even after that!

In March 1942 A. Dyson was concerned over the electrical supply and proposed that a start should be made on a changeover to A.C. at a cost of £1940 in preference to the Pipe Works linking cable, previously proposed. The production of pressed steel tank plates reached a record level in March when 3962 were completed.

On April 14 H.R.H. the Duke of Kent made a tour of inspection of part of the works, which is recorded on a rather jerky colour film and by his signature on a visitor's record.

In May 1942, A. Dyson prepared a further report on the Lloyds Class 1 welding list for pressure vessels. He envisaged an increase in demand for vessels in the oil industry due to enemy damage. To gain entry to the list three aspects had to be satisfied:-
1. Fully equipped Laboratory available.
2. X-Ray apparatus must be installed.
3. A sample vessel must be made.

The laboratory was included in the new office scheme. He urged acceptance or '...we shall be in a somewhat invidious position if we lag behind'. It is known that this scheme was proceeded with under Chief Development Engineer, J. D. Vaughan.

In May 1942 it was reported that six stern ends for tank landing craft had been completed and a further six were in hand. Fabrication of the bodies for the Beaverette tanks had benefited from visits by experts from the Ministry of Supply. Eventually about ten per week were built,

Work on the Canteen '...drags on very slowly', but it was opened with due ceremony on July 1st 1942 by Lord Dudley. Progress on Class 1 welding was reported in March 1943 when £2450 was required to purchase an X-Ray set and microscope. In April proposals were made to move the existing weighbridge and install it in the Pipe Works. A new 32ft x 10ft weighbridge was to be purchased and installed in its place. The total cost would be about £2,300.

The Ministry of Supply had asked that the pressed steel tank plates should be made to match those being produced by Braithwaite's to avoid problems of matching '...at the front'. Horseley retained their characteristic pattern of central design-essentially a raised circular rib. Members of staff, Coleman & Martin, had proposed a cheaper form of plate for A. R. P. Water Dams and a provisional patent was taken out. Seven tanks were ordered by the G. W. R..

Progress was again reported on Class 1 Welding. The X-ray set was to be housed in a building within the Welding Shop and the films developed in the new laboratory. Plant for the chemical and metallurgical laboratory was to be purchased. A decision was made to overhaul the old 50 ton Buckton tensile machine instead of buying a new machine.

Discussions were held with a Polish engineer, Spiwak in connection with ideas for steel framed houses. On 10 August, 1943 a 'Workers Playtime' concert was broadcast by the B.B.C. from the Canteen, which was attended by Lord Dudley.

The Mulberry Harbour project was envisaged in August 1943 when it was recorded that a large order for '...Special trestles for floating bridges' was expected from the Ministry of Supply. This would be '...very urgent work' and in September the Tank landing craft orders were on '...a most urgent' list.

An accident occurred when modifying a used petrol tank in the Welding Shop and two men were killed. They were John J. Bratt (28) and George H. Fellows (25). By November 1943 the directors were considering the likely effect of the cessation of the fighting, when there would be an immediate cancelling of many orders. Since the Essential Work Order required that the Company pay all the men, certain schemes which could be put in hand when labour became available were envisaged. These proposals included raising the roof of the Machine Shop to that of the Welding Shops which were raised in 1928; replacement of the timber roof in the Light Construction Dept. and modifications to the Water Gas Plant in the Pipe Works.

A. E. Dilley, Works Manager, a man of the old school, retired after 29 years service, he having started work at Piggotts. He was succeeded by J. H. Coughtrie, a Scot. At this time Arthur Deighton was still Foundry Manager and aged 68. He had been apprenticed in 1899 and joined Horseley in 1932.

In February 1944 the large Tube Association, formed in 1933 was in difficulty due to a claim by South Durham for an increase in their quota. The quotas in 1944 were:-

Stewart & Lloyds	50%
Claytons	11.5%
Horseley	16%
South Durham	22.5%

There were problems at Horseley due to a fire in the Light Construction Department. Horseley took over Factory '99' which was higher and on the opposite side of the road to Horseley. Meanwhile plans were made for re-building the Light Construction Shop.

The Minister of Fuel & Power directed a reduction in the consumption of gas & electricity. It was decided to cut out Saturday working, making the working week 47 hours and working until 7.00 p.m. on Tuesdays, Wednesdays & Thursdays.

Concern was expressed over the 100,000 tank plates sold to the Government when the war ceased, as after the first war surplus plates were sold to T. W. Ward Ltd. and for many years the tank plate trade was dead. Ideas for purchase were considered but A. Dyson considered it '...unwise to accept any financial responsibility'.

Spiral welded pipe, first considered in 1940 was raised again in May 1944, when it was believed that South Durham were considering it. 'Mephan Fergusson' pipe was being made in Australia and A. Dyson was to obtain details.

In May 1944 Factory '99' was in full production and the new laboratory was nearly complete. A new Avery testing machine was awaited and clearly the proposals for the old Buckton had been changed. As the end of the War became nearer, slackness in production and absenteeism increased. A new Absenteeism Committee was created to deal with the problem. Arthur Guest, a staff man with 29 years service, 16 with Piggotts, retired.

In June, the poor condition of plant in the Pipe Works was considered. In particular the hydraulic pumps moved from Birmingham were bought in 1919 from Harper Beans National Shell Factory, Dudley and had been in use for 30 years. A new set for 750 p.s.i. were to cost £3,500.

The Foundry and its equipment were considered to be '...very antiquated and practically worn out'. A new foundry on the site of the burned out Light Construction Shop was proposed. The demand for corrugated furnaces had fallen off and it was agreed that Horseley & Broomside Boiler Works should close their furnace department for six months and be compensated at the rate of £10 per boiler for their quota. The future prospects of the Scotch Boiler was considered to be doubtful.

Plans for the new foundry were submitted and were to cost £30,000. A. Dyson urged that the money be spent on a new welding shop which would be more profitable. The foundry '...in the past has always been looked upon as a necessary evil'.

In December 1944 there was hope that the tender for the new power station at Ocker Hill would be accepted. Its value was £150,000 for about 2900 tons of steel. About 1000 tons would be sub-let to Braithwaites. A similar contract for Walsall would be let in 1947.

At the end of 1944 the Horseley Home Guard was stood down and a special dinner and ceremony took place. W. T. Screen who for many years had been in charge of the Girder and Light Construction shops died during the year.

The major works reconstruction scheme is not mentioned in these reports until April 1945 when the foundations for the new shops are making good progress. They were to erect 270 feet of Building 'B' and 180 feet of Building 'A'. Permission was being sought for Buildings 'C', 'F' and 'G'.

They would then use the steelwork from the old tank shop to build a foundry on the Light Construction Shop site. This would enable them to demolish the old Foundry. They hoped to obtain a permit for the steel before 'V' Day so that they could find employment for the men '...during the hiatus which will follow cancellation of war contracts'.

The Large Tube Association was to continue for a further five years to end 31.12.1948 (sic). Boiler furnaces were in great demand – up from 320 for five months to 797 in 1945. Horseley were to start production again in July and Deighton & Broomside to stand down for three months. The Works reconstruction proceeded but approval was given only to replace the tank shop and build a new foundry.

Problems arose over labour, as the Government had decided to call all deferred men to the age of 30 whereas before it had been 25. Horseley found it impossible to replace the men lost. The demobilised men were given eight weeks leave and only one man – an electric welder had applied for reinstatement.

Immediately after the victory over Japan the Government cancelled most of their military orders, leaving only work on Tank Landing craft which were already two thirds complete. A further six men returned from the forces. An order was received for 700 tons of Calendar-Hamilton Bridge units for the Dutch Railways.

And so came the end of the Second World War.

Horseley Annual Accounts

No	Year end	Profit	Carry Forward	Reserve fund	Dividend Ord shares	Dividend Pref shares	Notes
2	31.12.1874	10,078-5-11	849-4-2	3,000	5%		
3	31.12.1875	6,034-15-6	646-9-8	+1,000 =4,000	5%		
4	31.12.1876	3,030-3-9	2,676-13-5	ditto	nil		
5	31.12.1877	(3,405-12-9)	(728-19-4)	-3,661-1-11 =338-18-1	nil		3,000 still in depreciation fund less loss 840-7-7
6	31.12.1878	4,242-19-7	4,242-19-7		2,498-10-6* nil		*to old Horseley shareholders
7	31.12.1879	3,745-0-10	7,988-0-5		nil		
8	31.12.1880	76-17-11	8,064-18-4		nil		
9	31.12.1881	7,242-19-8	8,010-8-0		6%		
10	31.12.1882	5,850-6-3	4,254-9-3	3,500 reserve	5%		
11	31.12.1883	7,860-4-2	2,508-8-5	3,500	5%		
12	31.12.1884	6,994-17-10	nil	+5,994-11-5	nil		3,508-14-10 bad debts w/o
13	31.12.1885	(7,828-2-10)		5994-11-5	nil		
14	31.12.1886	5,140-0-5	(6,884-3-9)	ditto	nil		
15	31.12.1887	14,474-11-7	1,049-15-4	ditto	5%		5,344-9-4 w/o
16	31.12.1888	11,537-1-2	6,046-4-0	ditto	5%		year to end 31st March
17	31.3.1890	15,125-5-6	6,046-4-0	+1314-6-9 =7,308-18-2	6%		
18	31.3.1891	14,961-11-2	6,046-4-0	+3,023-9-4 =10,332-7-6	6%		
19	31.3.1892	10,180-15-7	2,402-9-7	+4,667-12-6 =15,000-0-0	7%		
20	31.3.1893	9,690-13-0	1,936-5-1	+1,000-0-0 =16,000	7%		
21	31.3.1894	8,144-12-0	924-0-5	Ditto	7%		
22	31.3.1895	3,551-7-7	nil	-757-2-0 =15,242-18-0	4%		
23	31.3.1896	572-8-11	572-8-11	ditto	nil		
24	31.3.1897	6,285-5-3	317-1-8	15,242-18-0	5%		
25	31.3.1898	9,868-15-0	579-19-8	+1,757-2-0 =17,000	6%		
26	31.3.1899	17,319-4-1	1,817-18-9	+3,000-0-0 =20,000	10%		500 to Birmingham University Fud
27	31.3.1900	21,299-12-8	1,266-0-2	+5,000 =25,000	12½%		
28	31.3.1901	18,084-1-11	998-10-10	+2,000 =27,000	12½%		
29	31.3.1902	17,372-17-11	1,019-17-6	+1,000 =28,000	12½%		
30	31.3.1903	12,417-19-9	356-12-3	ditto	10%		
31	31.3.1904	8,907-16-0	107-10-9	ditto	7%		
32	31.3.1905	7,621-13-1	1,188-11-4	ditto	5%		
33	31.3.1906	5,887-8-10	1,843-10-2	ditto	4%		
34	31.3.1907	7,071-13-2	3,688-13-4	ditto	4%		
35	31.3.1908	(5,951-10-10)	(2,262-17-6)	ditto	nil		
36	31.3.1909	4,553-7-4	2,290-9-10	ditto	nil		
37	31.3.1910	773-15-8	3,064-5-6	ditto	nil		
38	31.3.1911	(2,510-12-2)	553-13-4	ditto	nil		
39	31.3.1912	7,492-10-10	18,13-14-2	+1,000 =29,000	4%		

Horseley Annual Accounts (cont'd)

No	Year end	Profit	Carry Forward	Reserve fund	Dividend Ord shares	Dividend Pref shares	Notes
40	31.3.1913	12,727-13-11	2,692-13-1	+4,000 =33,000	6%		
41	31.3.1914	18,275-6-1	4,157-0-5	+7,000 =40,000	7$\frac{1}{2}$%		
42	31.3.1915	23,264-7-5	6,956-7-10	+10,000 =50,000	8%		
43	31.3.1916	9,514-17-0	7,314-7-4	ditto	7%		
44	31.3.1917	17,948-9-9	9,797-17-1	+5,000 =55,000	8%		
45	31.3.1918	11,640-7-2	7,281-6-9	+5,000 =60,000	7%		
46	31.3.1919	23,789-8-8	10,605-15-5	+10,000 =70,000	8%		
47	31.3.1920	24,452-6-0	11,600-10-10	ditto	8%		HB & Eng. Co. Ltd.
48	31.3.1921	30,784-5-2	12,384-16-0	+10,000 =80,000	8%		
49	31.3.1922	19,189-17-11	9,074-13-11	+10,000 =90,000	5%		
50	31.3.1923	9,172-10-0	8,247-3-11	ditto	4%		
51	31.3.1924	(33,964-9-1)	4,282-14-10	-30,000 =60,000	nil		
52	31.3.1925	(4,257-17-6)	24-17-4	ditto	nil		
53	31.3.1926	6,017-1-8	6,041-19-0	ditto	nil		
54	31.3.1927	(10,398-6-2)	5,643-12-10	-10,000 =50,000	nil		
55	31.3.1928	12,406-10-2	8,050-3-0	ditto	4%		Take over of T. Piggott & Co. Ltd.
56	31.3.1929	12,597-6-8	8,647-9-8	ditto	5%		
57	31.3.1930	4,157-6-0	12,804-15-8	ditto	nil		
58	31.3.1931	864-3-6	13,668-19-2	ditto	nil		
59	31.3.1932	(11,424-12-4)	2,244-6-10	ditto	nil		
60	31.3.1933	(930-11-9)	1,313-11-9	ditto	nil		
61	31.3.1934	(2,186-10-6)	(872-18-9)	ditto	nil		Horseley Bridge & Thomas Piggott Ltd.
62	31.6.1935	1,103-15-5	230-16-8	ditto	nil		
63	31.6.1936	24,797-12-3	25,028-8-11	-21,912-8-3 =28,087-11-9	nil		Dispute Pending
64	31.6.1937	45,068-15-9	6,408-13-3	+21,912-8-3 =50,000	10%	5%	3$\frac{1}{4}$ yrs paid on Prof. Shares
65	31.6.1938	60,476	5,744	+40,000 =90,000	10%	5%	
66	31.6.1939	59,205	13,618	+10,000 =100,000	12$\frac{1}{2}$%	5%	
67	31.6.1940	52,634	25,625	ditto	12$\frac{1}{2}$%	5%	
68	31.6.1941	62,132	36,698	ditto	12$\frac{1}{2}$%	5%	
69	31.6.1942	77,149	52,417	ditto	12$\frac{1}{2}$%	5%	
70	31.6.1943	39,909	64,113	ditto	15%	5%	
71	31.6.1944	102,103	65,259	ditto	15%	5%	

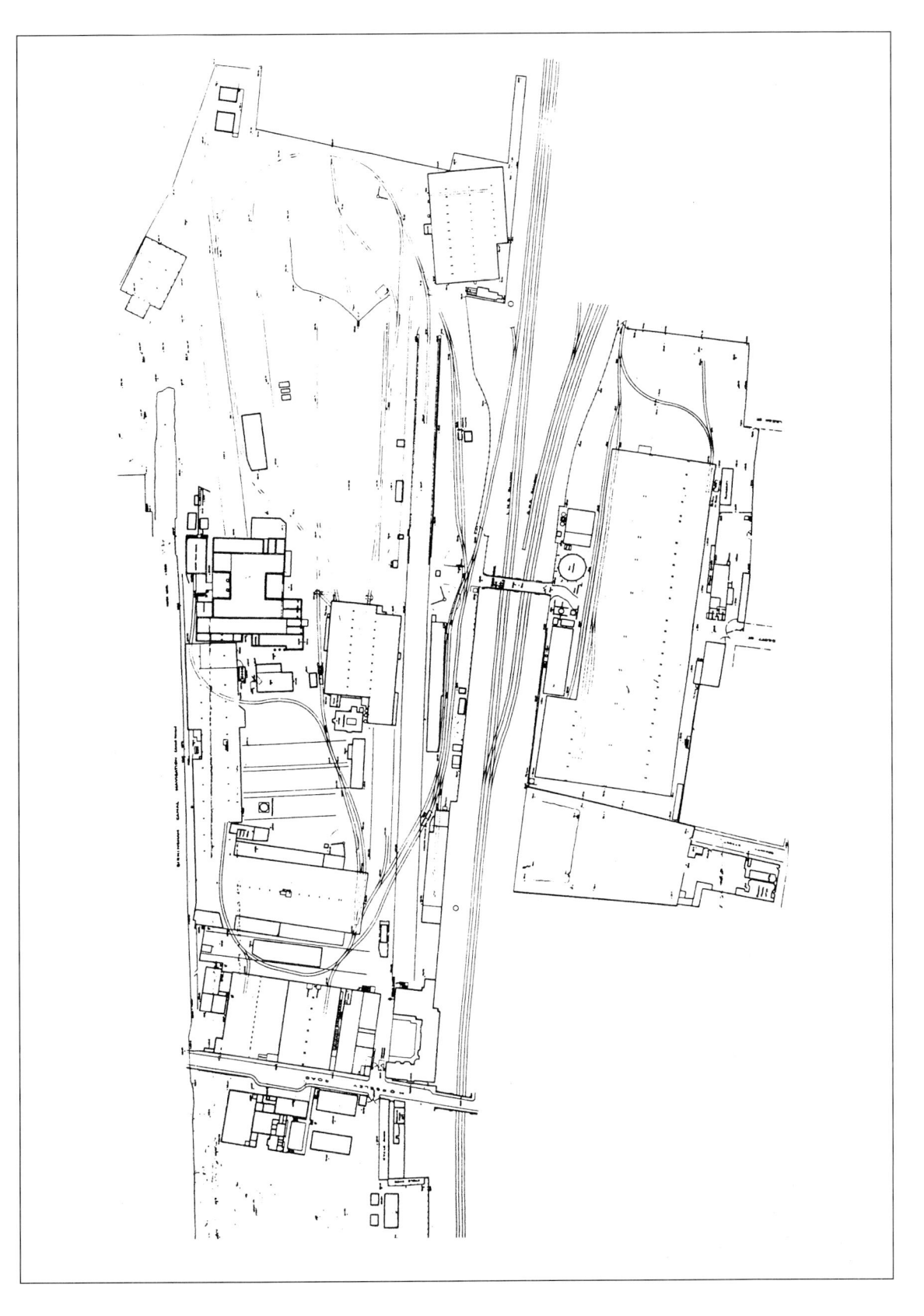

Horseley Works in 1943 prior to the works reconstuction

CHAPTER 8

THOMAS PIGGOTT & CO. LTD.

The Company claims that it commenced business in 1822. It appears that the early company was that of Joshua Horton who operated the Swallow Foundry at Spring Hill, Birmingham, but originally the land was owned by a boat builder James Taylor and his son, also James. Thomas Piggott was born in 1801 and would have been 21 years old in 1822. When he became involved is not fully clear but he was certainly the manager at the time that the business was operated by 'The Trustees of the late Joshua Horton' at Taylors Dock, Spring Hill, when thay were already building gas holders and boilers. References in papers prepared for the centenary celebrations in 1922 state that they first built canal boats and the first gas holder was in about 1826 for the Chartered Gas Co., Horseferry Road, London and was 40 feet in diameter.

The existing lists of Piggotts gas holders begin in 1845. A share certificate in the Newry Gas & Water Company dated 1848 is written in the name of 'Thomas Piggott, of Spring Hill, Boiler maker'. In 1853 Thomas Piggott was living in a house owned by James Taylor Beaumont who had inherited through the boat builder James Taylor the elder who died in 1827 and his son James Taylor the younger who died in 1852. It was a large house and garden with a small lodge house and part of the agreement allowed Thomas Piggott to take this lodge down. The lease was for 21 years at £50 year and commenced on 15 June 1854.

On the same date there was agreement that Thomas Piggott would take over the Boat Yard next to the house together with other property on the ground with permission to demolish buildings and fill in the large boat dock which led in off the canal, provided he built a canal wharf 60 feet long. Excluded from this permission was property known as the Dock Tavern with its brewery, which fronted Spring Hill and was run by William Clulo. The lease for all this land was for 21 years and the rent £150 year. The boat yard had been purchased by James Taylor from the Company of Proprietors of the Birmingham Canal Navigations on 8 June 1827 and was 1 acre 1 rood 2 perches in area.

In 1854 the land between what was described as 'Mr. Piggotts Boiler Works' and the then Workhouse (now Dudley Road Hospital) was being sold in plots for development and Thomas Piggott purchased in July 1854 those numbered 7 to 10 and 12 to 18 from John Scondrett Harford. All these plots were between a new road later known as Western Road and Piggotts Works and were used to enlarge the works area and later to provide the main works entrance. Plot 11 was in possession of John Battersby Harford and was conveyed to James Taylor Beaumont in February 1855, but was later included in the works area.

On 24 June 1859 Thomas Piggott formed a partnership with his sons George and Joseph to operate as Thomas Piggott & Sons. The notice claimed that they had then been in business 36 years. Thomas Piggott died on July 13 1869 aged 68 and was buried in the cemetery at Witton. Shortly after his death the business trading under the same name was leased on 28 January 1870 by the son George to Sampson Samuel Lloyd for a period of 14 years at a yearly rent of £720. S. S. Lloyd was the son of George B. Lloyd, a member of the Lloyds banking family. Born in 1820 he joined the banking business about 1842 shortly before they moved to 65 High Street Birmingham where they continued to the 1870's when they moved to Colmore Row. When they became a limited company in 1865 when he became Managing Director and three years later Chairman when they bought Barnetts Howes & Co., in London which he continued for 17 years and died 14 years later in 1899. Thomas Piggott's executors were his son George and Hubert Bewlay, senior, who had then been involved for 45 years and in superintendance for 12 years.

The lease is dated 28 January 1870 and contains an option to purchase within 7 years at a value of £20,000. The document refers to the Old Dock Tavern, the lease for which expired at Christmas 1873. The lease contains a coloured plan and inventory which includes:-

> Dwelling House Garden and premises.
> Public House called The Old Dock Tavern and Brewery.
> Malthouse buildings used as engine and boilerhouse, fitting shop and
>   pattern room.
> Entrance Lodge with general and private offices and drawing office
>   with hot water apparatus and iron chest.
> Shopping covering about 1500 square yards.
> Open sheds on iron pillars and against walls covering about 2000
>   square yards.

There were also a number of houses on both sides of Sampson Road, land in Farm Lane and wharf land at South Road. The total value was given as £11,706. 4s. 0d. with that of unfinished work at £1,633. 11s. 5d.

There is also a separate and full valuation of all the works, plant, fittings and stock of Swallow Foundry taken at the time. This lists:-

1. Levelling Shop.
2. Gas Holder Press Shop.
3. Pattern Makers Shop.
4. Striking out room.
5. Engine Shed with 5HP Engine and Boiler.
6. Gas Holder Shop.
7. Sheds outside Gas Holder Shop.
8. Smiths Shops – back.
9. Smiths Shops – front.
10. Fitting Shop with 6 hp Engine and pipes.
11. Upper Fitting Shop No.1.
12. Upper Fitting Shop No.2.
13. Pattern Stores.
14. Engine House.
15. Tool Room.
16. Room under Engine House.
17. Boiler Hole.
18. Yard Foremans Office.
19. Steam Rivetting Shed.
20. Press Shed.
21. Erecting Shed.
22. Furnace Shed Rolls.
23. Furnace Shed.
24. Hydraulic Press Shed. small
25. Hydraulic Press Shed. large.
26. Urinals and Rack.
27. Hyd. Engine House with 10 hp Hydraulic Engine.
28. Stores.
29. Rivet Room.
30. Washer Room.
31. Wheelwrights Shop.
32. Cart Shed.
33. Stables with Cart Horse 'Captain'.
34. Offices :- Drawing Office.
              General Office.
              Private Office.
              Landing.
36. Shed.
37. Store.

38. Foundry Engine House with 4 hp engine, boiler and fittings.
39. Foundry.
   Wrought iron tools.
   Hydraulic press tools.
   Site – tools at Rotterdam, Preston and Barnsley.
40. Foundry Shed.
41. Lower Sheds.
43. Yard.

Excl land and buildings £13,339-15s-5d.
Land and buildings £12,000- 0s-0d.

Total £26,339-15s-5d.

At the time the transfer was made there were two unfinished orders;-
   Preston Gas, telescopic gas holder 150 ft.x 30 ft dia.
   Birkenhead Gas Co. do do do 90 ft.x 24 ft dia.

Also there were a number of contracts with apprentices and workmen;-

Contract	Date & Name	Job & Length	Expiry
1865	Charles Collinson	Plater 5 years	13.4.1870
1865	Octavious Mason	Foreman Erector 5 yrs	20.5.1870
1866	Samuel Edwards	Rivetter 5 years.	30.5.1871
1867	John Day	Rivetter 3 years.	15.4.1870
1869	Samuel Parker	Foreman Erector 5 yrs.	14.1.1874
	F. W. Blake	Apprentice in the Office.	

Vessel by Piggotts on steam Waggon

Chapter 8 – Thomas Piggott Co. & Ltd.

> Piggott's undertake any size of contract. They keep a highly skilled staff constantly employed on welded work and are always ready to give sound and practical advice on the subject.

Transformer Tanks on Piggott's other steam wagon

The son of S. S. Lloyd, George Herbert Lloyd who was born at Lloyds Bank on the 8 March 1850 joined Thomas Piggott & Sons in 1871 and was to be responsible for many engineering improvements. In 1874 the Company built a novel lifeboat from wrought iron. She was known as the 'Petrel', shaped rather like a modern submarine, 25 ft. 6inches long, height 7 ft. 6 inches and three tons in weight.

In 1879 Hubert Bewlay junior, became a partner in the company with S. S. Lloyd, G. H. Lloyd, A. Ll. Lloyd and appealed for support which the company had had for the last 56 years. They had '...made extensive alterations, laid down plant and tools – of the newest design – and were in a better position than heretofore to turn out large quantities of work of the best possible quality'.

In 1881 the company purchased the Atlas Works of the Atlas Engine Co., Ltd., in Oozells Street, Birmingham. They were '...Hydraulic and General Engineers and Manufacturers of ice making machinery and successors to Siebe and West'. The Manager Samuel Puplett was retained but the office was moved to Spring Hill.

In the early 1880's G. H. Lloyd introduced the manufacture of large diameter steel pipes by water gas welding. They were in lengths of 12 to 15 feet and the tranverse joints were expanded or rivetted.

A stack of typical ships furnaces produced by Piggotts and later at Tipton

In 1892 they became a limited company as Thomas Piggott & Co., Ltd., with the works at Spring Hill then known as Atlas Works, and with George A. Everitt and his son Neville H. Everitt as additional partners. The first ordinary general meeting of the new styled company was held at Atlas Works on 20 October, 1892. The Directors present were:-

        S. S. Lloyd   Chairman   (Dec'd 1899)
        H. Bewlay (Son of Hubert.)   (Dec'd 28.8.1925)
        G. A. Everitt   (Dec'd 1900/1)
        N. H. Everitt   (Dec'd 1927)
        A. Ll. Lloyd   (Dec'd 28.3.1926)
        G. H. Lloyd   Secretary   (Dec'd 1914)

The book recording the proceedings of each of the annual general meeting deals principally with the annual accounts and the dividends paid on both the Preference and Ordinary shares. This information is given Table 1.

Some other information is recorded, however and from this it is learned that in 1899 G. A. Everitt resigned from the Board. In 1910 J. Maquire replaced G. H. Lloyd who was to die in

Chapter 8 – Thomas Piggott Co. & Ltd.

1914 as Secretary, a position he was to hold until his death in 1924 when his widow was awarded a pension of £50/annum for five years. In 1911 Thomas P. Barker was a director.

In 1918 an increase in capital was sought. It was decided to increase from £90,000 to £150,000 by the issue of 6000 new shares at £10 each. At this time there were 5,229 Preference shares of £10 and 3771 ordinary shares of £10. In 1919 Arthur Dyson was appointed to the board as Assistant Managing Director.

The Company letterheads state that they were iron founders, gas, hydraulic and general engineers and contractors; manufacturers of gas apparatus, welded and rivetted steel pipes. They produced constructional ironwork, petroleum and water storage tanks, steel chimneys, sugar, saltpetre and cassada pans. They also manufactured various profile boiler furnaces; Deighton Section, Fox corrugated and Morison Suspension type. The letter heads also proudly state that they are on the Admiralty list and also that they are members of the 'Engineering Employers' Federation 1896'. In 1915 new letter heads include reference to their being galvanisers and in 1916 an overprint states that they are a 'controlled establishment under the Munitions act 1915'.

A circular company logo is added to the letter head in 1920 and in 1926 they advertised sectional pressed steel tanks and included a logo of the 'National Scheme for disabled men'. These sectional tanks were developed from a Patent taken out by George Lloyd in 1901 numbered 22,900 and became known worldwide as 'Piggotts Tanks'.

In some years of high profit it was agreed to increase the remuneration of non- salaried directors by 50%. This occurred in 1919, 21, 22, 24 and 25. It was in 1922 that the Company celebrated its centenary with a dinner, speeches and much press attention. The

Thomas Piggott Ltd., works entrance

large production of gas holders was mentioned, with 600 built in the U.K. alone, including all the holders built in Liverpool (24) and in Belfast (10). Other cities with significant numbers were Leeds 9, Bristol 10, Leicester 7, Nottingham 9, Sheffield 6 and Vienna 5.

Very large quantities of steel pipes had been supplied:-

Birmingham Water	90.700 ft.
Manchester	7.350 ft.
Liverpool	1.500 ft.
Leeds	1.975 ft.
Bradford	15.850 ft.
Belfast	15.220 ft.
Newcastle	3.930 ft.
Seoul	25.000 ft.
Kolar Gold Fields	40.000 ft.
Harrogate W. W.	17.700 ft.
Johannesburg	68.660 ft.
Caracus	7.260 ft.
Campinas	56.753 ft.
Kimberley	68.600 ft.
Mazatlen	32.640 ft.
Montevideo	38.275 ft.
Swansea	104.300 ft.
Madras	4.350 ft.
Crown agents (Jamaica)	40.950 ft.
Vancouver	24.000 ft.
Pretoria	12.000 ft.
Llanelly	70.000 ft.

In addition they had built a semi-circular 'steel canal' in Egypt 19'-8" diameter, some 5185 feet long together with steel mains 6'-6" diameter, 3,100 feet long.

The long service of many employees was noted. A. H. Lloyd and H. Bewlay had served for 50 years. Other long service was listed:-

In 1922	A. Ll. Lloyd		45 years
	A. Bewlay		60 years
	N. H. Everitt		25 years
	T. P. Barker	Man. Director	40 years
	A. Dyson	Ass. M. Director	21 years
	Gilbert	Chief Draughtsman	25 years
	Teece	Chief Estimator	20 years
	Woodward	Leading Estimator	31 years
	Allen	Fitting Shop	27 years
	Edwards	Construction shop Foreman	24 years

On 29 January 1925 Piggotts formed an organisation by agreement with Guest Keen known as Guest Keen & Piggott with works at East Moors, Cardiff. The company had a

capital of £40,000 in £1 shares and 35,000 7% Preference shares. They were to produce '... mains, pipes, wires, containers and vessels of all kinds'.

In 1925 F. G. Holly became Secretary and in 1926 Hubert Bewlay junior had died. He was 82, being born on 8 December 1843 and having been articled to Thomas Piggott and Co had continued with them throughout his life. He became an Associate Member of the Institution of Civil Engineers in 1882 and a Member in 1901. He was always interested in politics becoming an Alderman of Birmingham in 1911 and Chairman of the Moseley Conservative and Joint Unionist Assosiations. He had retired from public life in 1923 due to his failing health. He left sons, Harry and Ernest. His wife a former Miss Ryland of Stourbridge had died in 1872.

F. Howard Hudson of Auditors, Caldicott Hudson & Caldicott who had acted as auditors each year had also died in 1925. The firm of Hubert Pepper & Rudland were appointed as auditors. In the same year T. P. Barker, Managing Director and A. Dyson his assistant were awarded a shared bonus of £625. On 28 March 1926 Arthur Ll. Lloyd died.

In 1927 the losses due to the General Strike and the Coal strike were noted and T. O. Lloyd loaned the company £20,000 at 6% to improve the capital situation. During the year, Neville H. Everitt died. From 1928 a second book records the discussions at the ordinary board meetings. It was at this time that the merger and final union of the Piggott company with Horseley Bridge & Engineering Co. took place and the minutes mirror the details recorded in the Horseley Bridge Minute books.

On 16 July 1928 the shares transferred to Horseley are recorded, a total of 5000 ordinary £10 shares and in the meeting of 27 July Sir Sidney H. H. Henn the Chairman of Horseley was welcomed to the meeting. At this meeting a special resolution was passed by which the directors other than the Managing Directors would receive £400 annum free of tax and the Chairman and Financial Director £150 and £100 in addition.

Early view of of Piggott's pipe delivery yard

In October 1928 A. Dyson discussed the development in gas holders where 'the ordinary gas holder with tank had been displaced largely in America and to a certain extent on the Continent by the Dry Gas Holder'. A company, 'Dry Gasholders Ltd.' with a capital of £5,000 had been formed and consisted of four shareholding companies:-

> Samuel Cutler & Sons Ltd.,
> C & W Walker Ltd.
> Ashmore Benson, Pease & Co. Ltd.,
> Newton Chambers & Co. Ltd.,

each having a licence to work the Klonne Patent. Horseley & Piggotts were to take one fifth share and contribute £500 towards preliminary expenses. Later the transfer of 250 shares from each of the other partners is recorded.

In October 1928 it was decided to capitalise £33,110 from the reserve fund and to pay a bonus to the ordinary shareholders. This was to be the issue of five new shares for every eight existing shares held.

A schedule is recorded which shows that the new shares were distributed, 3123 to Horseley and 31 each to T. P. Barker, A. Dyson, T. W. Horton, H. Bewlay, T. O. Lloyd and Sir Sidney Henn. In addition 189 new shares were issued for cash, 75 to Horseley and 19 each to the same individuals. The transfer of the Company Registered Office to 85, Lionel Street, jointly with Horseley is noted. In line with this change it was decided to have only one secretary and J. W. Baillie was appointed with F. G. Holly remaining as Assistant Secretary. It was recorded that this '...did not cast any reflection on Mr. Holly in whom that had the greatest confidence'. The formation of a Large Tube Association is recorded consisting of:-

> Leeds Forge Co., Ltd., Leeds.
> William Beardmore & Co., Ltd., Glasgow.
> John Marshall & Co., (Motherwell) Ltd., Motherwell.
> Deightons Patent Flue & Tube Co., Ltd., Leeds.
> Thomas Piggott & Co., Birmingham.
> John Thompson (Wolverhampton) Ltd.,

Reference to the Marine Furnace Association is also made in November 1928 when Leeds Forge had agreed to break up their plant for £5,000. Each of the remaining members of the Association were to contribute £1,000 and Piggotts had to find £500 with a further £500 taken from the Reserve Fund.

A pension was awarded to Josiah Green who was 69 years old and had worked at Piggotts for 56 years. He was awarded 10/- week. A pension previously granted to W. L. Ramsden of £52 annum was to be continued.

In January 1929 A. Dyson reported that the Lap Welded Tube Association '...had been revived from which considerable advantage should accrue to the Company'. The salary of J. W. Baillie, as Secretary was to be £150 per annum from 1929, presumably this being the contribution from Piggotts.

A Gas Washer or Scrubber was patented by Piggotts in 1929 and the benefits of the Marine Furnace and Large Tube Associations were noted as resulting in satisfactory orders. Indeed a new hydraulic flanging press might be needed at Hooper Street and it was agreed £2,000 could be spent if justified. Changes were also to be made to the frontage of Spring Hill Works costing £750 '...in order to afford light to the Machine Shops'.

Piggotts became members of the British Steelwork Association in 1929 and leased Work-

Large span transporter bridge by Piggotts

shop premises at Hooper Street to F. Willis & Co. A number of discussions concerning Guest Keen & Piggotts at Cardiff were recorded and eventually in February 1930 it was reported that as a result of an amalgamation between Guest Keen & Nettlefolds and Messrs. Baldwins Ltd. the pipe works at Cardiff might be needed for other purposes and a new site required.

A pension of 7/6d a week was granted to H. Ashmore who had been employed for 52 years. Further discussions were then held concerning the Cardiff works as to whether to transfer plant from Birmingham to Cardiff or from Cardiff to Birmingham or Tipton and whether a full merger with Horseley should take place. Eventually it was agreed the plant would go to Tipton.

With the introduction of Government Old Age Pensions the continuance in employment of men receiving such pensions was discussed as also was the question of stopping or reducing the pensions paid by the company to old servants. The matter was left in the hands of the Managing Directors.

The trading difficulties in the early 1930s were discussed and a scheme to reduce the salary of every member of staff on a percentage basis prepared and in July 1931 those between £52 & £156 per annum were reduced 5% and those over £156 by 10% with those under £52 remaining.

Piggotts were certainly using electric welding in 1931 when a semi-automatic welder at £200 and a welding set at £250 were authorised but problems arose over welded steel pipes supplied to the Lilleshall Co., Ltd. in 1925 as pump trees, presumably as lap welded pipes and claims were made in 1931 that two had defective welds. It was decided '...in order to avoid litigation which might affect our prestige, we would offer to replace one and recondition the other'. Later it was agreed that both should be replaced.

The resignation of T. P. Barker was recorded on 3 July 1931 when Sir Sydney Henn became Chairman, Barker being awarded a pension of £1,500 per annum with costs shared between Piggotts & Horseley. J. W. Baillie was elected a director to fill the vacancy and became Assistant Managing Director to A. Dyson who was made Managing Director. Baillie's salary was to be £1,250 per annum. Sir Sydney Henn was appointed to the Board of Guest Keen & Piggotts to fill the vacancy left by T. P. Barker. Pensions of 5/- a week were awarded to George Bailey and Joseph Marshall. A. Dyson reported on electric welding and stated that the Board would need to give consideration to this method of pipe manufacture at a later date. The depression continued and in December 1931 nine members of the combined Piggotts & Horseley staff were given notice.

It was reported in January 1932 that the Large Tube Association was in a precarious state '...owing to the introduction of electric welding by one of its members' but '...the question of the effect of electric welding on the trade was not considered to be sufficiently serious at present to warrant the Board giving attention to the installation of an electric welding plant'. Later it was reported the Association was being terminated but reformed on a quota basis.

The Directors' fees for 1932 were agreed as:-

Sir Sydney Henn Chairman	£300
T. W. Horton Vice Chairman	£200
H. Bewlay	£175
T. O. Lloyd	£175

A pension of 5/- a week was to be paid to W. Overton. An electric welding generator for Spring Hill was purchased for £220 in May 1932. Difficulties with Lloyds Bank over Piggotts overdraft occurred and coupled with uncertainties over the future of the company in the recession, resulted in a committee of Preference Shareholders being formed to discuss the situation.

A drastic staff re-organisation, salary reductions and dismissals took place. Horseley declared their inability to offer further assistance unless the complete merger of the two companies took place. Horseley offered to give each holder of the 5229 – 5% Cumulative Preference Shares of £10 each, ten 5% Cumulative Preference Shares of £1 each in Horseley. Also Piggotts Debenture Holders were to convert into like Horseley Debentures. This offer was accepted and the merger proceeded.

A Klonne gas holder was required by Guest Keen & Baldwins and Piggotts attempted to secure the order which was obtained in October 1932. It was to be built at Port Talbot. A. Dyson had visited Belgium to enquire into the cause of an explosion that had happened in a Klonne Holder. It was decided to cover all risks by insurance.

The problems with the Large Tube Association continued and Piggotts refused to accept a quota lower than that of the British Mannesman Co., Later, South Durham requested orders for steel to be placed with them an a quid pro quo basis for a reduction in their quota. Agreement was eventually reached.

The final acts of the Company concerned the winding up arrangements and a special resolution was formed in February 1933 by which J. W. Baillie became liquidator. The cleared land was sold to the City of Birmingham on 16 January 1934 for £15,489-15-0d for an area of 20,653 sq. yds. No further meetings are held until the final meeting which was on 9 May 1938 when the liquidation was concluded and all documents handed over to Horseley.

Piggotts Accounts

Year End	Profit (£)	Carry Foreward (£)	Reserve Fund (£)	Dividend Ord. Shares	Dividend Prof. Shares	Notes
28.3.1893	2408-0-4	785-13-5				
1894						
28.3.1895		98.12.9			2%	
28.3.1896					3%	
29.4.1897						
24.3.1898					3%	
13.4.1899		404-19-2			3%	
10.4.1900	18,828-13-11½	6,824-18-1½	+3,000	15%	5%	
2.4.1901	26,442-19-1½	8,536-0-9	+12,000	25%	5%	
8.4.1902	2,856-14-10½	7,673-16-3½		5%	5%	
11.12.1903	(5,011-17-11½)	208-1-11			5%	
23.11.1904	(5,405-10-6)	2-11-5	-5,200		5%	
19.4.1905	5,451-18-1	2,297-9-0			5%	
24.4.1906	175-5-1	2,472-14-1			–	
24.4.1907	3,171-4-3				5%	
29.4.1908	(12,626-2-9)				–	
27.4.1909	5,041-14-9					Plant reduced in volume by £10,000
26.4.1910	(664-18-9½)	1,893-0-5½				
11.4.1911	1,232-5-4½	1,818-1-2			2½%	
16.4.1912	4,430-7-10½	1,326-14-0½			2½ for 1905	
					5% for 1906	£10,000 to plant depreciation
3.4.1913	12,913-1-7½	4,396-5-8			5% for 1907/8/9	£2,000 to plant depreciation
30.3.1914	11,990-0-5½	9,157-6-1			5% for 1910	£2,000 to plant depreciation
25.3.1915	17,960-17-8	13,922-8-9½			5% for 1912/13/14	
20.4.1916	12,303-0-9½	13,948-0-1		10%	5% for 1915	Controlled Establishment 1915
17.5.1917	6,814-4-4½			10%	5% for 1916	
25.4.1918	34,722-12-8			10%+5%	5%	
16.4.1919	21,189-4-6½			10%+10%	5%	Share issue 2 new for 3 existing £10
19.2.1920	30,868-19-9			10%+5%	5%	
24.2.1921	28,197-7-8½			10%+5%	5%	
23.2.1922	25,419-0-2			10%+10%	5%	
22.2.1923	3,774-18-7			7½%	5%	
20.3.1924	(3,853-17-8)			5%	5%	Sec. J. Maguire dec'd
26.3.1925	17,095-18-6			12½%	5%	F. G. Holly – Sec.
25.3.1926	15,251-4-2			10%	5%	
25.4.1927	(?)		+2,820-14-5		5%	
3.4.1928	+?	6,084-6-1	+33,000	7½%	5%	
12.3.1929	+?	3,329-14-1	+5,460	7½%	5%	
4.4.1930	(1,123-16-8)	91-7-5	-500-0-0		5%	
14.7.1931	16,302-12-6	10,179-9-11			5%	
8.4.1932	(11,404-7-6)	3,275-2-5	-4,500-0-0			
10.3.1933						COMPANY WOUND UP

List of Gasholders 100ft. 0in. dia. and over, made and erected by Piggotts

Destination.		Diameter.	Depth.
Liverpool Gas Co.		104' 6"	26' 9"
Cardiff Gas Co.		150' 0"	32' 0"
Redhill Gas Co.		101' 11$\frac{1}{2}$"	25' 0"
Liverpool Gas Co.		112' 6"	27' 3"
Oldham Corporation		100' 0"	29' 0"
Ditto		200' 0"	29' 0"
Liverpool Gas Co.		165' 0"	30' 0"
Coventry Corporation		135' 0"	34' 3"
Bristol Gas Co.		104' 6"	24' 6"
Liverpool Gas Co.		212' 6"	41' 6"
Plymouth Gas Co.		120' 0"	26' 0"
Midland Railway Co., Derby		102' 0"	25' 0"
Bath Gas Co.		144' 6"	26' 3"
Bristol Gas Co.		144' 0"	26' 6"
Ditto		154' 0"	26' 6"
Wellingborough Gas Co.		110' 0"	30' 0"
Coventry Corporation		133' 0"	34' 6"
Brighton Gas Co.		126' 0"	30' 0"
Coventry Corporation		120' 0"	30' 0"
Gloucester Gas Co.		130' 0"	35' 0"
Coventry Corporation		110' 0"	30' 3" *
Brighton Gas Co.		101' 7"	36' 0" *
Brighton Gas Co.		124' 0"	30' 0" *
Brighton Gas Co.		100' 0"	26' 0"
Dudley Gas Co.		100' 0"	26' 0"
Cardiff Gas Co.	inner lift	145' 0"	32' 1"
	outer lift	147' 6"	32' 0"
Cardiff Gas Co.	inner lift	107' 0"	29' 0"
	outerlift	109' 6"	29' 0"
Cardiff Gas Co.	inner lift	147' 6"	27' 0"
	outer lift	150' 0"	27' 0"
Liverpool Gas Co.	inner lift	177' 6"	30' 3"
	outerlift	180' 0"	30' 0"
W. Coward & Son	inner lift	179' 0"	36' 0"
(Sydney Gas Co., Aus.)	middle lift	181' 0"	36' 0"
	outer lift	184' 0"	36' 0"
Leicester Gas Co.	inner lift	167' 6"	35' 6"
	outer lift	170' 0"	35' 6"
Salford Gas Works	inner lift	97' 9"	26' 3"
	outer lift	100' 0"	26' 0"
H. Williams & Co.	inner lift	100' 0"	29' 0"
	outer lift	102' 3"	29' 1"
Preston Gas Works	inner lift	148' 10"	30' 0$\frac{1}{2}$"
	outerlift	151' 2"	30' 0"
Stockholm Gas Works	inner lift	146' 8"	26' 2$\frac{5}{8}$"
	outer lift	149' 0"	26' 2$\frac{5}{8}$"
Brisbane Gas Works	inner lift	157' 9"	30' 8"
	outer lift	160' 0"	30' 8"
Liverpool Gas Co.	inner lift	162' 6"	30' 3"
	outer lift	165' 0"	30' 0"
Oldham Corporation (2 holders)	inner lift	98' 0"	29' 0"
	outer lift	100' 0"	29' 0"

* Prepared for extension

Destination.		Diameter.	Depth.
Liverpool Gas Co.	inner lift	195' 0"	40' 3"
	outer lift	197' 6"	40' 0"
Newport Gas Co.	inner lift	116' 0"	25' 3"
	outer lift	118' 0"	25' 0"
Bristol Gas Co.	inner lift	106' 0"	24' 3"
	outer lift	108' 0"	24' 0"
Ditto	inner lift	157' 0"	30' 3"
	outerlift	160' 0"	30' 0"
Belfast Gas Co.	inner lift	187' 0"	45' 3"
	outer lift	190' 0"	45' 0"
Reading Gas Co.	inner lift	125' 0"	20' 0"
	middle lift	127' 6"	20' 0"
	outerlift	130' 0"	20' 0"
Liverpool Gas Co.	inner lift	162' 6"	30' 3"
	outer lift	165' 0"	30' 0"
Ditto	inner lift	177' 6"	30' 3"
	outer lift	180' 0"	30' 0"
Brighton Gas Co.	inner lift	150' 0"	40' 2"
	outerlift	152' $4\frac{1}{2}$"	41' 2"
Leicester Gas Co.	inner lift	167' 6"	35' 3"
	outer lift	170' 0"	35' 0"
Salford Gas Co.	inner lift	149' 0"	40' 3"
	outer lift	151' 6"	40' 0"
Bristol Gas Co.	inner lift	157' 6"	30' 3"
	outer lift	160' 0"	30' 0"
Liverpool Gas Co.	inner lift	103' 1"	26' 3"
	outer lift	105' 0"	26' 0"
Leamington Gas Co.	inner lift	108' 0"	40' 3"
	outer lift	110' 0'	40' 0"
Sheffield Gas Co.	inner lift	150' 6"	37' 3"
	outer lift	153' 6"	37' 0"
Cardiff Gas Co.	inner lift	110' 0"	20' 0"
	outer lift	112' 0"	20' 0"
Wolverhampton Gas Co.	inner lift	107' 6"	28' 6"
	outer lift	109' 6"	28' 9"
Birmingham Corporation	inner lift	195' 0"	36' 0"
	outer lift	197' 6"	36' 0"
Gas Light & Coke Co., Beckton	inner lift	190' 0"	35' $10\frac{1}{2}$"
	outer lift	192' 8"	36' $7\frac{1}{2}$"
Sheffield Gas Co.	inner lift	150' 6"	31' 3"
	outer lift	153' 6"	31' 0"
Wigan Gas Co.	inner lift	149' 6"	30' 3"
	outerlift	152' 6"	30' 0"
Birmingham Corporation	inner lift	195' 0"	36' 0"
	outer lift	197' 6"	36' 0"
Gas Light & Coke Co., Beckton	inner lift	190' 0"	35' $10\frac{1}{2}$"
	outer lift	192' 8"	36' $7\frac{1}{2}$"
Liverpool Gas Co.	inner lift	150' 0"	30' 3"
	outer lift	152' 2"	30' 0"
Stockholm Gas Co.	inner lift	100' 6'	18' 0"
	outer lift	102' 6"	18' 0"
South Metropolitan Gas Co.	inner lift	177' 0"	45' 6"
	outer lift	180' 0"	45' 0"
Liverpool Gas Co.	inner lift	143' 0"	30' 3"
	outer lift	145' 2"	30' 0"
Bath Gas Co.	inner lift	147' 0"	26' 3"
	outer lift	150' 0"	26' 0"

Destination.		Diameter.	Depth.
Nottingham Gas Co.	inner lift	122' 6"	25' 7$\frac{1}{2}$"
	outer lift	125' 0"	25' 3"
Bradford Gas Co. (2 holders)	inner lift	118' 0"	24' 3"
	outer lift	120' 0"	24' 0"
Burton Gas Co.	inner lift	97' 6"	21' 74"
	outer lift	100' 0"	21' 3"
Rochdale Gas Co.	inner lift	98' 0"	30' 3"
	outer lift	100' 0"	30' 0"
Cheltenham Gas Co.	inner lift	126' 0"	24' 9"
	outer lift	128' 0"	24' 6"
Sheffield Gas Co.	inner lift	150' 6"	31' 3"
	outer lift	153' 6"	31' 0"
Rochdale Gas Co.	inner lift	124' 0"	26' 3"
	outer lift	126' 0"	26' 0"
South Metropolitan Gas Co.	inner lift	147' 0"	38' 3"
	outer lift	150' 0"	38' 0"
Liverpool Gas Co.	inner lift	138' 0"	30' 3"
	outer lift	140' 2"	30' 0"
Leeds Gas Co.	inner lift	177' 0"	24' 3"
	outer lift	180' 0"	24' 0"
Bristol Gas Co.	inner lift	157' 0"	26' 3"
	outer lift	160' 0"	26' 0"
Belfast Gas Co.	inner lift	177' 0"	32' 3"
	outer lift	180' 0"	32' 0"
Leicester Gas Co.	inner lift	147' 0"	30' 3"
	outer lift	150' 0"	30' 0"
Tynemouth Gas Co.	inner lift	98' 0"	26' 3"
	outer lift	100' 0"	26' 0"
Bradford Gas Co.	inner lift	118' 0"	24' 3"
	outer lift	120' 0"	24' 0"
Leeds Gas Co.	inner lift	103' 0"	26' 3"
	outer lift	105' 0"	26' 0"
Bristol Gas Co.	inner lift	147' 0"	26' 3"
	outer lift	150' 0"	26' 0"
Liverpool Gas Co.	inner lift	138' 0"	30' 3"
	outer lift	140' 2"	30' 0"
Bradford Gas Co.	inner lift	118' 0"	24' 3"
	outer lift	120' 0"	24' 0"
Plymouth Gas Co.	inner lift	118' 0"	26' 0"
	outer lift	120' 0"	26' 0"
Nottingham Gas Co.	inner lift	122' 6"	25' 7$\frac{1}{2}$"
	outer lift	125' 0"	25' 3"
Bradford Gas Co.	inner lift	118' 0"	24' 3"
	outer lift	120' 0"	24' 0"
South Metropolitan Gas Co.	inner lift	123' 0"	35' 3"
	outer lift	125' 0"	35' 0"
Belfast Gas Co.	inner lift	147' 0"	30' 3"
	outer lift	150' 0"	30' 0"
Liverpool Gas Co.	inner lift	103' 1"	26' 3"
	outer lift	105' 0"	26' 0"
Leeds Gas Co.	inner lift	147' 0"	24' 3"
	outer lift	150' 0"	24' 0"
Preston Gas Co.	inner lift	147' 9"	30' 0"
	outer lift	150' 0"	30' 0"
Liverpool Gas Co.	inner lift	138' 0"	30' 3"
	outer lift	140' 0"	30' 0"

Chapter 8 – Thomas Piggott Co. & Ltd.

Destination.		Diameter.	Depth.
Rotherhithe	inner lift	147' 6"	25' 6"
	outer lift	150' 0"	25' 0"
Horley Gas Co.	inner lift	98' 0"	24' 3"
	outer lift	100' 0"	24' 0"
Leeds Gas Co.	inner lift	98' 0"	26' 3"
	outer lift	100' 0"	26' 0"
Bolton Gas Co.	inner lift	138' 0"	30' 3"
	outer lift	140' 0"	30' 0"
Bradford Gas Co.	inner lift	126' 2"	24' 3"
	outer lift	128' 0"	24' 0"
Liverpool Gas Co. (2 holders)	inner lift	98' 1"	26' 3"
	outer lift	100' 0"	26' 0"
Leeds Gas Co.	inner lift	98' 2"	26' 3"
	outer lift	100' 0"	26' 0"
Sunderland Gas Co.	inner lift	117' 8"	25' 3"
	outer lift	120' 0"	25' 0"
Belfast Gas Co.	inner lift	98' 1"	26' 3"
	outer lift	100' 0"	26' 0"
Gas Light & Coke Co., London	inner lift	108' 0"	30' 3"
	outer lift	110' 0"	30' 0"
Leeds Gas Co.	inner lift	118' 0"	22' 3"
	outer lift	120' 0"	22' 0"
Bristol Gas Co.	inner lift	108' 2"	26' 3"
	outer lift	110' 0"	26' 0"
Bradford Gas Co.	inner lift	114' 2"	24' 3"
	outer lift	116' 0"	24' 0"
Liverpool Gas Co.	inner lift	103' 2"	26' 3"
	outer lift	105' 0"	26' 0"
Nottingham Gas Co.	inner lift	117' 8"	25' 3"
	outer lift	120' 0"	25' 0"
Glasgow Corporation	inner lift	160' 0"	26' 3"
	outer lift	161' 10"	26' 0"
Belfast Gas Co.	inner lift	108' 2"	30' 3"
	outer lift	110' 0"	30' 0"
Leicester Gas Co.	inner lift	128' 2"	28' 3"
	outer lift	130' 0"	28' 0"
Bristol Gas Co.	inner lift	98' 2"	28' 3"
	outer lift	100' 0"	28' 0"
Leeds Gas Co.	inner lift	98' 2"	24' 3"
	outer lift	100' 0"	24' 0"
Liverpool Gas Co.	inner lift	123' 0"	30' 3"
	outer lift	125' 0"	30' 0"
Bristol Gas Co.	inner lift	118' 0"	28' 0"
	outer lift	120' 0"	28' 0"
Dublin Gas Co.	inner lift	98' 2"	25' 3"
	outer lift	100' 0"	25' 0"
Sunderland Gas Co.	inner lift	98' 2"	20' 0"
	outer lift	100' 0"	20' 3"
Gas Light & Coke Co., London	inner lift	108' 2"	25' 3"
	outer lift	110' 0"	25' 0"
Belfast Gas Co.	inner lift	98' 2"	26' 3"
	outer lift	100' 0"	26' 0"
Liverpool Gas Co.	inner lift	118' 0"	26' 3"
	outer lift	120' 0"	26' 0"
Bradford Gas Co.	inner lift	118' 2"	24' 0"
	outer lift	120' 0"	24' 0"

CHAPTER 9
1945-1992

THE POST WAR YEARS

A special Victory Edition of the Horseley News was printed and this reported that A. Dyson had attended at St. Paul's for a Victory Thanksgiving Service. Ten men from Horseley had been killed during the hostilities and over 270 men had served in the Forces.

By November 1945 Factory '99' had been vacated and the light construction work sited in the new 'B' building but the changing situation with labour and the repeal of the Essential Works order caused difficulty. It was anticipated that higher wages would have to be paid to retain labour. A contract for a cyclotron was completed at Birmingham University and this was to be used for nuclear research.

On 26 November 1945 a special ceremony was held at which portraits were presented to both J. W. Baillie and A. Dyson. A. Dyson stated that he had started work as an apprentice at Piggotts on 26 November 1900 exactly 45 years earlier, and J. W. Baillie stated he had been Secretary for $26^1/_2$ years.

The death of Director H. D. L. Lloyd took place on 17 December He had been a Director since 1933. He had been born at the Old Vicarage, Sutton Coldfield in 1881, his father being George Herbert Lloyd the former Managing Director of Thomas Piggotts. His grandfather was Samuel Lloyd, the banker. H. D. L. Lloyd had started work at Piggotts in 1898, becoming General Manager when he left in 1911, returning in 1932.

The major order for steelwork for Walsall Power Station was received in May 1946 – 7,000 tons valued at £409,256. In addition following a plan to provide the steel frames for 4,000 houses Horseley agreed to make a small number. A large order for Shimshom Palestine Portland Cement Co., for buildings was obtained valued £186,000. Wages were increased costing £18,200 per year and 39 men had returned from the forces to the works and 12 to the staff.

Jim Bailey who had been in charge of the Stock Yard for many years retired in early 1946. He had 47 years service, had started with Piggotts and was also known for his blue jacket, so old that it had turned green!

With the success of the manufacture of the test vessel and the completion of all the tests the company were placed on Lloyds Class 1 list by September 1946 and looked forward to orders for that class of work.

A number of older men took advantage of the October 1946 increase in old age pension and retired. One retired moulder returned in order to train young men in the Foundry.

The five day week was introduced in January 1947 and higher salaries paid to technical staff in order to retain them. The staff unions applied for a 35 hour week but it was stated that '...this is the only country where there is any differentiation between staff and works hours, and manufacturers are of the opinion that further concessions cannot be made to a privileged class'.

A general works and staff outing

In February 1947 the Managing Directors gave details of the problems caused by the 'National Emergency' due to the very severe weather. The Ministry of Fuel & Power had announced on the 10 February that no electricity would be supplied from 18 February. The company decided to lay off all the men on Tuesday 18 February and 670 notices were posted to the men, leaving only 26 maintenance and four wagon unloaders. The foremen, charge hands and staff were not affected. The directors addressed a mass meeting of the men. By 19 February, 50 template makers, carpenters and pattern makers returned to work. Temporary diesel engines were brought in which provided some power and eventually the Prime Minister announced that power would be restored on the 24 February and the works was fully re-opened on that date. The costs of all this disruption was calculated at over £9,000 and there were to be 'power shedding days' to follow.

Supplies of all types of fuel were severely restricted and steel continued to be difficult to obtain although some had been delivered during the shut down. It was later reported that the power was not shut down again even on their official shedding days, but there were a few very short interruptions.

In February 1947 Thompson Bros. Bilston ordered a steel portal framed building, and in March 1947 an order was obtained for bridges at Hill St. and Navigation St. over the LMS at New Street. Station. 800 tons of steel was required with a value of £70,000. These bridges were the last to be built by Horseley of rivetted construction.

During the year ending 28 February 1947 the labour turnover was 40.3% due, it was believed, to '...dissatisfaction with wages and conditions'. The new shops were then nearing completion and the men would be under cover by the following winter. With the

Above: A pensioners' day excursion

Below: An early welded steel portal frame bridge at Walsall

whole scheme completed by the opening of the new Foundry (by the Earl of Dudley) a year later on 20 December 1948. The new works surgery was built adjacent to the main offices.

Another old servant Joe Wall aged 68 retired from the Repair Shop as did Len Harper of London Office. Problems with fuel & steel supplies continued into September 1947 and all this affected profits. With reference to the 1946/7 accounts it was noted that '...much of our war time 'fat' has now disappeared', and with regard to labour, they had men from Ireland, Scotland and the N.E. coast and had '...gained numerically but not in calibre'.

In November 1947 they gave notice to their South Wales Agent A. E. Smithson & Son Ltd. and appointed their Resident Engineer as Agent '...Mr. Smithson has served the Company well in the past for many years, but he is now over eighty years of age and he appreciates that the march of time cannot be arrested'.

In December 1947 John Thompson (Wolverhampton) Ltd. ordered their heavy portal frame building which became known as the 'Mars Shop' which was where they produced their heavy pressure vessels. This shop was so called because it was on the site of George Adams & Sons, Mars Ironworks (1866-1924).

Fuel supplies were still difficult but the problems of the previous winter were not repeated. Staggered hours were supposed to be worked but in the absence of any positive lead they continued to work normally. The supplies of steel were still very limited and it was believed many orders would eventually be cancelled on this account. Completed steel was being stored behind Atlas House and with the completion of Building A1, the old Girder Shop would serve as a Preparation Bay.

A new scheme of cost control was to be introduced in January 1948, and it was believed that '...the sellers market is shrinking' but lack of clear government guidance on appropriate export markets and continued problems with licences for steel caused difficulties. For example, contracts half completed, did not get a licence for the second half steel requirement. They did not anticipate supply of more that 19,000 tons of steel in 1948. On 31 March a new Iron & Steel Distribution Scheme was introduced and the outcome was awaited.

The Government had placed a ban on capital expenditure and a lack of encouragement on exports which made the Directors unsure of the future. Nevertheless a large order for the extension of Walsall Power Station was received, value £120,000 and tonnage 3575. As the year moved on the steel supply position changed dramatically and the works became flooded with steel. The complaint then was that certain sections and plates were needed.

The input of Polish men to the works proved very satisfactory and a further 20 were taken on. Visits were arranged by local school boys to encourage them to join the Company. A number of old employees were joining the Sports Club and that together with the Benevolent Fund might be a prelude to these men returning.

On Wednesday 30 June 1948 Arthur Dyson stood down as Managing Director but continued as a Director, and J. W. Baillie became sole Managing Director. Shortly before E. Trafford Willey had joined as personal assistant to the Managing Directors. Both J. Martin and J. Guy of the erection department left the Company and A. Gordon Osborne became Erection Manager.

There was still a need to stagger the working hours due to power supplies at the end of 1948. The Pipe Works went on to a night shift for three months, working a 10 hour shift – 8 p.m. to 7 a.m. and this enabled the Main Works to continue with normal hours. J. W.

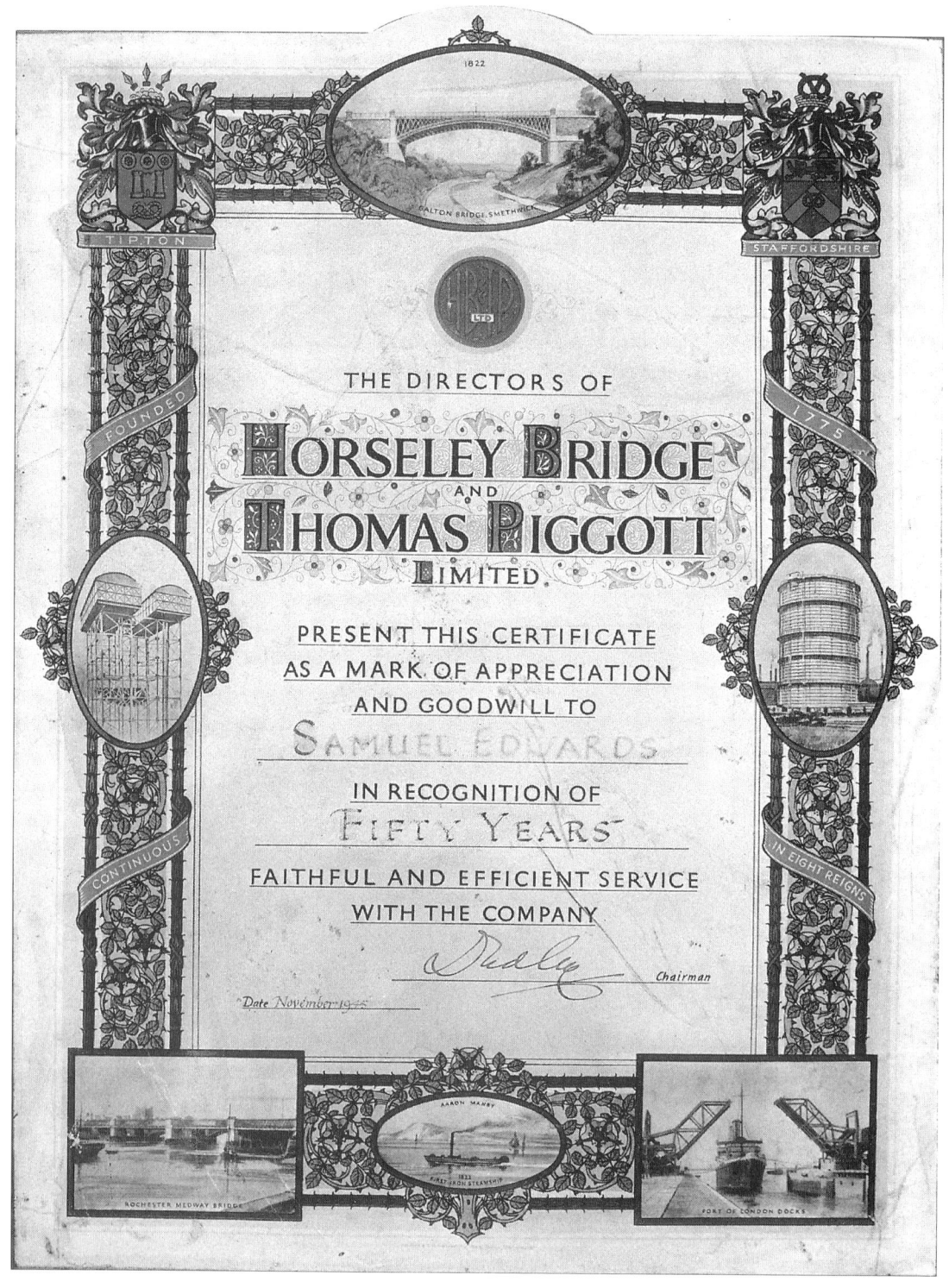

A long service certificate

River Great Ouse Flood Protection Scheme

Below: Complex Air Pipework for Mach 1.2 Wind Tunnel at Bedford. No repairs were needed to any of the shop or site welds on this complex fabrication

Complex pipe fabrication leaving the Pipe Works

Baillie had commented a number of times on low production rates and called in Urwick, Orr & Partners to survey and report. Steel supplies were still difficult and a total supply of 20,000 tons for 1949 was envisaged,

In April 1949 comments were made on some important contracts, Railway sheds for Egypt were in hand after many difficulties over steel supplies; Hill Street Bridge at Birmingham was about to be erected and included '...the largest built up girder ever made by the Company'; the 785 foot high, 80 ton B.B.C. television mast at Sutton Coldfield was proceeding and Walsall Power Station was nearing completion.

Labour continued as a problem during 1949 and two platers left '...who are practically impossible to replace'. An article by the Ministry of Labour stated '...there was no one unemployed in Tipton'. The labour problems led to the setting up of various internal committees which included the Shop Committee, the Works Council and the Joint Production Committee. Surprisingly an order for 200 – 1000lb. bomb casings from the Air Ministry was received as an experimental order.

In September 1949 J. W. Baillie noted that a quotation was being made '...for a very interesting contract which has considerable advertising value'. This was to be known as the 'Dome of Discovery' at the Festival of Britain; 365ft. dia. at the base of the supports, 342 ft. dia. ring girder 48 ft. high, with an aluminium dome 97 ft. high. 232 tons of aluminium would be needed, value £100,000 and 133 Tons of steel value £60,000 including £23,000 for erection.

Staggered hours still required to be worked over the winter months of 1949/50 with Departments alternating on day and night shifts, but this was later rescinded. The devaluation of the pound sterling was thought to give little benefit as only a small proportion of overseas work was in hard currency areas.

In November 1949 the order for the Dome of Discovery was received. Some aluminium would be fabricated at Tipton but the main quantity would be sub-let to Structural & Mechanical Developments Ltd. of Slough.

J. W. Baillie discussed the setting up of a joint selling agency with George M. Carter (Erectors) Ltd. an organisation which started in 1923. The Company was taken over by Horseley in October 1949 and became the

Original Sutton Colfield Television Mast

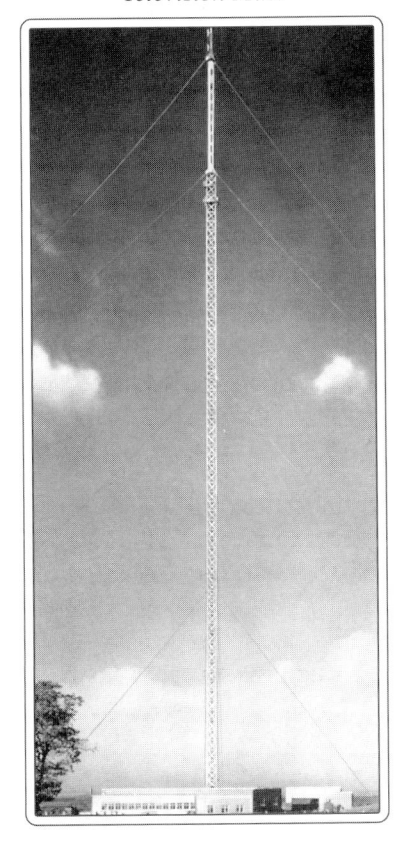

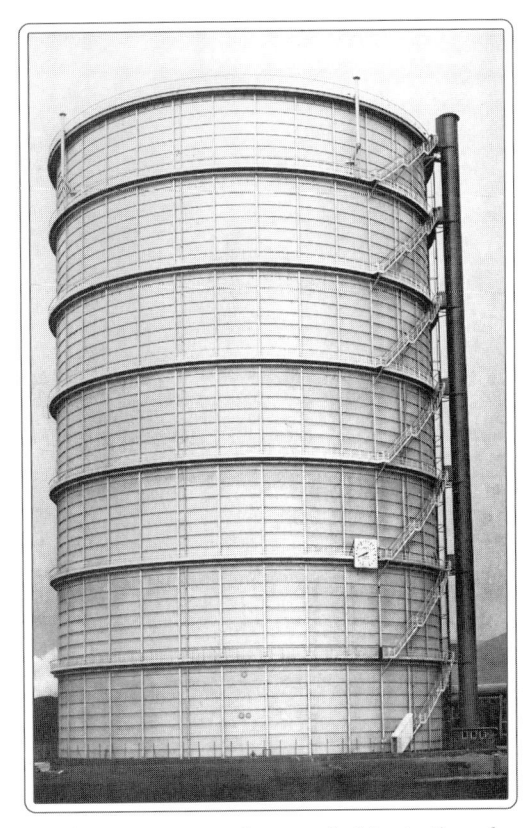

A Klonne type waterless gas holder built under licence from Klonne Ltd,, Germany

erection organisation known as Carter-Horseley (Engineers) Ltd., and it was they who would erect the Dome. They had Depots at Newcastle, Tipton, Sheffield, Cardiff and Croydon with selling departments at Manchester and London. J. W. Baillie and Commander Buist became Directors. Norman Gibb was responsible at Newcastle and R.W. Dewar at Croydon. A. G. Osborne became Midland Manager with J. S. Christie as advisor. John Vincent Sheffield became Chairman of Carter Horseley. He was a Lincolnshire man who joined John Lysaght Ltd. in 1935 and also in 1935 started his own Company. During the war he had various government positions becoming Secretary to the Ministry of Works. He had joined Geo. M. Carter in 1944 and when Carter died in 1945 he had taken over.

Part II – A History of the Horseley Company 1865-1992

Vincent Senior became Joint Managing Director of Carter Horseley. He had been with Robey & Co., Ltd., and then Francois Cementation Co. Ltd., as Outside Engineer before joining G. M. Carters, where he became Director in 1943 and Joint Managing Director with John Sheffield in 1947 and Managing Director in 1948.

At the end of 1949 reference was made to a further portal frame structure, this supplied to Edwin Danks at Oldbury where they extended their building and to an order for a 1 million cu. ft. gas holder to be built at Port Talbot.

At this point this series of Managing Directors Reports ends and reliance has to be placed on other sources including the Horseley Piggott News which appeared at least once annually.

On May 2, 1950 the King & Queen visited the site of the Festival of Britain and talked with the Horseley Directors.

Shortly afterwards James S. Christie was appointed Company Secretary. He had qualified as a solicitor in 1928 but joined industry in 1929. During the war he had been an Intelligence Officer with the Ministry of Security, Scotland and later Staff Officer to the Earl of Dudley and Assistant Chief of Staff when in 1945 he joined Horseley as Personal Assistant to the Managing Directors.

Works Manager W. J. Coughtrie left during early 1950 and Basil Vincent Smith became Northern Director of Carter-Horseley. He had a degree from Durham University and after being associated with Sir George Canning became Outside Technical Engineer for Wolverhampton Corrugated Iron Co., Ltd., before joining Carters in 1941 and becoming Northern Manager in January 1947 and joining the Board in November 1947.

Aerial view showing the final extent of the works prior to the demolition of the Pipe Works

Template Shop with George Downton supervising

Towards the end of 1950 Albert E. Edwards the Pipe Works Manager celebrated the completion of his 50 years of service, but decided to continue work for a while longer. He had started work at Piggotts aged 13 with A. E. Dilley and moved to Tipton for the official opening of the Pipe Works in July 1935.

In July 1950, J. D. Vaughan, M.Sc., M.I.C.E., M.I. Struct. E., became Chief Engineer and James Sim was appointed Production Manager.

On 4 November 1950 a visit was made to the Dome of Discovery at London by those who had been involved in its construction, where they were met by John Allen who was acting as Site Engineer. On 4 May 1951, the Festival of Britain was opened and a number of Horseley people including A. D. Orton (Responsible for the contract in the Drawing Office), E. Salt (Carter-Horseley), R. Barry (Shop Forman), J. Kennedy (Carter-Horseley), A. Pritchard (Preparation Bay Foreman) and J. S. Allen were presented to the King & Queen and the Duke of Gloucester through the assistance of the Earl of Dudley and Commander Buist. In September 1951 a full works trip was made to the Exhibition.

During 1951 J. W. Baillie undertook a world tour and W. Cyril Hammond, Foreman of the Tank Shop visited the States to study their methods on a six weeks tour. Lord Lloyd who had joined the Board in July 1946 resigned as he had been appointed Lord in Waiting to the King. A bonus was paid to the employees and an increase in pensions allowed.

By the Summer of 1952 Llewellyn Cartwright, a long serving plater, achieved a remarkable 60 years of service having commenced work in 1892. His father had also been with the Company having started work at the time of Robert Broad.

During 1952 the Company purchased the new Sports Field from Triplex Co., it having been shared for five years. A lift bridge at Millwall Dock was completed.

Above: Works locomotive J. T. Daly by Bagnall, Stafford, 1936 under repair at Tipton with driver Arthur Cyril in attendance

Below: The Comptometer office

Roger Lloyd, who had been accountant for some 18 months left and was succeeded by Geoffrey Plant. J. P. O'Callahan who had been involved with Water Treatment and also for a time acted as Editor of the Horseley-Piggott News died on 14 September 1952. He had joined the company in 1933.

During 1953 the works was busy with the construction of Ince Power Station. At the end of the year J. W. Baillie retired after some 35 years in management. He had joined the Company in 1919 and was appointed to the Board in 1927. He had recently been unwell but had recovered. Jas. S. Christie and Vincent Senior became Joint Managing Directors. Sadly J. W. Baillie had only a short retirement, passing away in July 1954. He had indeed played a leading role in the control and development of the company.

The year 1953 also saw the demolition of the railway bridge at Shifnal which had been cast by the old company in 1848. A section was presented to the Company and was located in front of the offices. During the Spring of 1955, J. D. Vaughan became an Official Director. He had been educated in Germany and joined Horseley in 1924, becoming Chief Draughtsman in 1925. Richard J. Fowler then joined the Company as Chief Engineer. In 1945 he had become Welding Engineer to John Thompson Ltd. and later spent seven years in private practice.

An early type welded portal bridge was completed over the canal at Walsall and a large fatigue testing tank for aircraft was built at Farnborough. During early 1955 the death of the old Works Manager A. E. Dilley is reported. Lt. Col. Ronald Degg became Personnel Manager.

Medium Structural Construction Bay 'B' with Pressure Vessel Bay 'A' on right

The Cost office

At Christmas 1955 H. E. Lewin of London Office retired. He had joined Piggotts in 1906 at the age of 13 and rose to be London Manager after serving under Len Harper as assistant. During 1956 the head-gear at Ryhope Colliery was completed as was the 3 million cu. ft. Klonne Holder at the Steel Company of Wales. This was 141'-9" dia. x 223'-3" high. A. A. Taylor became Assistant Secretary and Chief Accountant and Douglas E. Moyle Chief Accountant to Carter-Horseley. R. A. Rubenstein was appointed to Overseas Sales.

During 1957 Horseley took over the Scottish Company, Mechans Ltd. on the Clyde. They had been established in 1862, settling on their then site of 18 acres in 1898. A working arrangement was also made with Blythwood Shipbuilding Co., Ltd., on the Clyde.

At Tipton the completion of the 100th Powermaster Boiler Body was celebrated. These were package type boiler bodies produced for G. W. B. Ltd. of Dudley. A pipe bridge and pipe work for the River Dove near Repton, Derby were completed. L. R. Meek became manager of the Gas Plant Division and with the final retirement of A. E. Edwards, John G. Jope became Pipe Works Manager.

On 14 November 1958 the death of J. D. Vaughan was reported, following only a short retirement. He had been a well respected engineer and known to the leading Consultants in London. He left a widow but no family. The author records his indebtedness to J. D. Vaughan who was most helpful during his early career.

New pipe making equipment was being installed using the sub-merged arc welding process, when Arthur Dyson finally retired from the Board and Basil Vincent Smith was elected in his place. During 1959 A. B. S. Young, who had been at Mechans and joined the Horseley

Board, retired and during 1960 J. S. Christie, V. Senior and B. Vincent-Smith became joint Managing Directors.

Lord Dudley who had been Chairman from 1937 to 1955 resigned his seat on the Board. Later J. S. Christie resigned to become Deputy Chairman of Scotcross a holding company which had been set up by John Sheffield. J. S. Christie was appointed as Deputy Chairman of Mechans Ltd. and a substantial interest in the shareholding of Mechans was sold to the Union Tank Car Company of Chicago.

A company, Concrete and Structural Products Ltd. were bought and placed as a subsidiary to Carter-Horseley. This company had their base at Crawley and it was decided to close Waddon and move the whole organisation to Crawley. Two directors of this unit F. Marriage and Ronald Penfold joined Carter-Horseley as senior executives Norman Gibb moved to Tipton as Sales Manager and Local Director of Horseley, Norman Renney taking over at Newcastle. Ernest Salt who had resigned some time before from Sheffield was replaced by Philip Baldwin and Fred Elliott replaced him at Tipton as Commercial Manager.

It was during 1960 that the first all welded high strength steel bridge of 270 foot span was built over the River Thames at Maidenhead and the Head & Tail Sluice gates were completed on the flood control scheme at Denver and Kings Lynn.

In 1961 The Earl of Dudley's brother the Rt. Hon. Viscount Ward of Witley joined the board and J. S. Greenhalgh became Managing Director of Mechans. Horseley absorbed a small engineering company G. H. Whitehouse & Son Ltd. who were located near the Pipe Works entrance. The then owner was H. Gurmin Whitehouse son of the founder. They

Mechanical Test House, a part of the Laboratory block

eventually became the machine shop facility for Horseley and moved their plant to the main works but H. G. Whitehouse retired during 1962.

Horseley supplied the steelwork for two major power line crossings, one over the River Severn and one over the River Thames. A site visit was paid to the Thames Towers which were 630 ft. high, by some members of Horseley during the summer of 1961.

In 1962 in order to strengthen their market in specialised pressure vessels Horseley-Piggott (Water Engineers) Ltd. became changed to Horseley-Piggott (Process Engineers) Ltd. Dr. G. J. Shaw became General Manager and he was assisted by M. G. Wright. Ian Adams became Group Secretary and Vincent Senior and B. Vincent-Smith continued as Joint Managing Directors. V. Senior was also Chairman of Carter-Horseley & H.P. (Process Engrs) and a Director of G. H. Whitehouse & G. M. Carter (Agencies) Ltd. New offices for Carter-Horseley were built at Tipton.

Significant decline in shipbuilding and activity on the Clyde forced the closure of the Mechans site on 30 September 1963 but some products such as watertight ships' doors were transferred to Tipton. During 1964 there was significant investment in new plant at Tipton and the end of the old Dixons Branch of the Canal was removed to increase the tower storage area.

A 2,000 ton press was installed in the Hydraulic Shop; a Merlin Autoscan gas cutting machine some 30 ft. in length was installed in the Pipe Works and this was used to cut the mild steel chain links for the reconstruction of Marlow Bridge. The low pressure 800 lb. hydraulic system in the Pipe Works was upgraded to 1500 lb./sq. in.. 'A' Bay was converted to a Class 1 Welding Shop and an X-Ray shed built at its end using $^3/_4$" lead sheets for protection. A new X-ray set of 300 kv was purchased and installed. A number of new welding sets were installed and a hydro test pump purchased. During the year three – 60 foot diameter radio-telescopes were built for Cambridge University and these were the equivalent of a single telescope 1 mile in diameter.

During 1965 an additional expenditure of £150,000 was made on plant including:- Shanks lathe with 10 foot diameter swing, Pipe Works lathe 17" centres, radial drills, Jones KL 77 Rail Crane, Tractor and Trailer, Welding rotators, 600 amp welding sets, Fusarc Deck Welder and a hole cutting machine. The layout of the Hydraulic Shop was revised and the roof of parts of the new main bays were re-sheeted. The principal contract was Rugeley 'B' Power Station. During the year there were three notable retirements. Reg Barry the Structural Shop Foreman with 50 years service; Harry Green born 1898 who joined Horseley in 1925 but was away from 1949-1962; and M. S. Scrivener, born 1897 who joined Piggotts in 1919 and was Purchase Manager at Horseley.

The Company was now much involved in the building of pressure vessels, heat exchangers and process vessels in a variety of material types including stainless steels. Many of the vessels were very large and some heat exchangers had tube plates up to 12 inches thick. In order to cope with this work further plant was purchased in 1966. A plasma arc torch was added to the Pipe Works Merlin gas cutting machine to cope with stainless steels, two horizontal borers, a new 5 ton crane, Wadkin numerically controlled tape drill for tube plates, argon-arc and MIG welding sets, 300 cycle grinding machines, PEP gas cutting machines, the 55 inch gas cutter refurbished and an X-ray van for site work set up. The old welding shop was converted to Special Products and the Unionmelt vessel welding machine with new rotators set up in 'A' Bay. The main shops were equipped with gas heaters and the old coke braziers which polluted the shops removed.

Rebuilt Fitting and Machine Shops

    A new system of pipe coating having been invented, Horseley-Piggott (Coatings) Ltd. was set up and J. J. Heilker became Manager. During the year two moving footbridges were built for Madras Port Trust, one bascule and one swing. Marlow Bridge replacement work was completed. Vincent Senior became Deputy Chairman, I. G. Adams, Managing Director of Coatings, & D. E. Moyle, Secretary. Commander Buist retired as Deputy Chairman but remained a director.

    Horace Irons retired from the Works. He had joined in 1940 becoming Chief Time Supervisor, and had been a Tipton Councillor and Mayor. Stan Prosser also retired. He had joined Piggotts in 1926 and was involved with the setting up of the Cardiff Works as a duplicate of the roller welding set-up at Birmingham. From 1929-32 he was on outside work including time in Egypt. He was involved in setting up the Pipe Works at Tipton and an was an expert in pipe lining and sheathing, and was finally Chief Engineer to Horseley-Piggott (Coatings) Ltd.

    A significant financial change was made on 29 March 1966 when a Holding company was established as Horseley Bridge Ltd. and the units became classed as manufacturing units. During 1967 a sole U.K. Licence was obtained from Process Engineering Incorporated of Boston, U.S.A. to manufacture their range of cryogenic storage transport and converter vessels and this increased the type and sophistication of the Company's products, including the manufacture low temperature double wall transport vessels for low temperature liquid gases such as oxygen, nitrogen and argon.

    The spiral pipe welding machine was fully in production. This had been supplied by Driam of Friedrichshaven, Southern Germany. An exhibition having been organised by the Institute of Welding and the British Welding Research Association at the Science Museum, London, Horseley provided an exhibit featuring pipes and pipelines and the spiral welding process.

General improvements were made to the works buildings and items of new plant purchased. With the arrival of natural gas, arrangements were made to feed this into the Pipe Works. Those who had the old Mond Gas supply were the first to be supplied.

The old heavy travelling portal crane on the Main Race which had served for so many years, became unsafe and was demolished. It had originally been steam driven. A number of developments took place in welding using the TIG process automatically on tube end welding and new handling plant for welding was installed. A new automatic telephone exchange was installed which enabled many more extensions to be added. Carter-Horseley Engineers moved to new offices at Wordsley, near Stourbridge.

The last issue of the Horseley News Magazine, then known as 'Horseley Group News' was at Christmas 1967. Amongst details of long serving staff were those of George Downton, then in charge of the Template Shop who started at Piggotts in 1916, his father having worked there for 30 years before. He had moved to Tipton in 1933 as Foreman of the Tank Shop.

Chauffeur Harold Harding had 40 years service and Chauffeuse Hilda Scriven 26 years. Ralph Allbut, Senior Project Engineer had joined Horseley in 1925 and held various positions in the Drawing & Design Offices.

A new building was set up as a training school in the old Carter- Horseley Offices and John Allen was presented with a watch for 25 years service.

It was in 1969 that a major change took place during a period when company mergers were considered advantageous. Following enquiries from sources considered to be

The Dome of Discovery and other structures for the 1951 Festival of Britain during construction

The first all welded high tensile steel bridge over the River Thames at Maidenhead in 1961

unfriendly, Horseley merged with the John Thompson organisation of Ettingshall, Wolverhampton. Thompson were an old established boiler and pressure vessel manufacturer engaged in early nuclear power station work, and agreed to aquire the whole of the issued capital of Horseley Bridge Ltd. The agreement was announced at the Board Meeting on 26 September 1968.

There was at about this time a major proposal to merge John Thompson Ltd., Clarke, Chapman & Co. Ltd., International Combustion (Holdings) Ltd. and Horseley Bridge Ltd. However International Combustion (Holdings) Ltd. had encountered a major loss on a nuclear contract and at a meeting held on 20 November 1968 the proposal was deferred.

By this time Horseley had probably reached the pinnacle of their technical and production abilities. Class 1 pressure vessels in complex materials and of large size were being produced. Many major contracts were completed, such as the construction of Maidenhead Bridge over the River Thames, the first all welded, high tensile steel bridge; the reconstruction whilst still in service of Marlow and Hammersmith suspension bridges, complex pipework for the supersonic wind tunnel at RAE Bedford and a pipe bridge and road crossing of the River Severn at Hampton Loade. At the same time pipe production and the supply of pressed steel tank plates continued. Shortly afterwards the order was received for the Milford Haven High Level Box Girder Bridge.

Nevertheless, although initial work with John Thompson was friendly and a number of Horseley people were involved, later the joint organisation was taken over by Clarke Chapman of Gateshead who commenced an asset stripping exercise.

From this time decline set in which was to prove terminal. The pipe industry itself declined due to proposals for nationalisation and rather than invest in new plant to produce longer pipes and compete in the market a decision was taken to close the Pipe Works and the site was later sold to a supermarket distribution organisation.

Above: All welded Maidenhead Bridge during consturction
Below: Pipe Bridge over River Severn at Hampton Loade

Rationalisation was the order of the day and the accountant mind became ever more in evidence. Horseley were to concentrate on structures, cranes and bridges and allow other units to produce vessels and special plant.

This smaller and more difficult market, as a study of the company history would have shown, was to prove an increasing problem.

The 1,000 ton centre section of the high-level box girder bridge at Milford Haven has just been lifted into position

The new Foundry building which had reverted to Light Construction was demolished and the lower part of the yard fenced off – Horseley was back to its 1865 area. Attempts to sell this area failed.

The Works continued to produce many large and important structures and bridges against a falling and increasingly unprofitable market. Very little investment took place and one major installation was ill chosen – the purchase of a sawing and drilling line for light structures – never the real forte of Horseley in latter years, put them in competition with smaller fabricators with lower overheads.

With the creation of Northern Engineering Industries (NET) the positon of Gerneral Manger was established and those who served were Dr. Salmon, Jim Nock, W. C. Holliday, G. H. Butler, Roger Simpson, Cedric Birch, Norman Hodgkiss, John Leeson, Bill Cox and Stuart Price.

Works Managers included F. J. Daniels, Jim Hay, John Jope who moved up from the Pipe Works, Don Macintosh, Phin Butler, John Harris and John Parker with John Harris returning at the close. Bob Wild acted as welding Engineer and Michael Jones was respoonsible for Testing and Quality. For a period John Lewis acted as Production Director.

The land across the road with the canteen and garage was sold and the company then a unit of NEI Thompson, struggled. NEI became a division of Rolls Royce Engineering and the original office block was demolished leaving a disgraceful and unrestored entrance.

Against the deepening depression and a series of major losses by Rolls Royce, early in 1992 it was announced that the company did not feature in Rolls Royce plans, and was to be put on the market. It was not surprising that in a depression and with an order book

A typical heavy Class 1 pressure vessel

containing many loss making contracts, that this did not succeed. The final blow then fell – Horseley was to cease trading and close. Ironically the shops were very busy with many orders, but taken at a loss. The structural and bridge industry had finally cut its own throat by quoting ever lower prices, no less than 190 structural fabrication companies closed in the 15 months prior to April 1992.

No attempt was made to save the company by suggesting wage cuts and taking other drastic actions. The opportunity to concentrate on other types of production, always a Horseley strong point, had been lost by earlier decisions. Little thought was given to the 350 employees and the possibility of their ever finding other work. The site was more valuable for the building of houses and the demolition contractors were being appointed before the works closed formally on 15 May 1992, although a few continued to oversee the last rites, and were to be at Horseley on 18 July 1992 at what should have been a triumphal celebration of the 200th anniversary of the founding of the Company.

Those who have studied this later history and the earlier paper covering that of the first works will appreciate the vast range of construction worldwide in which the company was involved for almost two hundred years. There can be few companies who have contributed more to development worldwide.

It is these works which will stand as a proud memorial to the men and management of the Company and remain in the memory of those many dedicated people who were proud to know that they were HORSELEY.

BY THEIR WORKS SHALL YE KNOW THEM.

NOTES & REFERENCES

This history is based essentially upon deeds, Company books catalogues, balance sheets, photographs and documents deposited at the County Record Office, Stafford. The deposit reference numbers are D1288, D3142, D4819 et al, much material being deposited in 1992 at the closure of the Works and not yet calendared.

To give detailed references would prove most laborious and repetitive. The principal works quoted are given below and those seeking further information will need to refer to the relevant dates either in the Board Minute Books or the Managers Day Books or to the relevant Deeds. Later information is taken from the various issues of the Horseley News (Horseley-Piggott News).

Information on Thomas Piggott Ltd. is taken from the surviving Board Minutes and from their catalogues.

Horseley Bridge

1. Foundry Pattern Book   1865-1879
2. Board Minute Book Nos. 1-6.   1873-1941
3. Directors Day Books Nos. 1-5.   1875-1928
4. Minutes of General Meetings   1874-1904
5. Minutes of General Meetings   1905-1942
6. Private Minute Book   1874-1923
7. Managing Directors Report Book   1878-1885

Thomas Piggott

1. General Meeting Minutes   1892-1933
2. Board Meeting Minutes   1928-1938

This history is written in extenso and attempts to record all matters of principal relevance in company development, engineering, social and wage structures, labour problems and names and details of personnel. Readers with particular interests will need to extract relevant information.

During the majority of the history recounted imperial units of measurement and the system of pounds shillings and pence were in use. It is pointless to convert the sterling into the current system since inflation renders this meaningless. Units adopted in the original documents have therefore been quoted throughout.

The classical spelling of 'riveting' is with one 't', however it has been normal in the local area and trade to use double 't' and this has been so in all the documents on which this history is based and has thus been adopted herein.

The spelling of place names are quoted as in the documents quoted.

ACKNOWLEDGMENTS

I would like to record my sincere appreciation of the many hours spent by my wife, Joan, in committing all these words to the word processor and for tolerating the office cum-sewing room being so full of ancient volumes. Thanks too to son, David, who assisted when the processor decided to misbehave and for making additions to the text.

I am also most grateful to the late W. K. V. Gale for studying the draft and for his assistance and comments which have been incorporated.

A version of the first section of this book was read by the author to the Newcomen Society at the Science Museum, London as his Presidential Address in April 1987. The agreement of the Council of the Newcomen Society to the inclusion of this paper is gratefully acknowledged.

The work is dedicated to my many colleagues at Horseley whose friendship and assistance over 50 years is most gratefully acknowledged.

Index

1924 British Empire Exhibition Wembley Park 98
85, Lionel Street, combine the staff 104

A

Aaron Manby 19
Accident and a Sick Fund 61
Acid Open Hearth 63
Acton Town footbridge 108
Adams, George, & Sons, Mars Ironworks (1866-1924) 153
Adams, Ian, Group Secretary 164
Admiralty Mooring and Dragging Buoys 76
Agent General of New South Wales 80
Airship Hanger, Karachi 99
all welded high strength steel bridge, Maidenhead 163
Allen, Fitting Shop 140
Allen, J. S., Apprentice 128
  Site Engineer 159
Allen, K., Drawing Office 82
  Draughtsman 79
  Chief Draughtsman 99
Allen, T. H., Order Dept. 79
  Company Buyer, died 102
Allen's Patent Portable Rivetting Machine 56
Ammonia Stills at Belfast 106
Amphlett, E. G., Worthing 13
Amphlett, Joseph, Dudley 8
Angus Sanderson, car 94
Antofagasta Railway, Bolivia 55
Antofagasta Railway Viaduct 48
Aqueduct 83
Arc Manufacturing Co. 121
Arroll, Sir William 107
Artisans and Machinery 20
Ashbury Railway Carriage & Iron Co. 65
Askwith, Sir George, Employers' Federation 73
Associated Firms' List 124
Association of Employers 64
Aston, Mr., Agent of the Canal Company 15
Atlas Engine Co., Ltd. 137
auditors 141
Automatic River Control Gates 109
Avery, Foreman 66
Avery testing machine 130

B

B.B.C. television mast, Sutton Coldfield 156
B.I.F. 122
Babcock & Wilcox, John Thompson Ltd., Lloyds Class 1. 122
Backhouse, John, crushed 66
Bagnalls of Stafford 107
Bailey, George 144
Bailey, Jim, Stock Yard, retired 150
Bailey, Michael R. 37
Baillie, J. W., Secretary 85, 90
  Assistant Managing Director and Sec. 103
  Director 157
  retired 161
  passing away 161
Baillie, Mrs. A. M. 85
Baldwin, Philip 163
Barker, John, Civil Engineer 61
Barker, John William, son of John Barker 61
Barker, Thomas P., director 139
  Man. Director 140
  resignation 144
Barnes, J. B., agency 97
Barnsley, Horseley Company's Engineer 24
Barrages Automatiques S.A. 109
Barry, Reg, Structural Shop Foreman 159
  retired 164
basic Bessemer Steel 63
Basic Open Hearth 63
Batting, H. L., London Office 90, 104
  retirement 98
Beardmore, William, Glasgow 142
Beaumont, James Taylor 134
Beaverette tanks 126, 128
Beckton Gas Works 63
Beckton Retort Work 61
Bedford, William 12
Benfield, J., retired Foremen 113
Bengal and Nagpur Railway 55
Bennett, Harry S., General Manager 55
Bennett, Peter Duckworth, Ironfounder, Oak Farm Iron Co. 46
Bennett, Sandwell Park Colliery Co. 54
Benson, Ashmore, Klonne Patent 142
Benthall, Sibella 71
Berry's portable hydraulic rivetter 58
Bewlay, H. 138
Bewlay, Henry 103
Bewlay, Hubert, died 141
Bewlay, Hubert junior, partner 137
Birch, Cedric 169
Birch, Draughtsman 79
Birmingham Canal company 7
Birmingham University 150
Bituminous Pipe Linings Ltd. 114
Blackwall Extension Work 61
Blake, F. W., Apprentice 136
Blaw Knox Limited 105
Blythwood Shipbuilding Co. 162
Bodmer, John George 15
Boer War 66
Boiler Furnace Co Ltd. 114
Boiler House 63
Boiler Makers Association 66
Boulton & Watt Engine 12
Boulton and Watt 6
Bourne, J. W., grants 121
Bowater, John J., West Bromwich 56
Bowen, apprentice 66
Bowen, London Office, retired 83
Braithwaite and Co. 73, 112
Bramah, Cochrane and Deeley, Messrs. 18
Bramah, J. J. 17
Brannan, John 111
Bratt, John J., killed 129
Bridge & Construction Industry Association 71
Bridge Building 25
bridge, River Itchen 80
bridge, Upton on Severn 120
Bridges at Hill St. and Navigation St. 151
Bright, John 59
British Constructional Steelwork Association 124
British Electric Ray Ltd., A.R.P. Shelters 122
British Foreign Colonial Corporation Ltd. 89
British Mannesman Co. 144
British Steelwork Association 105
British Thomson-Houston Co. Ltd. 93
Broad & Tierney 17
Broad, Robert, Ironmaster, Tipton 43, 44, 45, 159
Broadwaters Branch 7
Brookes Meadow 7, 10
Broomside Boiler Works Limited 115, 130
Buck & Hickman 120
Buckton tensile machine 129
Buenos Aires and Great Southern Railway 101
Buist, Lieutenant Commander Colin, director 121, 157
  Deputy Chairman, retired 165
Bull, Mr., Canal Company 11
Bullivant Company 76
Bullock, Edwin, Ironfounder 47
Bushell, J., Wages Clerk 79
Bute West Dock Lock Swing Bridge 106
Butler, G. H. 169
Butler, John, & Co., Ltd., Leeds 104
Butler, Phin 169
Butler, Thomas, Kirkstall Forge 15
Bye, Simms & Gifford 120

C

C Type Hangars, St. Athen 120
Cadburys, steel framed buildings 119
Caledonia Engine 24
Calendar-Hamilton Bridge units 130
Calley, John 6
Cambridge University 164
Canning, Sir George 158
Cape of Good Hope Jetty 59
Capewell, George, pensions 113
Cardiff Gas Works 126
Carpenter, William, crushed 65
Carter-Horseley Engineers 166
Cartwright, injured 69
Cartwright, Llewellyn, long serving plater 159
Cashmore, J. 92
cast iron houses 99
Central Argentine Railway 55
Central Bridge Building Association 83

Central England Electricity
    Scheme 105
Chaloner and Henderson 20
Chamberlain, Neville 79
Chapman, Clarke,
    Gateshead 167
Charing Cross
    Railway Bridge 49
Charing Cross Station Booking
    Hall, purifier for 102
Chartered Gas Co. 134
Checketts, transport horses 47
Cherrington & Stainton 96
Cherrington, J., Cashier 79
    retired 80
Cherrington, T.,
    Draughtsman 79
Cherrington, Tom,
    Port Harcourt Drawing
    Office 99
Christie, J. S., advisor 157
    resigned 163
Christy Brothers 118
Civil Defence Bill 122
Clark, J., old servant 120
Clarke, Chapman
    & Co. Ltd. 167
Clarke, Charles A. 68
Clayton Son & Co., Ltd. 113
closure 164
Clulo, William,
    Dock Tavern 134
Cochrane, John, Hyde Park
    Gate, London, Ironmaster
    17, 45
Colbourne, John, and Sons 17
Coleman, member of staff 129
Collins, H,. Joint Committee
    representative 85
Collinson, Charles, Plater 136
Columbo Harbour Jetty 63
Commission on artisans and
    machinery 31
Company of Proprietors of the
    Birmingham Canal
    Navigations 134
Compeigne, bridge 76
Concrete and Structural
    Products Ltd. 163
Cook's stationary rivetter 58
Cooksey, Joseph, and Son 49
Cort, Henry 8
Cory's 75
Coughtrie, J. H. 129
Coughtrie, W. J., Works
    Manager 158
Coventry and Oxford
    Canals 25
Cox, Bill 169
Craig & Donald 58, 65
Cutler, Samuel,
    Klonne Patent 142
cyclotron 150

D

Daly, James T., Director 55, 87
    retires 103
Daniels, F. J. 169
Danks, Edwin, Oldbury 158
Daventry & Leamington
    Railway 63
Davis, James 21
Davis, John, Foreman 71
Day, John, Rivetter 136
de Horseley, John 7
de Horsley, Thomas 7
Deeley 17
Degg, Lt. Col. Ronald,
    Personnel Manager 161
Deighton, Arthur 129
Deighton Flue & Tube
    Co Limited 115
Deightons Patent Flue,
    Leeds 142
Deloitte, Plender,
    Griffiths & Co. 107
Dempsey, C. W. 59
    death 68
Dempsey, Mr., death of 63
Dempsey, William,
    engineer 44
Denver Bridge, River Ouse 69
Derby Locomotive Works 101
Dewar, R.W. 157
Dilley, A. E., Works Manager,
    retired 129
    death 161
Dixon Amphlett
    & Bedford 13, 45
Dixon, Edward, Dudley 8
Dixons Branch canal 48, 164
Dixon's Horseley Colliery 67
Dock Tavern 134
Dodds, Isaac 32
Doughty House 126
Downing, G. and
    W. E., Malsters 56
Downton, George 166
Dowson Gas Plant 61
Driam of Friedrichshaven 165
Dry Gas Association 104
Dry gas holders,
    Klonne Type 111
Dry Gasholders Ltd. 142
Dublin and Kingstown
    Railway 24
Dudley Guest Hospital 70
Dudley, Lord 119, 163
Dudley, Thomas, Shutt End 7
Dunn, J., assistant 64
    Works Manager,
    resignation 82
Dunn, L., D.O. 79
Dunn, Mr.,
    Works Manager 77
Dyson, A.,
    Ass. M. Director 139, 140
    Managing Director 103

E

E. W. Peacock, Dixon House,
    Tipton, Estate Manager 13
Earl of Dartmouth 94
Earp 100
Eastbourne Pier 97
Easthope, H., Junior Clerk 79
Ed. Sockett, accident 67
Edwards, Albert, E., Pipe
    Works Manager 159
Edwards,
    Construction shop 140
Edwards, Samuel,
    Rivetter 136
Electric Construction Co. 67
electric welding 143, 144
Elliott, Fred, Commercial
    Manager 163
Elliotts Metal Co. 70
Ellis, W., Cost Clerk 94
    Prime Cost Clerk 79
    Cashier 102
Embleton & Co. 93
Engineering Joint Trades
    Movement 116
Essential Work (General
    Provisions) Order 1941 126
Evans, E., Draughtsman 79
    pensioned 108
Evans, James 54
Evans, Joseph, & Co. 58
Evans, Junior D.O. 79
Evans, W. E., Invoice Clerk 79
Everitt, G. A. 138
    resigned 138
Everitt, N. H. 138
Everitt, Neville H. 138
    died 141

F

F. C. Construction Co., Ltd.
    119
Factory '99' 129
Fearn, C., Draughtsman 79
Fellows, George H., killed 129
Fellows, Noah 100
Fenton, E., Wages Clerk 79
Fergusson, Sir John 95
Field, Joshua 13, 28
Finch, John 7
Finches Mill 7
Finch's Devisees 7
fire engine 58
Fish Market, Preston 97
Ford Motor Co.,
    Dagenham 117
Fordson Tractor 98
Founderie Anglais 21
Fowler, Richard J.,
    Chief Engineer 161
Francois Cementation
    Co. Ltd. 158
Friendly Society of Iron
    Founders 75

Frost, Messrs., and Sons 106
Fryer, David, killed 96
furnaces and production at the
    Horseley Company 36
Fusarc Deck Welder 164

G

G.W. B. Ltd. 162
G.W.R. Shifnal Bridge 26
Gale W. K. V. 26
Galton Bridge 25
gas holder 126
gas holders, Horseley
    Company 37
gas lamp columns 106
Gas Light & Coke Co. 69
Gas Light & Coke Co.,
    Beckton 94
Gas Trade Association 98
Gay, Fitting Shop Foreman 98
Gibb, Norman,
    Sales Manager 163
Gilbert,
    Chief Draughtsman 140
Golding, H. 12
Government Old
    Age Pensions 143
Great Eastern Railway 63
Great Indian Peninsula
    Railway 55
Great Western Railway 68
Green, Harry, Midland
    Representative 117
    retired 164
Green, Josiah, pension 142
Greenhalgh, J. S., Managing
    Director of Mechans 163
Greiner & Erpfs 58
Griffiths, Norton, M.P. 72
Group Pension Scheme 120
Grymoff, works and offices in
    Scott St. 121, 125
Gt. Eastern Railway 69
Guest, Arthur, staff man 130
Guest, Keen & Baldwins 112
Guest Keen & Nettlefolds 112
Guest, Keen & Piggotts 107,
    109, 140
Guy, J., left erection
    department 153

H

Hammersmith
    Rail Bridge 108
Hammersmith Station,
    steelwork 108
Hammond, W. Cyril 159
Hampton Lucy,
    Stratford on Avon 25
Handyside, Andrew, & Co. 63
Harding, Harold,
    Chauffeur 166
Harford, John Battersby 134
Harford, John Scondrett,
    plots 134

Harper Beans National
  Shell Factory 130
Harper, Len 162
  outside sales
    representative 93
  London Office
    Manager 121
  Director 125
Harper, Len,
  Repair Shop, retired 153
Harper, Leonard 98
Harris, G. H., old servant 120
Harris, H., dismissed 99
Harris, John 28, 169
Harris, painter 67
Harrison, Fitting Shop
  Foreman 98
Harrison, Richard,
  Horseley Partners 21
Harrison, Richard,
  Wolverton 12
Harrison, Thomas,
  Storeman 72
Hay, Jim 169
Hayward & Co. 67
Haywood, W. J., & Co. 68
Head & Tail Sluice gates,
  Denver, Kings Lynn 163
head-gear,
  Ryhope Colliery 162
Heilker, J. J., Horseley-Piggott
  (Coatings) Ltd., 165
Helsby, C. 110
Henleys (1928) Ltd.,
  aeroplane hanger 105
Henleys Telegraph Co. 101
Henn, S. H. H.,
  Director 77, 87, 103
  Chairman 141
  chaired meeting, died
    suddenly 118
Hill, Ben, lost a leg 66
Hill, Rowland 64
  Director 72
  death 76
Hill Street Bridge,
  Birmingham 156
Hirons, H. 44
Hobden, H., reporting
  agent in China 117
Hodgkiss, Norman 169
Hoggins, R., patent 113
Holcroft, Charles, brother
  of James Holcroft 46
Holcroft, G. H. 87
Holcroft, James, Stourbridge,
  Iron & Coal Master 45
Holcroft, Sir Charles 73
Holcroft, Sir George 103
Holland, F. H.,
  commissioned report 116
Holliday, W. C. 169
Holly, F. G., Assistant
  Secretary, resigned 111
  Secretary 141

Home Guard 126
Hood, Mr.,
  Canal Company 12
Horbury & Wakefield,
  widening, Thornes Lane
  100
Horbury Bridge 99
Horse Ambulance 70
Horsehay Company 71, 93
Horseley Branch 11
Horseley Bridge & Engineer-
  ing Company Limited 109
Horseley Bridge & Thomas
  Piggott Ltd., 1934 111
Horseley Bridge Ltd. 165, 167
Horseley Coal and Iron
  Company 21
Horseley Colliery 11
Horseley Group News 166
Horseley Home Guard,
  stood down 130
Horseley House, Tipton 8, 10
Horseley Patent Bearing 65
Horseley Patent Flooring –
  Wadsworth Patent 95
Horseley Piggott News 158
Horseley platoon 126
Horseley Road 6
Horseley-Piggott
  (Coatings) Ltd. 165
Horseley-Piggott
  (Process Engineers) Ltd. 164
Horseley-Piggott
  (Water Engineers) Ltd. 121,
  164
Horseleye, Ph'O De 7
Horton, Isaac 37
Horton, Joshua, Swallow
  Foundry 133
Horton, T.,
  Thomas Piggott & Co. 102
Horton, T. W., died 120
Hubert Pepper &
  Rudland 141
Hudson, F. Howard, Auditors,
  Caldicott Hudson
  & Caldicott 141
Huffer, D. M. 28
Hughes, Thomas 70, 102
  Secretary, retires 84
Humpage, T., Clerk 79
Humphreys & Glasgow Co.
  106, 116

I

Imperial Airways Ltd.,
  new headquarters 119
Ince Power Station 161
Indian Midland Railway 55
Inman, Cecil D. 62
Institute of Welding 121
Institution of Mechanical
  Engineers 65
International Combustion
  (Holdings) Ltd. 167

iron furnaces 12
Irons, Horace, retired 165

J

J. Maquire 138
Jacob, W., Hamilton Iron
  Works 54, 63
Jaffray, Sir John 70
James, A. J. 93
James, L. H., pupil 93
James, R. T., & Partners 93
Jessop & Son, Leicester 58
Jetty at Port Elizabeth,
  South Africa 70
John Lysaght Ltd. 157
John Marshall & Co Ltd. 115
John Thompson
  (Wolverhampton) Ltd. 115,
  153, 167
Johnson, Ekin & Keeling,
  Solicitors to the
  Company 85
Joint Stock Bank 70
Jones, Arthur,
  leading plater 84
Jones, George Edward,
  Works Manager 45
Jones, Michael 169
Jope, John, G., Pipe Works
  Manager 162, 169
Jukes, F., widow 122
Jukes, N. H., plater 81
  Works Manager 90
  Works Superintendent 96
  Structural
    Superintendent 116
Junkers & Zollbau
  Syndikat 105

K

Kaloriferwerk Hugo
  Junkers 105
Keep & Hinckley 70
Keep & Son 70
Keep, John, Scrivenor,
  Birmingham, Director
  Midland Wagon Co. 45
  Chairman 55, 70
Kell, W. V. W. 87, 102
Kendall & Gent, Salford 59
Kennedy, J.,
  Carter-Horseley 159
Kenrick, A., & Sons 56
Kent, G., pensions 113
Kettle, assistant 98
Kidson, Draughtsman 79
King Edward VII, funeral 72
Kingston Bridge,
  River Thames 81
Kitely, Richard,
  Stoney Stratford 12
Klonne Dry Gas Holders 115,
  117, 144, 162

L

Lamella construction,
  Apex Motor Co., Ltd. 125
Lamella Construction Co.,
  (British Proprietary) Ltd 105
Lamella construction,
  Meteor Garage 125
Lamella hangers,
  Air Ministry 117
Lamures system 64
Lap Welded Tube
  Association 142
Large Tube Association 114
Law Accident
  Association Ltd. 66
Lawrence, T. 111
Leach, J. S.,
  Draughtsman 79, 82
Leeds Forge Co., Leeds 142
Leeson, John 169
Leicester and Swannington
  Railway 25
Lester, Thomas, Horseley 21
Lewin, H. E., retired 162
Lewis, John 169
lift bridge, Millwall Dock 159
lift bridge, Litherland 112
Lilleshall Co. 95
Lincoln automatic welding
  plant 120
Littleton Colliery 68
Liverpool Overhead
  Railway 63
Liverpool St. Station 63
Lloyd, A. Ll. 138
Lloyd, Arthur 66
Lloyd, G. H. 138
Lloyd, George B. 134
Lloyd, George Herbert,
  born 137
Lloyd, H. D. L., death 150
Lloyd, Henry D.,
  Warrington 108
Lloyd, Lord 159
Lloyd, Roger, accountant 161
Lloyd, Sampson Samuel 134,
  138
Lloyd, T. O. 103
  resigned 108
Lloyds banking 134
Lloyds Class 1 150
LNWR 65
locomotive 'Pioneer' 76
Lofthouse, N.,
  Wages Clerk 79
London & N.E. Railway 97
London Brighton & South
  Coast Railway 69
London County Council 121
Lovesey, E., Typist 79, 102
Lucigen Light 58
Lyles Furnace 58
Lysaght, J., Ltd., Bristol 99

M

Macartney, Frederick Newton 62
Macintosh, John 169
Maddocks & Walford, Birmingham 120
Madras Port Trust 165
Maidenhead Bridge, River Thames 163, 167
Manby, Aaron 15
Manby and Smith 15
Manning Wardle & Co. 76
Manning Wardle & Co., engine 83
Manufacturers Association 94
Maquire, J. 138
Marine Furnace Association 111, 114
Marlow and Hammersmith suspension bridges 165, 167
Marriage, F, Senior Executive 163
Marshall, John, Motherwell 142
Marshall, Joseph 144
Martin, J., left erection department 153
Martin, member of staff 129
Mason, Octavious, Foreman 136
Massey, H., Draughtsman 79
Mechans Ltd., Clyde 162, 164
Meek, L. R., manager of the Gas Plant Division 162
Mephan Fergusson pipe 129
Midland Auxiliary Shipbuilding Committee 82, 93
Midland Electric Corporation 97
Midland Federation of Employers 73
Midland Structural Association 83
Midland Wagon Co. 70
Miles, G. 66
Milford Haven High Level Box Girder Bridge 167
Milliken Bros. 105
mine sinkers 79
Minister of Fuel & Power 129
Mitchell, Pullan, Chief Engineer and Works Manager 96 resigned 101
Mond gas 126
Montevideo Water Works 63
Morgan, Wm., & Co. 105
Morris, Weigh Clerk 82
Mortar Mills 64
Mortgagees, James T. Daly, William Dempsey, Chas. 55
motor car, Austin 12 HP 99
Mould, Arthur, E., Chief Engineer 56, 62
Mountford, J., grants 121
moving footbridges 165
Moyle, Douglas E., Chief Accountant for Carter-Horseley 162
Munitions Act 1915 76
Muntz, Frederick E., Chairman 70, 71 died 93
Muntz, George, Frederick, Chairman of B'ham Joint Stock Bank Ltd. 45, 55
Murray, David, builder 44
Murray, James Douglas 65

N

Napier, Captain (later Admiral Sir) Charles 19
Nash Mills, London-Birmingham Railway 26
Nasmyth and Co. 18
National Association for the help and protection of fabricators 71
National Coke and Oil Company 115
National Insurance Act 100
Nechells Power Station 100
New English Glass Co. 75
Newcomen, Thomas 6
Newhaven Bridge 106
Newry Gas & Water Company 134
Newton Chambers & Co., Sheffield 95
Nock, Jim 169
Nock, John 47
Nottingham Station 66, 69

O

O'Callahan, J. P., Water Softening Plants 109 died 161
Ocker Hill Power Station 73, 93, 130
Oldhams patent paddles 20
Oliver, John, Banker of S toney Stratford 12
Onions, W., Foreman 113
Orton, A. D., Drawing Office 159
Osborne, A. Gordan, Erection Manager 153 Midland Manager 157
Osney Bridge 55
Outwell, Birmingham Corporation Gas Works 83
Overton, W. 144

P

Paddington Station 75
Page, Works Manager 56
Page, Arthur, pensioned 108
Page, G., Draughtsman 79
Page, Jacob 63
Parker, John 169
Parker, Samuel, Foreman 136
Parker, Winder and Achurch 101
Parker's mines 68
Parkes 7
Parsons, Leonard, specialist 106
Partridges Mill 7
Partridges Mill Pool 10
Patent Copper Tube and Wire Co. 56
Patent Shaft and Axletree Company 73
Pattern Store 63
Paxman, Davy, & Co., Colchester 56
Payton, old servant, eleven horses 98
Peacock, F. W., Dixon Amphlett & Bedford 68
Peacock, Thomas, Managing Director, Guest, Keen & Nettlefolds Ltd. 99
Pels Folding Press 119
Pemberton, Thomas, Brassfounder 47
Penfold, Ronald 163
Peninsula Railway 55
Pensions 144
Pensions Act 1925 102
Perks, D. 85
Perks, F. D., Assistant Secretary 102, 111 dismissed 121
Perks, Frank 85
Perks, M., Typist 79, 102
Perks, Walter, General Manager 78, 85, 90 resigns 103
Petrel, Company built novel lifeboat 137
Peyke, Mr., Horseley 15
Phoenix Assurance Co. 120
Picture Houses 105
Piggott, T. W. 54
Piggott, Thomas and Sons 7, 54
Piggott, Thomas, born 134
Piggotts Tanks 139
Pigott Smith, map, 1825/6 17
pipe bridge and road crossing, River Severn at Hampton Loade 167
pipe bridge, River Dove 162
Pipe Works, closed 167
Pirelli Co. 105
Plant, Geoffrey, accountant 161
Platt, Samuel, Wednesbury 59
Polish men 153
Port Elizabeth, piers 55
Port of London Authorities 75
Power Distribution Ltd. 97
Power line crossings 164
presented to the King & Queen 159
Pressed Steel Tank Association 111
pressed steel tank plates 128
Price, Stuart 169
Prince of Wales National Relief Fund 76
Pritchard, A., Preparation Bay Foreman 159
Process Engineering Incorporated, Boston 165
Prosser, Stan, retired 165
Provident Surgical Appliance Society 59
Prudential Assurance Co., Ltd. 116
Puplett, Samuel, Manager 137

Q

Queen Victoria, funeral 67

R

radio-telescopes, built for Cambridge University 164
Railton, Leonard, agent for South Wales 95
railway bridge, Shifnal 161
Ramsden, W. L., pension 142
Randall, G., Repair Shop 120
reconstruction 167
reconstruction of Marlow Bridge 164
Rendel, Sir Alexander 63
Renney, Norman, Newcastle 163
Richards, H., employee of Horseley 107
Riddell, C. J., Works Manager, resigned 96
Riddell, C. S. 81, 82, 85, 90
Ritchie 101
'River' 83
River Loa Bridge, Bolivia 80
River Severn 164
River Thames 164
Roberts, R., & Co. 93
Robey & Co., Ltd. 158
Robins, Mr., Canal Company 11
Robinson, A., employee 120
Robinson, W. W., grants 121
Rogers, S. 70
Rogers, Samuel, death 87
rolling lift bridge, Manchester Road, Mill 102
Rolling Mills Association 99
roof collapse 125
Roper, J. S. 28
Rose, Bill, works engineer 126
Round, Mark, & Sons of Dudley 73
roving bridges, Oxford Canal 36

roving bridges supplied by Horseley 35
Rowley, George, works engineer 126
Royce crane 73
Rubenstein, R. A., Overseas Sales 162
Rubery Owen 96
Rugeley 'B' Power Station 164
Ryhope Colliery 162
Ryland, Miss, Stourbridge 141

S

Salmon, Dr. 169
Salt, E., Carter-Horseley 159
   resigned 163
Sanders, Foreman Fitter 65, 81
   resigned 81
Sanzer bucket pump 72
Sash shop 63
Scherzer lift bridge 121
Scotcross 163
Scottish Employers Liability and General Insurance 66
Screen, W., Foreman of the Light Construction Shop 120
Screen, W. T., in charge of Girder and Light Cons 130
Scriven, Hilda, Chauffeuse 166
Scrivener, M. S., Purchase Manager, retired 164
Select Committee 20
senior executives 163
Shakespeare, W., military record 87
Sharp, Roberts, and Co. 18, 93
Sharrock, Hamiltons Windsor Iron Works 54, 66
Shaw, Dr. G. J., General Manager 164
Sheffield, John Vincent, Chairman of Carter Horseley 157
Simpson, Roger 169
Shimshom Palestine Portland Cement Co. 150
Short, Thomas, London and Birmingham, East India Merchant 45
Siebe and West 137
Sim, James, Production Manager 159
Simcox, Foreman 56
Sirius Welding plant 73
Smith, Basil Vincent, Northern Director of Carter Horseley 158
Smith Brothers & Co., Glasgow 62
Smith, Joseph, Coseley 12, 15
Smith, William, Toymaker 47
Smithson, A. E., & Son Ltd., South Wales Agent 153

South Durham Steel & Iron Co. 104
South Staffordshire Mond Gas (Power & Heating) Co. 85
Southern & Grice, accident 66
Southern Railway, six bridges 100
Spencer, J., Piggotts 66
Spencer, John, Secretary 45
spiral pipe welding machine 165
Spiral welded pipe 129
Spon Lane Foundry 47
Spring Hill Works 114
St. Helens and Runcorn Gap Railway 21
Stacey methods of welding 117
Staffordshire Steel & Ingot (Iron) Co. 63
Stanton, Edward, died 69
Stanton, Miss. A., pension 122
Star Locomotive, 1833-4 22
steam boats supplied by Horseley 30
Steel Company of Wales 162
Stephenson, Robert 37
stern ends 128
Stockport Gas Engine 67
Stonehewer, Thomas 45, 68, 72
Strong Room 67
Structural Steelcrete Ltd. 101
supersonic wind tunnel, RAE Bedford 167
Swannington Incline Engine, 1833 23
swing bridge at Lowestoft 69
   Barry Docks 119
   Beccles 97
   Exeter 116
   Folkestone 105
   GWR, East Bute Dock 102
   River Dee near Chester 80
   St. Olaves 97
   Upton on Severn 117

T

Table Bay, jetties 55
Tangye, Messrs. 61
tank landing craft 126, 128
Tank Loco 65
Taylor, A. A., Assistant Secretary 162
Taylor, James, boat builder 134
Teece, Chief Estimator 140
Teeside Bridge & Engineering 104
Telephone Exchange 73
Telford, Thomas, Smethwick 25
The Horseley Bridge & Engineering Company Ltd. 79

The Liverpool and Manchester Railway 23
Thomas Piggott & Sons, George 133
Thomas Piggott & Sons, Joseph 133
Thomas, William, land 72
Thompson Bros. Bilston 151
Thompson, John, (Wolverhampton) Ltd. 142
Thomson-Houston 73
Tilbury Docks 101
Timmins, George, Button maker 47
Tinsley & Meadow Hall, Sheffield, LNER 106
Tipton Gas 61
Tipton Wake 66
Toll End Branch 11
Tooby, F., old Horseley workman 115
Tower Bridge 63
Townsend, G. E. C. 26
Treorchy Bridge, Rhondda Council 97
Triplex Co. 159
Troath, J., Contract Clerk 79
   General Office 99
Turner, A. E. P., Accountant 121
Turner, William, Wolverhampton 21

U

Umberslade 72
Underhill, Dr. 69
Union Street, Tipton, damage and loss of life 77
Union Tank Car Company of Chicago 163
Unity 98
Urwick, Orr & Partners 156

V

Van Wart Kell, Washington 76
Vaughan, J. D., Chief Draughtsman 99, 121
   Chief Engineer 159
   Official Director 161
   death 162
Vignoles, C. B. 25
Vincent Senior, Joint Managing Director of Carter Horseley 158

W

Walker, C & W, Klonne Patent 142
Wall, Joe, Repair Shop, retired 153
Wallis, H. E. 45
Walsall Power Station 150, 153
watertight ships' doors 164

Watt, James, & Co. 54
Webb, rivetter, fell from crane 82
welded gas-holder, Tipton Gas 123
Weller, John 44
West India Docks, P.L.A. 101
Western Road 133
Westwood, Alfred, Foreman Moulder 65, 71
Westwood's (Foundry Foreman) 56
Wheale, W. 44
Whitehouse, G. H., & Son Ltd. 163
Whitehouse, H. G., retired 164
Whitehouse, H. Gurmin 163
Whitehouse, William, Whitesmith 47
Wild, Robert 28, 169
Wilkins & Mitchell 124
Willey, E. Trafford 153
Wilson Gas Generation Plant 71
Witley, Rt. Hon. Viscount Ward of, joined board 163
Wolverhampton Corrugated Iron Co., Ltd. 158
Wood, Edward, Contractor of Derby 61
Wood, Tom Percy 61
Woodward, J. T. 111
Woodward, Leading Estimator 140
Wordsley 166
Workers Compensation Act 66
Workers Playtime 129
Workman, Wm., pensions 113
Wright, J., & Co., Tipton 56
Wright, M. G. Assistant General Manager 164
Wright, S., manager of the Chemical and Industrial 117

Y

York, Harrison and Co, Messrs. 18
Yorke, John, Horseley Partners 21
Young, A. B. S., Mechans, retired 162

Z

Zeppelin raid 76